GENGHIS KHAN BURIAL METHOD

By William G Ellis Jr

I hesitated entering the Allen Brother's Funeral Home casket display for it was something I didn't want to do, but at seventy I must. I was greeting my Charley who asked, "Hello William, so you finally going to take my advice about paying for a casket now. We been having a special buy one get another at half price or buy four and get one free."

"I'm just checking," I answered paying no attention to his joke as I rub my hands over the soft material in the all-white interior of nearest black casket. I felt of the small pillow my head would be resting upon thinking good enough for my dead body.

Charley waited till I had examined the casket before asking, "I'm telling you William, I think this one to me is the best for the money at just $4695.00. We have others from forty-two hundred to ten thousand.

"It looks like a good one as any," I answered. "That is a lot of money, but it will be the last bed that I'll ever sleep upon. Might as well be a good one."

"You want to look at another," Charley asked pointing to the other six or seven caskets in the room.

"Ney," I answered, "I'll take your word that this casket here is the best for the money but personally wish I was having a Genghis Khan Burial."

"If you are satisfied, let us go into my office and fill a few forms," Charley said motioning for me to follow him.

As I took a seat across before his desk, Charley asked, "I was wondering, what is this Genghis Khan Burial you mention earlier. It just now caught on what you said. What is it, I'm curious?"

I joking, said, "You mean, you have never heard of the Genghis Khan Burial Method." "Nope," he answered.

I lean back in my chair and smiled as I said, "Well, what I heard and not going to say it is true, the Mongol Nation in China long, long time ago would place someone that had died on a cart which was being pulled by a donkey, cow or a goat and allow to roam free with the cart and body behind it. I'm not sure and could be way off, but I think it had a name like "Last Ride" or something like that. Anyway, they place the body upon the cart and the donkey was free to feed and travel the plains and where the body fell off the cart that where the body is buried. It was said a donkey who has been chosen to pull the "Last Ride Cart remains attach to the cart its whole life always remaining people death is coming to us all.

Charley, as I finish said, "I don't think I would do that, myself."

I leaned forward and picked up the brochure on the casket saying, "Charley, I would, for when I'm buried like that and grass cover's me and there no indication I'm buried there, I know for sure the only one that knows where I'm buried would be the Lord."

THE PONY TAIL THAT WON

"Hello Mom, I just had to call and tell you what happen last night at the dance." Lisa said and her Mom instantly could tell Lisa seem to be quite excited about something.

"Now clam down Lisa and speak clearly," her Mom asked while all the time thinking, "I just got to hear this. It ought to be a good one. The last time she calls this excited was when Taylor tripped and fell through the kitchen screen door."

As Lisa still seem to be gathering her thoughts, her Mom asked, "Dance, you telling me they are having dances here in Marshall," "Mom, it was not a club kind of dance, it was a dancing contest over at the Grand Opening of William's, the new dance hall that was built where the old action barn was located. It cost us $1000 dollars to enter the contest and William told us the money would help to get the dancehall going."

This is getting more interesting by the minute her Mom thought just before she asked, "Ok, I want to hear every detail and leave nothing out."

"I'll try not to Mom," Lisa stated before she said, "I think the real reason we won is what Taylor and Stefanie did to my hair when I was getting ready."

Her Mom broke in asking, "You telling me they cut your beautiful hair?"

"No Mom," Lisa answered and her Mom could hear a little frustration in her voice and a few giggles in the back ground.

"Well what happen," her Mom returned.

Lisa was silent for a second before she answered with, "You know how I like to wear my long hair braided in a ponytail. Often when I am preparing my hair, Stefanie would help me making sure I had no lose hairs. Well last night as I prepared my hair, I had her help me and check real good for

1

any lose hairs especially since I was going to be in a Dancing Contest and I wanted to look my best. Anyway as she finished, Taylor sneaked a bottle of some kind of washable glitter solution to her and unknowing to me, Stefanie covered the whole length of my pony tail with it and did not tell me what she had done. I knew something was up for I heard them giggle and it was not till Steven told me how beautiful I looked with the glitter in my Pony Tail did I find out. Then Steven told me my glittering Pony Tail would diffidently be the star of the dance floor for sure."

"Did you get mad," her Mom asked trying to visualizing the glitter in her Pony Tail.

"Not after what Steven said about me looking so beautiful with it. I gave Taylor and Stefanie a hard look while acting like that I had asked the children to do it not wanting to cause a yelling scene before we left the house. Besides I kind of like it, especial while dancing as I spun around, my pony tail would flash in the lighting. Steven said that it gave me a more graceful appearance as he spun me and diffidently added to my beautiful body. We were number eleven and was I ever surprised when William call out our number as the winner of the contest and as he handed us what we had won, William told us my flashing Pony Tail was one of the reasons we did for it added grace and beauty to our dancing making us stand out above all the other dancers."

"What did you win," her Mom asked thinking twenty dollars. "A 2014 Infiniti," Lisa answered.

"Yea right," her Mom answered adding, "I'll believe that when I see it."

Then her Mom heard nothing but laughter for a second before Lisa calm down enough to say, "Mom, come out the front door for me and your two wonderful Grandchildren are waiting outside to give you a ride in it and I want to show you my glittering Pony Tail that helped Steven and I win the Dance Contest."

THE BULL RING

When I was fifteen, Mother and Dad decided for reasons I will never know to send me off to Military School. I guess because of my wild running around I did. In many ways I'm sorry they did and in many ways I'm not. It placed my wondering mind in a more stable situation to learn. I think I graduated tenth my senior year and I still hardly cracked a book. Of course I did my usual trouble making or I really think I was tricked. I became a great Guide Arm Barer who was the guy that carried the flag in front of a Company of marching boys. Besides marking who the company was, it was the method in a parade for the company to perform a command together as they march passed the General such as the command, "Eyes Right."

Now my senior year I had become a Sergeant and could no longer carry the flag. Somehow I got myself into a card game and got busted claiming it was my card deck and such. If I think back, I think I was the only one got busted for that and I assure you it was not my cards or my game.

I really was glad in a way for I did not like being in charge of a group of boys anyway. Got me out of that for I just did not want to lead and I have never really wanted to. Some of the Guys did and made good ones. I guess I was and always will be a boy at heart to do my own thing. But there was an event at Allen Academy that I would not do and that was the Bull Ring.

It was simple enough. Just a caulk off twenty-foot circle of mud, where three boys from each company walk in and the last company's boy still in it at the end was the winner. If I was thrown in, I would have found a way to get pulled out quickly.

Now the boys that entered the Bull Ring were covered with grease and for days before the event the ground was water soak. A twenty-foot-wide caulk circle was place around the mud hole and if even a finger hit that

3

caulked line they were out of the battle. It began with the boys becoming a mass of bodies in the middle and of ring and there were those that wonder outside trying to pull one of the boys out of the pile to place a boy's foot over the caulk line. But the mud and grease made that almost impossible. I've seen boys pass out, yelling, fighting and even biting. It lasted for several hours and I remember the only reward a Company received was bragging rights.

I remember one big muscled up boy who was on the bottom of the piled picked the whole pile upped yelling. Sometimes boys from different companies would work together to get a big boy's foot or hand over the caulk line. There was much yelling and from those gathered around the caulk line especially when one boy was fighting not to be pulled out of the pile or across the caulk line.

I often wonder how many of those young men upon leaving the Academy, join the army and died in Vietnam. I hope myself not one of them.

NO TRUCK DID NOT STOPPED MOTHER

Daddy liked to get drunk and not always at home either. He sometimes would drive down to Ronnie's who always had moonshine hid out somewhere. Well one drinking night, I guess Daddy fell asleep or was just too drunk and wreaked the truck while coming home. He just left the truck in the ditch and staggered home and in the morning we found him sleeping on the couch out on the porch snoring away.

Later that day he and Grandpa took a couple plow horses and fetched the truck. It was all torn up on one side where he walked the ditch with it. As he walked into the house Daddy said, "I guess we either walk or stay at home for a while."

Truck or not that did not stopped Mother, if she wanted to go somewhere she walked down to the mailbox with us five kids and hitch a ride. For some reason it was mostly with Uncle Johnny. I think she knew what time he would be passing going to work or something. Not all the time. In fact, I think I rode in back of every truck in Searcy Country. Some had hay and it would get all in our hair and cloths and stay there all day until we got back home. If Mother wanted to travel somewhere she went rain or shine. It was mostly to town where we would stay there all day and Dale Horton at the Variety Store always gave us a ride back home with her few Groceries and us kids wore out and the twins asleep.

Now every Sunday morning, Mother had all of us put on our nice Sunday Meeting Dress. That is what she called it. Mine was full of ruffles and lace all over the shirt and I always hated to take it off when we got back home. I think Grandma made it. She would make us stand still while she measured us and every birthday we would get ourselves a new pretty dress.

Anyway one Sunday Morning, Mother had a time with us either fighting or crying. We still went and at the mail box got our usual ride with Dale Horton and his wife Emma and his four kids. He took it real easy going down that old dusty dirt road. After church that day and I still remember it clearly. When we got home Russell was missing. Mother went bananas asking us questions where we seen him last for

that Sunday Elaine, who usually watches after the twins, did not go with us for she was over at one of her girl friends.

Mother turned to Dale and wanted him to take them right back to church. While he was backing back into the drive way to do so, Ezra and Lou Horton came driving up with Russell in the back seat. I don't think I ever seem Mother as grateful as she was to them as Russell jumped out of their car running to catch upped with us as we heading for the house. After that she kept one eye on Russell at all times whenever we would catch a ride at the mailbox. She learned right then and there Russell was a wonderer and of course he never stopped his wondering even after he was grown.

Barbara then turned to me and said, "You know what, William. I wonder if today Mother could catch a ride at the mailbox with us five kids as she did back then. I wonder?"

THOSE DARN BOOKS

I was just sitting here thinking about me and how I lived my life and I guess I did what I had to do at the moment. One thing I never had was a simple stationary view of life and thinking back, it was the books that I love and I like to read as a child. Adventure novels, I would disappear into them for hours. It was an escape from how I was made to live. I can still remember the whippings I would get. Mother gets a belt and had me bend over the bed. Then she would start in on me taking all her frustrations out on me for doing something I absolutely don't remember what it was for. There could have been other reasons, I don't know and I will never know. Many a time I would go into my room afterwards and bang my head on the wall killing the pain that was in me. So I read any and everything that, for just a little while, I would escape my surroundings and that includes Westerns.

For all I know I needed the whippings. I was a wild child seeing just what I could get away with. Even now at sixty-six still have urge's even though I can now pay for it. I remember I found a check upon the ground as a freshman in collage right after I got out the Army at 23. I cash it, not that I needed the money of $23.75 but to see if I could.

This view I have and is still with me just had to come from reading those darn books.

I guess I try to keep the childhood way of life. For 12 years we go to school moving from one class to another doing as many as six subjects a day most of the time. Then all of a sudden we find ourselves forced to attend one class. It could be a well-paying job but it the same dam class day in and day out. It appears that most people like it that way. But not all and that includes me.

Sometimes I had a job so I could play at different adventures. I go to work which was in away adventure itself. Then off to do this or that when I was not working. One thing I loved was basketball and three times a week was a joy. I loved to travel to different courts around Houston. I was the only white guy there and the players respected my style of playing.

If something new came along that allow me to be adventurous I took it. Doing the same thing without an adventure in it always loses

my appeal and I'm quickly off to fine another. But now I guess I've having as much fun as I ever had. I write, I paint, I garden, I play games at the center and I have a good friend and lover. That is five subjects a week I'm doing and I'm telling you it all started when I began reading those darn books.

MY TWIN BROTHERS

My twin brothers, Russell and Reynolds, were identical twins. They were a wild pair when they were young boys and even wilder as young men. There was a difference between them Mother knew and us Girls knew also but the community around us did not. Russell at time would take Reynolds place and vice versa. Especially, if one of them they got themselves in trouble and that was mostly Russell. What also help they also talked like each other.

I remember one time Russell was arrested and instead of using his name he used Reynolds name. There he was in jail and Reynold had to use Russell's name to visit him. We all had to do that when we visited him.

There was another event with the law when they both got drunk and while Reynold was driving had an accident and were both arrested. The arresting officer did not who was driving and neither Reynolds nor Russell volunteered the information so he gave them both a ticket. Now Russell had been cut from hitting the windshield which did not come into play as they stood before the Judge. With the officer not knowing who drove the car and both of them looking identical the Judge could only dismiss the charges they had against them and set them free.

Now girl friends were another story between them. I remember Reynolds had a girlfriend name Susan and Russell call her upped and made a date with her. Took her out and who knows what and for as I know she never knew that Russell was not Reynold.

The only difference between them was their heath as Russell developed cancer later in life and finally during his last days, he lived with Mother. One of the things Russell like to do was grow vegetables and did it wherever he lived. He would sit at the picnic table in back of the house and watch over his garden. I remember Roy Ragland would come by to visit and every time he did, Russell would load him up with zucchini and some of the other vegetables he had grown. I remember one time Russell gave Roy so much zucchini Roy ended up giving most of it away but never did tell Russell.

I miss him for as the years went by, he still stayed wild and I had many of laughs watching him get out of trouble not only with the law but with many a girlfriend also.

Reynolds on the other hand has Grandchildren now and I'm sure his wild side still shows as he still likes to ride motorcycles with a few friends that in many ways were and are still as wild as he was.

Thinking back, I think their wild nature really came from Uncle Johnny. He started doing wild things with them when they were quit young. I remember they had a small wagon and Uncle Johnny pull them up the hill near the house and let them fly down the hill in it. Over and over he did that. But one day he got very mad at them and hung them upon the nails located in the wall around the pouch and left them. They stayed there for several hours and that was the last time Mother ever bought overalls for them.

They were wild alright but kind also and have looked after me when I had needs so many times I can't count them.

PHIL'S MERCURY

Phil wrecked his Blue Ford trying to drive to school when the road was real icy. He was able to trade it in for 54 Mercury that was pink on the bottom and white on the top. It ran and drove Ok but did not have a lot of power.

Now soon after Phil got the Mercury, he came by to pick Lorraine up for a date one weekend and Lorraine would not go with him unless our Cousin, Gary Horton and I went also. We quickly climb into the back seat and away to the Buffalo we went. As he dove, of course Lorraine move real close to him and soon after we arrived at Taylor Bend, him and Lorraine stroll off with Lorraine hanging all over him. Of course I quickly notice he had left the keys in the ignition.

I look at Gary and Gary look at me and soon we were heading back to town for I was thirsty for a Coke. Back in town there were two areas us kids hung out at and our stop was the Wick Snack. The Daisy Queen was for the Smart Elects and we stay away from it most of the time. Not always, for we would go by drive threw but we never went inside. Anyway, I guess we stayed longer than we thought and figured Phil would be mad at us. But when we returned, neither Phil nor Lorraine was mad at us only seen to be happy we returned. I still think he left the keys in the car for us to take it hoping we leave them alone.

Now Phil at this time live pass Leslie and that Mercury being a heavy car didn't have the power to climb Alberta Mountain unless he had a running start by running every stop sign in Leslie. After Phil drop us off back at home that day, he told us later when he got to Leslie and was just about to give that Mercury a run for the money when the Leslie cop stopped him. He was expecting a ticket but the cop instead told him his mom had called him and for him if he saw Phil, to stop him and tell him to get home.

I remember Phil came to visit and at this time Lorraine wanted to learn to drive and would Phil teach her. He said yes and of course I jump into the back seat. Phil fussed but gave in and away we went. I guess as Lorraine weaved all over the road it caught the attention of the local Sheriff and he pulled us over. He told Lorraine she was not doing a very good driving and looking at us three young teenagers

asked did anybody have a driver license. Phil answered he did. After he took over he drove out onto one of the dirt roads and let Lorraine drive. I begged and pleaded after Loraine became more comfortable behind the wheel to let me drive. Eventually he gave in only after Loraine asked him too.

The last I heard of Phil's Mercury was it broke down halfway up Alberta Mountain and left out in the field behind Phil's parent house. I'm not sure but I think it still out there.

MY FRIEND PAUL

Looking back to my child hood I can't help but remember Paul Skipper. He was a very smart and love to invent or experiment. He lived next door and he was my age. His older brother Carl was two years older than us who also lifted weights. Paul and I would wrestle him and he just throws us around like rag dolls.

Now their Father was a Chemical Engineer for Shell oil and I really do not know his influence over them, especially Paul. For as long as I lived next to them, I have never been in their house. Their Mother was German and no kids other than theirs were aloud in the house. Carl slept outside in the garage side room and that where we played many of game.

Paul in away was like me and maybe a lot of him rubbed off on me and I on him. I was always after some kind of work around the neighborhood to have an extra quarter. Paul did not but somehow was able to obtain a scooter to deliver newspapers after we moved away. Even though we had moved to Waller, Paul would come and stay and we would spend time together playing and doing things out at the Farm. One summer we redid all the fences around the Forty Acres. But, as things happen we moved into High School and I never saw Paul again. By then my world or playground was at Waller and we never went back to town.

What I really remember about Paul was the time we made balloons out of Dry Cleaning Bags and filled them with Hydrogen and set them loose. I believe we were about twelve or eleven and Paul had learned from his Father to create Hydrogen out of Water using Lye and Aluminum. It was simple enough to make. First you mixed a good solution of Lye into warm water. Throw in a ball of Aluminum Foil and the reaction generates very hot gases. We simply cover the reaction and using a vacuum cleaner hose which we ran through a container of ice water and slowly filled Dry

Cleaner Bags. Then we tied a post card with our name and address on it and let the Cleaner Bags fill with the Hydrogen Gas free. They caught the wind and were soon gone from sight. I don't remember exactly how many we did but it was at least five or six.

We did this in early summer and my Dad's ship was in dry dock down in Tampa Florida. So we left to stay there with him while they work on his Ship. While I was gone someone almost sixty miles north of Houston found or caught one of these Cleaner Bags that so happen worked for the local paper. They came to Paul's house to find out who had released the balloons. Of course I was gone and when the story came out in the newspaper I was not even mention.

I often think back to what if we had never moved to the country and continued to live on Amherst beside Paul. There would have been a big difference in my life. I might even have had a chance to enter their home. For I know Paul was always giving me a mental challenged and that ended when we no longer walked and played together. I guess I got this view point from him, "I know what I know and what I don't know I make up."

WE WERE MISCHIEVOUS

I have to admit us nor our cousins were really bad but there were times we were I assure you. I guess it was more mischievous than anything else and it was the adults of the family we seem to aim for as much as we aim for each other. Of course there were times we had to run, I assure you, for I know I had to run several times.

I remember the doctor gave Daddy a special test for diabetics because of his drinking to use to test his blood sugar where one would pee on the strip and if it turned Green your sugar was high. I remember Daddy called it his Diabetic tape. Well in our mischievous way we girls and I don't remember who, came up with the idea of using green coloring on the tape. Well Daddy was drunk when he saw how green the tape was, he cried.

Now us Girls love and had learn to leave blind Aunt Flossy alone but not Earl and my other cousins. If they were out playing and saw her heading for the outhouse, they would get her off the path and she would take her walking stick after them and hit them if she could. I know it hurt for it has gotten me several times. Once she was inside, they might hit upon the outside of the outhouse and diffidently hide when she came out yelling "If I catch you, you are going to get it" while swinging her staff around. The cousins just laughed.

That was not the only time the outhouse was use for mischief. I remember Russell was in the outhouse and him being small could not reach the lock and usually left the door open. Lorraine and I lock him in the outhouse and would only let him out if he could spell toilet. He tried but eventually Mama had to come and save the day as he cried so loud she heard him. Of course Mama fussed on us.

A SMALL COKE BOTTLE WAS BIG

During my early childhood years, we live in a two story white house that had four large columns station in front of the house. Around the house, Daddy planted a field of at least twenty Pecan Trees. I was free to wonder the yard and visit the chicken yard. We had a dog that lived outside. If you open the top floor windows, the Gulf breezed would blow through the house while on the ground level there were none.

Daddy had to return to sea and I remember while parked by his ship waiting for him, I noticed a man floating in the water below. I told Mother there a dead man in the water and she had the guard called the police. For many years after that, I thought when you die you turned black.

Living by the Galveston Bay, Mother and Daddy also loved to fish and crab. They often took us to a small bayou where they could fish and crab from the bank. I remember once when Daddy had caught a big blue crab and thrown it upon the bank, I took a small coke bottle tried to stop it from going back into the water. The darn thing reaches up and pinches me on the hand. I cried and held my hand out for them to look at. Yep, those were the days when I thought a small coke bottle was big.

MOMENTS LIKE THAT

When we moved to Waller TX, I was so out of place moving from a large city to the country. When I entered school I was met with a great hostility but on the school bus I met Milton Thomas that changed everything. He taught me to live and work around the community of farms in the area. At first we hung out at school until Dad let me drive the old 52 Dodge pickup. I would drive to Milton's house and during the summer find old jobs. Sometimes it was picking vegetables such as cucumbers or water melons.

But to me the best job was hauling hay. I remember stacking hay in a barn that was so hot inside we would have to hold our breath as we ran with a bail and stacked it in the barn. My arms would get all scratched up while hauling cane hay and try hard to keep the bail from coming apart with coastal hay. Peanut hay was the best. You could stack it ten high on the truck and get at lease fifty bails on the old Dodge Pickup. I remember one of the few times in my life I ever worked with Dad, beside doing chores, was his words as I showed off to him while loading bales of hay. He told me, "You must work like the black man. You must work the fields at a pace that want wear you out. That way when tomorrow comes to you are still able to work."

The best moment while working these odd jobs in the heat of summer was when a thunder shower would appear out of the north. There nothing like it as the air would change directions and the cool ozone filled air hits you filling you with its' energy. Before the rain wall hits, we would dive into the pickup or run like crazy to the house hoping the lighting does not strike us. Moments like that travels with you all the days of your life.

AMERICA HAS A CALLING

It was just before sunset and I was just finishing loading the car with my fishing gear and my ice chest full of the fish I had caught when down the sand came a stranger praying as he walked along the edge of the wave wash. I notice him a long way off and forgot about him and now thinking, "I waited too long."

As he came nearer, I calmly asked, "What you praying about and would you like a soda or a beer?"

He stopped and looked out into the Gulf and in the hesitation I had a chance to study him and his highly windblown hair sticking out from around his straw hat. He had a highly tan face, arms, and legs. He had on a bright white shirt with big blue dots loosely scattered upon it with matching shorts. And here I was thinking I had a very religious man here when he turned toward me and said, "A beer would be great."

I could not help myself and laughed as I reach into the ice chess, and pull two beers and held out one to him which he calmly took saying, "Thanks." Popped the top and took a big guzzle of the beer dwelling on the taste and his image to me was of one really enjoying how good the cold beer felt going down his throat.

"That is just what I needed," he said as he held out his hand toward me and added, "My name is, Rick Paine."

I took his hand and said, "Just call me William and do you need a ride are something."

"Oh no," Rick answered quickly, "I have an RV's coming for me now and if the mosquitoes get to bad, I run calling them to come get me. With the Sun setting I know those buggers be out soon so I've already called them."

After I took a drink of my beer, I asked, "What are you doing anyway

way out here in the middle of nowhere praying and what you praying for anyway?"

He took another swig of his beer before he answered and almost as an afterthought said, "I'm praying for America is what I'm doing. I'm running the complete outer border of America from California to Maine while praying America would not turn from her calling."

Now his words perked my interest, I asked, "What is America's calling?"

"That answer is simple if you know the Nature of Jesus," he answered noticing his transportation coming toward us on the payment. Finish off his beer and said, "America is the image of Jesus to the world and the countries that have chosen to follow her image has been set free."

"Well, she has not been perfect," I added.

He handed me the empty can saying, "Thanks, I got to go before those blood suckers get me."

Then as he left me he said, "I know she not perfect. That is why I'm praying as I'm walking around America's borders. That she will stay upon the path God has called."

As he left me at a run, I called out after him, "I hope so too."

LORRAINE'S AND HER SOAKIES

I never did like Soakies but my sister Lorraine sure did. I mean if she could, she would have one every morning ever sense she started to drink coffee. She would get a biscuit and after sweating her coffee with sugar and cream pour it onto the biscuit and munch away. Daddy sometimes join her and I guess that where she learned to fix them. But then she could learn it from almost anyone in the family. I remember going with Mom and Daddy on many of a breakfast gathering before Church at the Café and I'm sure almost all the men would order a biscuit and take their coffee and make Soakies. A few of the Aunts join them also.

I mean she like then so much sometimes Lorraine would get up in the middle of the night and if there was any good and dried out biscuits around grab the instant coffee and make a helping of Soakies. She loved them and I know Mother put on extra biscuits just for her Soakies and Daddy's also. I'm sure of it.

I remember one night she prepared a couple Soakies on the stove and before they were warm, she wondered back to her room and forgot about them. Well, in the early morning Mom entered the kitchen full of smoke. She found the biscuits burning and the coffee kettle empty. I assure you Lorraine did not do that again after all the fussing she got from both Mom and Dad. Especially Dad for she had gotten into his Nescafe Coffee and that was a big giant NO, NO.

I remember during all the yelling Lorraine said, "I know one thing when I get married, my husband going to like Soakies."

Anyway a few years later Lorraine married and the first morning I ever saw them together at breakfast, there they were, both making Soakies out of Mothers freshly baked biscuits. As I watch them fix their Soakies each adjusting to their own taste, I remembered back to Lorraine's words years earlier just who her husband would be and sure enough he was.

DADDY'S PIG SLOP

As Barbara waited at the domino table, WT Treat entered the room and seemed frustrated. Placed his coffee on the table and as he sat down across from Dempsey said, "I just bought a load of Pig Shorts and they have raise up the price again. If this keeps up I think I'll stop raising any kind of pig."

"What would you raise then? Hogs" Dempsey joked.

"Funny, Dempsey." WT answered. "I usually raise only a couple for us and the boys and I have been thinking I will just stop completely. I'm not young anymore and the boys never come by to help anymore. They are always too busy doing this and that. Shoot, it has been over a month sense I seen either of them are their kids."

Rex started to shuffle the dominoes when Barbara asked, "Is Pig Shorts the only thing you feed the pigs?"

WT answered, "Now I do."

"Did you ever make your own Pig Slop? Barbara asked as she turned over a 6/4 to determine who would down first.

"Sometimes," WT answered.

As Dempsey shuffled dominoes, Barbara said, "My Daddy always made his own type of slop."

Dempsey stopped his shuffling and asked, "His own pig slop?" Barbara answered, "He sure did. He always started with the dish water from the night before. He had us to put it in a 5 gallon bucket he had sitting by the back door. Then he added a bar of Mon's and Aunt Flosey's lye soap, potato peelings and any food we or the dogs would not eat. In the summer he added snap bean, over ripe tomatoes, corn cobs and anything else he could think of from the garden. Then he would add the pig shorts and you could hear those pigs a hollering as he carried that bucket out toward the pig stall."

WT Treat while drawing his dominoes said, "I have to admit, Barbara. I never did that. Corn Cobs were about all I added."

As Barbara placed the double five to start the play said, "Milking cows, raising pigs, raising chickens and raising kids Daddy did that for sure and not one time did we ever go hungry."

WT play the five blank and said, "I do believe you, Barbara. I do."

UNCLE JOHNNY'S HUGE HAT

Lorraine opened the screen door to let Doc out and said, "It getting time for me to go home and fix supper."

Barbara swatted and just missed one the flies Lorraine had let in and said, "Do you remember Uncle Johnny and his enormous hat he wore when he stop by this time of day when we were kids."

"Uncle Johnny," Lorraine said taking her eyes off of Doc and onto Barbara. "I sure do. He was a character, that for sure. Him and that huge hat he always wore. He would come walking up the road from his house down near Cottontail Hollow at least once or twice a week seeking something."

"I like him myself." Barbara said, "He made me laughed and show us games we could play.

"Do you remember when we tried to knock his hat off with rocks down at the creek crossing?" Lorraine asked. "I do and he would dodge the rocks yelling, "Is that the best you can do? Come on just try to knock my hat off. I double dare you. We just laughed."

Laughing, Barbara said, "He sometimes would play hide and seek with us. He would look for us with that huge hat of his flopping back and forth. It always gave me away because I could not help laughing at him. He was so funny."

Lorraine sat back down in her rocker and as she picked up the fly swatter said, "I never been to his house but I remember Mother saying he slept with chickens, dogs, cats and even had a goat in his house."

Barbara after taking a sip of her ice tea said, "Me either. But I do remembering him showing us how to swing on grapevines."

"I don't remember that." Lorraine said as she calmly swung at a fly that flew to close.

"I do." Barbara said. "He showed us which grapevine we could swing on and how and where to cut them for swinging. I remember you were not with us for that was the one and only time I went Grapevine Swinging I'm telling you. It was the last time."

Lorraine looked at smiling Barbara and knowing she shouldn't but asked, "Why was that?"

Barbara set her tea down and laughed as she said, "Over by the creek bank he took Rita and I and showed us how we could swing across the creek on grapevines. Well we did exactly as he told us and upped the tree we went with our vines. We settled somewhere on that tree and both of us just knew we could swing across the creek to the other side. Uncle Johnny and His huge hat smiling up at us from below telling us we could do just that just building our confidence up. Well we said, "One two three go" and off that tree we flew. We did not even get close to the other side and there we were hanging onto those grapevines over that cold creek water just a hollering. Uncle Johnny stood on that bank laughing at us with his huge hat bouncing up and down as he did. I never forget his words as he said, "Girls, you should have let go when you were over on the other side. Bye." Then he was gone leaving us a hanging over that cold creek water."

"Well what did you two do?" Lorraine said knowing good and well they ended up in the water.

Barbara stood to let Doc back onto the porch and as she did said, "We tried to swing ourselves to the bank but both of us eventually got tired of hanging on and into that cold water we went. I still think he did that on purpose because we tried to knock his huge hat off of him."

Lorraine laughed as she stood to leave. "You could be right there. Anyway, I got to go. Besides, I know for a fact that was not the last time you swung on Grapevines."

Barbara held the screen door open and said, "Well, almost last time."

"Yea, Right," Lorraine said as she left the porch with Doc just a barking following her out to her car.

NIXIE TRIXIE DIXIE BRIKIE

Elaine had a girlfriend just down the holler, our cousin Brenda. They would go to each other's house and play and during the summer sleep together. Of course I also played with them and of course the dogs got themselves comb and brushed and tied with colorful strings or whatever we could we find that could fit on their tail or around their necks.

Now Daddy had a squirrel dog name Nixie and down at Brenda's house they had one name Trixie. Brenda's Dad and Daddy during squirrel season would get Nixie and Trixie and away they would go into the woods somewhere and bring home a meal or two of fat squirrels with sweet potatoes.

Well just before school started in fall, Brenda started to add names to Trixie's name. She started simple, "Trixie Dixie," then move to Trixie Dixie Brikie and when Elaine was there they would play at adding names to Trixie's and of course Trixie seem to enjoy it.

Now when they were at Elaine's house, old Nixie name became long also and guess what happen. Those dogs answered to those long names. Now Mom and Dad did not think anything of it until Brenda's Dad and Daddy took Nixie and Trixie squirrel hunting.

It was one of those early cold spells in October. Them, with the two dogs barking out of the truck bed left the house for "Squirrel hill" as Daddy called it. When they got there and wondered into the woods they began to have a problem calling the dogs. They would not answer to just Nixie or Trixie.

But Daddy remembered the first three names Elaine and Brenda used and was able to work the dogs. But having to use three names resulted many a time having both dogs answering his command for the Nixie and

Trixie was always getting mixed while trying to add the other names the girls had use.

When Daddy arrived home, Elaine was on the porch begun hollering for Nixie with all the added names she had placed upon poor Nixie. Daddy climbed out of the truck knowing he had to stop her calling Nixie by so many names and as he places his Four/ten against the porch said, "Elaine, come here a minute will you."

"What is it Daddy?" Elaine said as she sat down beside the shotgun.

Daddy looked at his lovely daughter and gently said, "These adding names to Nixie's must stop."

Elaine look at Daddy and a tear could be seen forming at the edge of her eyes and asked, "Why do I have to stop, Daddy?"

Daddy looked down at the tears forming and suddenly realizes the dog was not his. Nixie was hers and for him to force her to stop would be like taking Nixie away from her.

"I'm sorry, Elaine." Daddy said, "I meant to say Nixie and I had a good time today and those added names really help us and I sure had a lot of fun using them. For while I was calling to Nixie or Trixie with the long names you and Brenda gave them, here came the squirrels trying to see who had such a long name and everyone of them are ready for our supper.

"Oh Daddy, they did not." Elaine answered shyly.

Suddenly Nixie came wagging upped wanting to be petted. Daddy smiled and was glad for the interruption as he left them and went on inside the house he stopped at the door and said, "Elaine, they did. They surely did."

INDIAN JOE

When I was a child my Grandfather was a great story teller. I don't remember any of them except the one about Old Indian Joe. He always began with, "Now when I was your age I live in a true Wild West Town name Hardrock. I mean it was so wild it took three days to pump sunshine in and right in the middle of town stood old man Daniel's Hardware store and lumber. I like him and he often gave me money to make a delivery to someone around town.

Well, he kept noticing a few things keep coming up short from his Lumber Yard so he bought himself the meanest watch dog he could fine. In the day time, it just lay around the Lumber Yard and anyone could pet it. But when Mr. Daniels let him loose in the yard at night it was another story and no longer were items coming up short after that.

Now Mr. Daniels had one fault. He liked to gamble and The Game of Poker was his first love. At least twice a month he would have a big game in one of the back rooms of the store and as they were playing the Guard Dog came up into their conversation.

Mr. Springer said, "Are you telling us no one can enter your Lumber Yard once you let Samson loose in it at night?"

Mr. Daniels smile as he said, "That is right and I'll bet anyone here a hundred dollars they can't find a man brave enough to enter the Yard after I let Samson loose at night. All they have to do to win the bet of hundred dollars is to him remove the marked two dollar bill I place within the collar round Samson's neck. In fact, I give whomever you choose a week, no two weeks to accomplish that."

Now Mr. Springer thought of his friend Indian Joe over at Wet Rock and said, "You have a bet Mr. Daniels."

Now Mr. Springer informed Indian Joe of the Bet and told him he could have Daniels hundred dollars if he could get the money from the Watch Dog.

Indian Joe just smile. The next night he came to the Lumber Yard around 10 o'clock and sat down cross legged beside the gate entrance and watch Samson pace eying him and every once in a while he could hear a faint growl warning him not to enter. After about an hour, Indian Joe lean back his head and howl for several minutes just like the Coyotes did in the wild. There was no response from Samson only a little more growling.

The next night Indian Joe came to the entrance a Howling. Samson response was still a faint growl. By the fourth night Samson had stopped his growling and there was a slight wag in his tail as Indian Joe appeared. On the seventh night, Samson started to howl with Indian Joe but still would grow at him if he started to open the gate.

Indian Joe started to stay longer in the night on the eighth night and would sit and call to Samson as well as howl. By now Samson no longer growl at all and would wag his tell when he saw Indian Joe coming and would howl like a coyote did when meeting a friend. Then on the eleventh night Indian Joe was able to open the gate and enter the Lumber Yard. Samson appeared a little nervous for without really knowing why, he had become a member of Indian Joe's Dog Pack when he joined him in his howling. Indian Joe in fact had become his fiend and true Master.

Indian Joe after entering lowered himself upon one knee howl and called for Samson whom quickly came to him wagging his tail. As Indian Joe removed the money, he smiled and petted him and he told him he was a good boy. Before standing, Indian Joe started a long coyote yell and was quickly joined by Samson. For several minutes with their mouths lifted into the air they continued to howl before Indian Joe stood to leave. But as he left through the open gate, Indian Joe just could not help smiling as Samson led the way.

AND WOODY HOLLERED, "PUSH"

As Barbara was clearing customer's dishes and wiping off the table, Charlie, who lived across the street from Woody and Elaine, entered. As he took a seat at the table near the door he said, "Morning Barbara, how you feeling this morning."

"Just fine Charlie," Barbara answered as she started to wipe down another table and as she was cleaning she said, "I'll get you a cup a coffee in a moment just as soon as I finish this table."

"Did you know Woody and Elaine traded their old car in and got themselves a new car?" Charlie asked as he started to reach into his pocket.

Barbara stopped her cleaning and looked at Charlie and said, "No, I didn't. When they do that?"

Charlie set a dime on the table as he said, "Yesterday and I think it is about time too. You knew Elaine had to push their 53 Chevy to get it started every morning. I've watched her push that car out on the road. Then she would get behind it and when Woody inside the car would holler, "Push," Elaine give it all she was worth. I mean this has been going on for over two months."

Barbara returned to cleaning the table and said, "Yea, I knew that and Elaine told me they were having a hard time saving enough money to get another. What happen? I know Woody didn't want to get a loan for one I'm sure of it. So, sometime must have happen?"

"I think it all started too happened last Friday morning." Charlie said.

Barbara finish cleaning then as she started to fetch Charlie his coffee she asked, "And what may that be?"

Charlie kind of laughed as he said, "Well last Friday, I heard a knock at my door and there was Elaine in her Pajama's all frustrated wanting to use the phone to call Woody. It appears after pushing the Chevy to get it started she could not get back into the house for all the doors were locked. I believe that was just the start of her problems. For Saturday, I saw them out working out in the garden and Woody got Elaine to pull the plow. I was amazed she could do that. But, it did not last long for Woody started to holler, "Gee and Haw," at her and she quit telling him she was no horse. Then yesterday it came to the head when she pushed and pushed that car and it would not start. I stood on the porch and just laughed as Elaine pushed that car up and down the street for at least an hour trying to get that car started and Woody inside hollering "Push." I guess that broke the camel's back and she ordered Woody to get them a new car for she was never going to push that car again."

Barbara sat Charlie's coffee down and as she picked upped the dime off the table asked, "If it didn't run, how they were they able to trade it in?"

"They pushed it." Charlie answered. "I mean they push it up to the top of the hill between us and town and at the top they coasted right down to the car lot. Traded it in and you would have never seen a happier individual then Elaine when they came back with that brand new white 65 Mustang she was driving."

Barbara left Charlie to put the dime in the cash register and said, "I bet Elaine is happy. I better call her up and see what happening. What do you think?"

"I guess you better," Charlie answered with a snicker. "That is if you can get her out from behind the steering wheel of that new Mustang you will."

NOT THE CHICKENS

When I was born, Daddy said, "If that another split tail she's not mine." I was the seventh girl born before Mama had a set of twin boys. We lived in a Share Cropper's house at the edge of a cotton field in east Arkansas. At picking time, all girls had to be out in the field picking cotton. About noon time, Mama would stroll out onto the field and come to me. You could tell she had just gotten out of bed for only the very front of her hair was fixed and her clothes were all wrinkled. She would say, "Now Honey, I just about got everything fixed now. Just go in and finish lunch for me." I would go home and there would be nothing.

Daddy liked to gamble and drink. We would raise pigs and chickens and just when they were laying good and the pigs was fat, Daddy would go to town and gamble and come home drunk. The next day here came many of the farmers and take a pig, the milk cow, but when someone came for the chickens, Mama Said, "Not the chickens. I'm going to bed and never get up." She didn't either until the chickens came home.

THE BASE BALL GAME

Lorraine handed Barbara her cup of hot coffee and as she sat down said, "Never guess who I saw yesterday?"

Barbara, as she took a drink of the hot coffee said, "Was he good looking?"

"It was our cousin Paulette and she looking as old as we are." Lorraine answered.

"Paulette," Barbara said, "Shoot, I've haven't thought of her or her sister Rita in a long time. When we were young we were always doing something together. I remember it was always Rita and I against you and Paulette in our games we played. We were always the Indians and you and Paulette the cowboys and I bet we died a hundred times."

Lorraine laughed as she said, "We sure did. Do you remember when you got Rita to walk out onto that shallow pond to ice-skate and she went through the ice."

"Well, she really did not really walk out onto that ice." Barbara said with a snicker, "I kind of push her out onto it and was she ever mad. I remember I ran home and hide in the closet under a blanket. We sure were wild bunch alright. Do you remember when we wanted to go somewhere once and we got Daddies' old truck and Rita drove and I shifted and you and Paulette road in the back. Did we ever get in trouble over doing that?"

"We sure did." Lorraine added. "I remember we would go Crawdad hunted, Snake hunting, and bug Mom and Dad for this or that. I wonder how they were ever able to put up with us. Do you remember the baseball game we played?"

"The baseball game, I sure do." Barbara said slowly. "We had set up a small baseball field in the back yard and I remember if one of us hit the ball over the fence we could run around and around the bases getting as many runs as we could before one of us could fetch the ball. Shoot, there were as many as four or five runs at times before the ball was fetched. If I remember right, Rita and I hit the ball over the fence most of the time."

Lorraine reached and petted Doc before she said, "I believe you did at that."

Barbara leaned back in her chair and took a drink of her coffee before she said, "Yea, we kind of drifted apart as we grew older. You and Paulette grew into a couple beautiful young women a lot better looking than Rita and I."

Lorraine laughed as she said, "But, look at me now. I do not have that long black hair and blue eyes now."

"That remains me." Barbara said. "What were you doing while you were within that crane that were working on the bridge near the house with your long black hair and blue eyes?"

Lorraine laughed as she sat her coffee cup down and said, "Just having fun like we always did when we were young. I remember I asked the operator if could I watch him work and he let me. Let me get right into that crane he did."

"You were in there a long time." Barbara said eyeing Lorraine seriously.

Lorraine looked down at Doc who wanted more petting thinking back to her time in the crane before she said, "He had cold cokes to drink and sense we never had any at home I kept talking him into letting me stay to drink a couple. I think I had four and only left after I had to pee"

"Yea right," Barbara snickered.

"I did," Lorraine answered as she continued to pet Doc not looking over at Barbara. Then she said, "To bad we grew up and got old."

"I guess so," Barbara added looking out into the yard still thinking back to her childhood not really believing Lorraine's story.

THE PROFESSOR'S INVENTION

Professor Wilson set the very old rusty sword upon the table before me saying, "Is this worth anything?"

I glanced over the rusty sword a second as the Professor walked over to fetch himself a cup of coffee. Then looked at him saying, "I believe it could deliver a great deal of money if I think this is what I think it is, "An old Spanish Sword."

"Good," he said and after a taste of his coffee Professor Wilson said, "This sword is my last auction piece I'll be bringing you. I'm going on eighty and my old body saying enough. I found this sword close to two miles out on Galveston beach and it almost killed me fetching it from the bottom for it was buried about three feet down in the sand."

I reach for my camera and place some our standard forms before him to fill out concerning the sword its beginning value and just had to asked, "Professor, now that you are quitting, I just got to know how you were able to fine such artifacts in the mud and sand. I've action whole Armors you discovered to a hand full of jewelry. There must be a secret here for I know there not a seeker out has ever discovered what you found over the years."

He just smiled at me saying, "I have at that. Haven't I?"

"What is your secret," I asked putting the sign documents in my briefcase.

"I use nature is all," he answered.

"Got to more than that then just nature," I asked leaning back in my chair looking upon Professor Wilson who I've learned was quite a brilliant inventor over the years for the Space Industry. But now he over eighty and I always secretly assume he was using some invention he created and kept for himself.

"I guess it is a little more than nature," he answered before taking another sip of hot coffee.

He gave me a serious look before saying, "I guess it want hurt if you knew."

I answered serious saying, "You know us Auctioneers are a close mouth bunch unless it will help in selling a product to make it more valuable."

Professor Wilson appear to look off in the distance before he said, "About thirty years ago I was place in charge of a project for developing a system that could analysis the reflection of radio waves as it travels into the Earth and determined all it properties. I formed a team and we after couple years had a functioning operation in theory only the computer systems were not fast enough to analysis the Data to bring forth a visual image or any information at all. So they scraped the project and I took what we have developed home until computers operation speed became capable to analysis the Data. I modified the system to work with a Laptop. It is simple enough. I just send a strong radio wave into the Earth and through trial and error I learn how to handle the Radio Waves Data. Using my programming basically I was able to remove the water, mud, and sand's radio reflections till only what I was left brought forth an image I could see like rings, swords, and lots of other types of material. You never know how many bottle caps or under the beach sand for example. That where I started. I mean I started walking the beach and I found rings, necklaces, bracelets and even guns which you know of one that brought us over ten thousand."

"I remember that one alright," I answered. "So, that how you find things you bring here using space industries developments."

"I guess you could say that," he answered. "Anyway, I name the thing "My Seeing Eyes" and the beach was just the beginning,"

Professor stopped a second as he took a drink of his coffee before continuing saying, "I then tested it upon the bay waters and discovered my radio wave went farther into the ground than expected. I'm talking close too fifty feet of water and two feet in the mud or sand bottom and in shallow water close to ten feet in the mud or sand. I mean I found lots of goodies way too deep for me to bring into the boat. I can only gather as long as it is not too deep in the sand or mud. This sword was in ten foot of water and close to three feet in the ground. It about did me in getting it out of the mud. There was more metal around the sword like an old suit of armor but I wanted the sword and it about did me in getting it too."

"You do have the movie documentation of where and how you dug it up," I asked handing him his copy of our agreement.

Professor Wilson set the coffee cup upon the desk as he took the documents saying, "That I did. You can find it in the envelope on the sword."

"Thanks," I answered as I watch him leave. I open the envelope to discover a video chip and wondering what I'll see as I plug it into my computer and call it up.

It began with an image of the sword outlined on the bottom, which I now knew was from his image device. The screen with blank for a second before it returned showing him starting to dig which cause a cloud of muddy water hiding the Professor. Slowly the tide pushed the muddy water away and we find Profess or Wilson holding his chest and I'm thinking heart attract. It appeared to take a deep breath of his air supply before bending over and reaching way into the hole he had dig and slowly brought out the Spanish Sword trying not to disturbed the mud. Then he calmly brought the sword toward the camera for a close up view of the sword follow by the location off the beach."

After I pulled the video chip from my computer, I marked it with a yellow M and as I place a C on the five copies, I got to wondering about Professor Wilson and his invention. I wonder if it will die with him or will he make sure it lives on. At lease it has made me quite a bit of money over the last few years. That it has.

ADAM'S SWIMMING HOLE

Lorraine swatted at one of the darn August flies as Barbara called them saying, "At lease it is cooler out here than in the house."

Barbara started to answer her when Alice and Raff drove up and as they exited the car she could see both of them were wearing a very colorful swimsuit and flip-flops. Raff followed slowly behind Alice as she said, "Hello Grandma, Aunt Barbara, we were going swimming and Raff here," pointing in the direction of Raff, "wants to go swimming in the coldest water around here. I told him you and Aunt Barbara would know. Do you know where the coldest swimming hole is?"

Lorraine looked over at Barbara who was swatting at the fly that came near her that Alice and Raff let in and asked, "Barbara, I believe on Big Creek has the coldest water. What do you think?"

"I have not thought about the Adam's Hole in a long time." Barbara answered.

Alice took a seat beside Lorraine and motion for Raff to sit saying, "Might as well sit down. They are about to tell us a story before they will ever tell us where this Adam's Hole is."

Lorraine laughed and said, "You learned haven't you." Then turning toward Barbara said, "Barbara, you went there more then I. Tell them about Adam's Swimming Hole over on Big Creek."

Barbara rocked back and forth looking off thinking before she said, "Over on Big Creek where Long Creek flows into it is the clearest and coldest water your will fine coming right out of a big spring. There is only one place deep enough to swim and it was call "Adam's hole." It has everything you would want it a swimming hole. It has a sandy beach on one side and a big buff where one could jump into the hole from the other."

Lorraine, as she shooed a fly away said, "Aunt Barbara is telling you the truth. It had the clearest and coldest water you will fine but you cannot drive to it, you had to walk."

Then looking at Barbara asked, "Isn't that right, Barbara."

Barbara finally got that fly and smiled as she answered saying, "That is right, Lois. I'm pretty sure it was about half a mile of walking to get to it and we teenagers followed a deer trail right to it. I guess they still go to it."

Raff, who was standing a little behind Alice suddenly spoke as he placed his hands upon Alice's shoulders and asked, "You said there was a bluff there. Can you jump off it into the water off it?"

Barbara stopped her rocking and laughing said, "You sure can but you got to be careful if you do. I still remember the first time Phil Read jump off it and came real close to hurting himself. I mean close. You see Raff, at the top of the bluff is an old oak tree with the number fifteen carved into it and that is where you are suppose jump off. Any place else you might land on rocks. Anyway, after Phil and I had climbed the bluff to that tree, Phil began to hound me to jump. Him not knowing that I had already done it many times. I think I was laughing when I did jump knowing I surprise him and I did remember you had to hold your arms above your head to keep from stinging your arms and hands when you hit the water. After I swam to the beach and yelled for him to jump. Of course I tease him calling chicken and such. Well he took a few steps backwards and at a run, off that Buff he came which was a big "No, No." Well Phil landed right at the edge of the deep hole just a few feet from being really hurt but still the water was pretty shallow. He said he was ok but there for a second I thought he broke every bone in his body."

Lorraine did not stop her rocking as she added saying, "Barbara is right. If you do fine Adam's Hole, you better be careful jumping off that bluff. Anyway, I also believe if we were to tell you how to get there we would get you lost. Why don't you stop by the Library? I believe they have a good map that would show you where it is at. That is if you want to swim in the coldest water in the county."

Alice turned and grabbing Raff by the hand said, "Come on Raff, let's go fine where this Adam's hole is."

Lorraine and Barbara watch them leave before Barbara said, "I bet it is filled in by now?"

"Could be," Lorraine added just before she popped one of them darn August Flies that Raff and Alice had let in as they left the screen porch.

IN THE WATER BUCK NAKED

Swimming was something I have always enjoyed and I guess most young boys and girls have the same opinion. Diving into the water, splashing your friends, and racing from one side of the swimming pool to the other was always fun. I guess I started to learn how to swim before I even started first grade. We live in a housing division called South Side and located in the center of the small community was the local swimming pool and there I was call a Tadpole, then a minnow, a trout and then a shark. By the time I was thirteen I had my Junior Life Saving License. Then we move to the country.

My swimming did not stop. I had a friend name Milton Thomas and often in the summer after hauling hay we hit the local Pond and go for a swim. Having no swim trunks did not stop us and there we were playing in the water buck naked. I remember one pond was a new pond and the water was shallow only about waist deep. We place a barrel in it and we would battle to be on top of it for an hour are more.

I remember one very large lake lined with willow trees and we would climb the trees and dive into the water. What I remember about the water was it was hard to stay afloat and the water had an almost a white appearance to it. But that did not stop us from diving off the willows.

Of course I grew up and swimming the ponds and such ended as I went off to war and schooling. But the heart of my short story and I guess I will one I will never forget was the day I ran through a rain storm buck naked. I was alone at home and one of those good summer storms came. It was one of them that had no lighting but a real heavy downpour. I watch the heavy rain and just could not help myself. I stripe and ran around the yard in the downpour buck naked. Those very large rain drops hitting me as I wave my arms and turned round and round letting the rain wash me. I guess God wanted to baptize me and what better way than to have me run around naked in a good downpour saying, "I the Father baptize thee in my son's name for the remission of sins from this day forward."

AFTER THE WEDDING MARCH ALLY

The crowd roared as Lisa held her arms up waving and showing herself off before taking her position before the array of targets. She slowly shut out the noise of the crowd yelling out for her to win or for her to lose. This was her only time she was ever to compete in a Hair Wiping Contest and she was thinking and hoping that all the practice at wiping her hair into targets at home was going to come into play ahead of her. I mean she has chase Taylor and Stefanie around many of time popping them in the butt and they soon learned it hurt and whatever they were doing that was wrong they quickly stopped. Now all that practice will come into play as she performed her only attempt at hitting all targets before the time of 79 seconds runs out.

She took eyes off the twenty targets and again lifted hands into the air waving at the crowd which answered and roared even louder. After several turn a round's of waving, she again focused upon the targets moving her head and shapely body preparing her for the target run. Her very beautiful hair shining brightly against the all-white wedding outfit with all its fancy white lace which moved with her but was specially design not to interfere with her hair wiping into the two lines of targets ahead God had named "After the Wedding March Ally" and smile to herself as she watched Steven suddenly show himself at the far end of the targets and was he ever dressed in the best bright red suit with white outlines she ever seen him in. Then as he stopped to face her, his reached out with his left hand toward her and in her mind it was the image of pure love.

Slowly the crowd around her became quiet and looking up, the thousands of Angels were gone. She was alone facing the Targets and her handsome Steven waiting at the end. Each target was important to her and each journey was with her love. She closed her eyes reaching out for the strength and wisdom to hit each target not just the edge of but right smack in the middle.

Then she bowed her head as God's voice come saying, "Lisa my child. I will always be with you and help you to hit each target right smack in the middle."

When she opened her eyes, the starting bell ran out and as the time ticked, her hair song out love right smack into the middle of each target she came to. Soon it was like rifle shots which ended as Lisa collapse into the waiting arms of her Steven having the image of her Savior behind him.

Steven, after giving her a kiss of a life time, asked, "Did you get them all?"

"Sorry dear I did not," Lisa said with a smile. "I diffidently miss the one said we would work in a garden together."

"Oh," he answered, "And I guess there were others."

Lisa answer was only a smile.

IT'S ALL IN THE QUEEN

Living down the road half mile or so lived old man Mr. Jean and as a boy, I would mow his yard and get myself two bucks off of him. He was eighty-one and must have been a big strong man when he was young. I still could see the strength in his body and him being over eighty. He also was a fairly smart man and told me many stories of his life. He also gave out wisdom and it was always in story form. That is where "It's all in the Queen" came from and what he taught me from it.

Only thing he raised beside cats was Honey Bees and he had several Honey Bee Hives in an area I felt was way off limits to me located along a fence row just pass the gate leading out into the pasture. The story of the Queen is still with me and still do not know if it was the truth or some story he just made up.

Now Honey Bees have always been around and even as a very young boy I was never scared of them. I do not remember who, but someone showed me how to catch a Honey Bee and it would not sting as long as you left a clear hole for it to escape. I guess I was pretty shaky the first time but it got so I would for over an hour place myself beside a large clover patch in full bloom and cuff my hands on one after another and never did get stung. I always thought they gave me a good cussing before they flew off thou.

When I rode up with my bicycle to see if I could do his yard, I could see several Jars of honey on the porch table and sitting behind the table in the shade was Mr. Jean with that big smile of his as I dropped my bike on the ground. If fact, he always gave me a big smile when I would stop by.

I, before climbing the three steps to the porch, asked, "Came to see if your lawn needed mowing, Mr. Jean."

Before he answered, I quickly glance around to what I needed to do to get the lawn back in good shape for it has been almost three weeks since I last mowed it and was now a little bit overgrown.

Mr. Jean motion for me to come and join him before he said, "You know you can come over and mow anytime you think the lawn needs mowing and I will pay you the two bucks we agreed on."

I thought of sitting in one of the lounge chairs across the porch as Mr. Jean added, "Bill, why don't you take a jar of Honey home to your mom and if you are going to mow the lawn, you better be careful over on the right back corner. There a bee swarm and they piled up in that big willow."

"They are?" I said and from deep inside of me I was getting this I got to see this feeling.

"I wouldn't get to close to the Bees if I were you." Mr. Jean quickly answered already reading my mind.

"But," I asked.

"There no but to it," Mr. Jean said looking at me for a second. I could see he had his thinking face on before he said, "Do you know why they swam, Bill?"

"Sure," I quickly answered, "To keep the queen safe while other workers are out looking for a new home."

"In a way you are right." Mr. Jean answered, "But the main reason is for the worker Bee's to swarm is to obtain the scent of the Queen. It is by her scent upon them that marks the bees that can enter the hive. But the same scent also calls for the Drones to mate. But to get there the Drone must enter the swarming bees, and battle their way to the Queen. Thus, only the strong make it which assures the colony of good strong workers."

As Mr. Jean finish, he took a drink of his ice tea, and I asked, "I thought the Queen was mated first before they swam and now you tell me that is not true?"

"They do mate but not for the reason you think." Mr. Jean answered, "It is to open the scent pouch before she leaves the bee hive and it is said she always kills the Drone that did it. If her scent pouch was too opened within the Bee Hive all hell would break loose. But once she outside Drones attack her and one of them opens her scent pouch. The scent then scatters out from her bringing in all the workers marked by her as she made her way out of the Bee Hive Colony and slowly begin to swarm around her receiving a good dose of her scent. While the scent is marking them it is also calling for the Drones and in her scent the drones could be from any Bee Hive around."

"Very interesting, Mr. Jean," I said as step toward the edge of the porch. "I'll be careful and leave that corner alone I assure you."

I quietly jumped off the porch and as I took hold of my bike I heard Mr. Jean add, "There is a theory that the Queen had already chosen the Drone and it is the only one they will let through to her. I personally feel it was the Drone that broke her scent pouch."

"That is nice," I replied as I pushed down on the bike petal to leave and added, "Sorry Mr. Jean, I would chat but need to mow before it gets too hot."

Suddenly from behind me came, "Remember stay away from the bees." Mr. Jean called out as I wheel around the corner of the house. But as I flew toward the barn for his mower I was thinking, "I may be dumb but I'm not stupid."

WILLIAM'S EYES

"Peekaboo, you want out," Barbara said as she slowly walked to the screen door and all the while Peekaboo was doing his little turn around on two feet. But Barbara was thinking, "I bet I let in twenty flies."

Lorraine and Elaine just laughed as Peekaboo was quickly followed by Princess and Boldee and Barbara all the while trying to keep the flies from coming in as they exited.

Barbara turned and was relieve to see only ten flies had entered said, "At lease swatting flies keep us entertained."

"It will at that," Lorraine said as she picked up the fly swatter and quickly swatted a fly that came near her.

Elaine, after taking a drink of her wine asked, "Barbara, where is William."

Barbara regained her seat and said, "I gone to play dominoes over at Dempsey's place by the Berry Shed." Then as she picked her glass of wine from the table beside her said, "Do you know how you can tell when William is about to cheat."

Both Lorraine and Elaine could not help themselves as both smile and Elaine laughed as Lorraine said, "William cheats?"

Barbara just smile as she took a drink of her wine letting the question sink in their being when Elaine finely asked, "OK Barbara, tell me how can you tell he is cheating?"

"His eyes change colors. It is a dead giveaway," she answered which only brought more laughter among the three sisters.

As they returned too drinking their wine Barbara said, "His eyes are normally green until he gets carried away doing something he is not supposed to do. They then change to blue. You can see the change through the Bi-Focal's of his glasses."

Elaine quickly swatted a fly that wondered near her and almost laughed as she asked, "What else about William we don't already know?"

After taking another sip of her wine she said "He does not hear a thing I say. I have to repeat myself several times before he'll hear me and he is also a big blabber mouth."

Again the sisters laughed and as they settle down Lorraine asked, "I guess you got that off your chest. What did he do today?"

"Dance with that MaryAnn." Barbara said with a little heat in her voice.

Elaine and Lorraine all they could do was laughed almost spilling their wine.

"I told him so too." Barbara continued. "I told him I can tell where his mind is by just looking into his eyes."

'Did he believe you," Elaine asked.

"Nope," Barbara answered, "He didn't even hear a word I said for I could see his blue eyes were telling me his mind was still on that Maryann."

BLACKMAN SCARE

Barbara set the glass of green tea on the small table beside Elaine asking, "What brings you to Marshall?"

"Woody getting stuff to fix all the water leaks," she answered. "Water leaks," Barbara question as she sat down grabbing the fly swatter.

"Pass me that other fly swatter, Elaine asked and as she took it from Barbara she said, "I catch them if they come my way and you catch them if they come yours."

"Sounds good to me," Barbara answered just missing a fly before she asked, "Well, what happen that Woody out fixing leaks,"

Elaine popped the fly Barbara missed before she said, "You know we put a new floor in the house last year preparing it to move in this summer. Well, I noticed areas of the floor was buckling and Woody checked and he found out the freezing weather of last winter froze the waters pipes up under the house and there no telling how many leaks there are down there either. Woody right now is morning and groaning so I'm staying out of his way."

"I would too," Barbara answered taking a drink of her tea along with Elaine and as she popped a fly that landed close enough, Barbara said, "Elaine, I been thinking about the time we hide the first time we ever saw a Blackman."

"Oh, I remember that," Elaine answered. "Were we ever scared?" "Were we ever," Barbara added before saying, "That was when they were running the water lines and there was several Blackman working the equipment that summer and we were so scared we hide in the closet."

"We sure did," Elaine laughed.

Barbara ignored her laughter saying, "What has got me, I remember hiding and being scared but I cannot remember why we were scared."

"I do," Elaine said while settling down. "We thought they were going to steal us if they saw us."

"Oh yea," Barbara answered happily. "I remember now. I thought they were going to get us and carry us away if they saw us. So we hide."

"We were so young," Elaine laughed. "I wonder who gave us that idea that those Blackman would steal us if they saw us."

There was silence a second before almost as one they said,

"Mother."

FISH ARE PICKY EATERS TOO

Grandpa Horton watch Billy and Wesley leaned their poles against the Red Barn. They both seemed to be very frustrated and as he watched, he laughed to himself as Billy placed the box of worms in the shade. Then under his breath, Grandpa said, "The Fish didn't like their worms."

Then as Billy and Wesley entered screen porch letting the screen door slam behind them, Billy said, "No fish supper tonight. Neither Wesley or I even got a nibble for over an hour."

"Yea," little Wesley sputtered out as he opened the cooler for a soda. "I mean we fished every good spot there is on your pond and nothing."

"Yea," Billy added just before he took the soda Wesley held out, "Nothing."

Grandpa looked upon his young great grandsons and laughed at their love of hunting the wild being only around seven but a hunter has to have patience and it was obvious these two did not have any. But Wesley to him looked to have the most promise of two. He could see it in his eyes."

"Grandpa," Wesley said breaking Grandpa's wondering mind which allowed him to say, "What the matter boys. Fish not biting your worms?"

"Not even a nibble," Billy answered with Wesley agreeing.

Grandpa stopped his rocking saying, "Would you like for me to tell you why and I'll do it in a way your minds can understand."

"Oh Grandpa," Billy answered.

Grandpa quit his rocking again but this time he leaned forward in the rocked before calmly saying, "Now you know living here with us is Peekaboo and Princes and you know how picky those two dogs are when it comes feeding time, do you not? That one day they like one kind a food and the next want eat it and I must throw it away."

"I know that," Wesley answered with Billy agreeing.

Grandpa check to if they were still listening before saying, "Now listen closely and your grasp one of the secrets about fishing. Now I know you already know it is best when fishing Grandpa's pond, you need to sneak up to the pond and had to be real quiet or the fish hear

you coming and want come near your baited hook. But fish in Grandpa's pond are also very picky eaters just like Peekaboo and Princes. If there are a lot of grasshoppers around, what do you think the fish might be eating that interest them more than that old worm there hanging off your hook?"

Wesley caught on quickly answering, "Grasshoppers."

"That is right, Wesley," Grandpa answered while leaning back into his rocker. "But it could be butterflies, June bugs, crickets..." But his words seem to fall on deaf ears as both Billy and Wesley left the porch at a run letting the screen door slam behind them heading for their fishing poles.

Grandpa Horton took a sip of his hot coffee while he moved back into his rocker saying under his breath, "That worked better than I thought. That should keep them busy all day chasing bugs and stay out of my hair."

"I heard that," Barbara yelled from the kitchen followed by lots of laughter.

HANAHAHA AND I AND BOWLING

After Vietnam, Frank, John and I began installing cables and power to Radio Equipment around the bases overseas, Specialist Five Hanahaha was one of the advisors or instructors we had when we went to Turkey to learn as you do kind of teaching.

Now running cable, we talked, and Hanahaha never stopped talking about bowling and bragging most of the time of him winning games when he should have lost and about those he slaughtered. It was alright the first week he talked about his bowling but the second week came. Now he was beginning to repeat himself for the hundredth time and I for some reason, I spoke up and challenged him to a Bowling match.

He quickly humble himself and we discuss the issue with Frank and John putting their quarter worth in also and the outcome in which we all agreed that Hanahaha never again talk about him and his bowling. He was a sport and agreed. In fact, it was kind of funny and we all laughed. I like Hanahaha and I'm sure he thought I was crazy for taking him own at his game.

That night, after eating I have no idea what, we met in the bowling alley there on the base. The walk there appears to have warm me up and I think help my bowling for did I ever bowl as both Frank and John was given me the "Go get him speech."

But Hanahaha gave no indication that everybody was against him as he picks his bowling ball upped to start the game. Before he turned away to concentration on the bowling lane, he gave us a smile and I knew the two black strip pins in the strike zone was his aim. Position his ball and in a fluid motion he sent that bowling ball right into that strike zone and I watch him stare with mouth open at a nice set of split pins was left which only a little luck able to knock both of them down for a spare.

I took my turned and I was quite surprise to receive a Strike my first throw and I'm telling you that is how it went the whole game. I'm getting strikes or spares and Hanahaha getting splits and spares and all Hanahaha could do was laugh with us as the final score was 230 to 140.

I have to admit that Specialist Hanahaha was a good sport and took our ribbing we gave him as grain of salt. At least it shut him up about him and his bowling. Still, we went bowling several times together before we left Turkey and I do admit he was a good bowler. It just was not there on the day he had to prove himself to us three GI's.

KING WESLEY

Now I have been a Bible pusher for the Holly Roller Church over on Heaven's Door Avenue for close to twenty years and I've knock on doors all around Little Rock. Made many trips out into the wild areas of the Ozarks and Yesterday, Frank and I made a trip around Rainbow near the head waters of the river flowing through Clinton. Little Red River I think what it is called. Anyway, we came across the strangest group of people I ever met. Really I did.

Frank drove his truck and we split the gas and with our map in hand out into the country we went. We stopped at several houses and talk about our Lord and gave them one of our Bibles and everybody told us to stay away from crossing the Iron Bridge. I asked why of course and they answered it's the King Wesley's Clan is all I got. I dug but they were mum on telling anything else.

Now curiosity after about the fifth house got both of us and it was not long till we found the Iron Bridge and across it we flew both thinking we might have a good place to hand out a lot of Bibles. We followed the Dirt road, cross a low water bridge and up the other side came across a well-organized group of parked cars and there across a large field was a path leading straight to a large two story white house with four large pillars across its front and on each side of the well-kept driveway were many pathways leading out to many House Trailers of all kinds on cinderblocks scattered among many Spring Gardens that was across the pasture with a nice well-kept walkways among the Trailers which were outlined with many colorful Spring Flowers. We stood with our mouths open at the view for it was so peaceful.

Frank parked the Truck and we both grabbed a bag full of Bibles and had just started walking up to the well-kept driveway leading to the house when we were greeted what must have been a guard dressed in a T-shirt and shorts stopped us saying, "Welcome to King Wesley's Kingdom, my name is Peter and may I ask, "are you seeking the King?"

Frank and I looked at each other and with our best smile said, "Sure."

He smiles and he walked over to a gong hanging from a tree and banged it five times. Each bong echoed among the trees after each hit. Slowly from the among the many trailers families began to gathered along the well-kept driveway and they all seem to be very excited and the children fought over a position beside their parents. Their dress is what you see anywhere and a hush filled the air as the two massive doors of the house open and out walked a well-built man I would call a woodsman from the looks of him with his long bread, longhair and dress in camouflage pants and shirt and was just darning his jungle hat as he walked down the massive steps follow by a mix breed dog wagging its tail.

As he entered the line of followers, the families and friends bowed down before him and King Wesley at times would say something to the man or women bowing before him. As we watched those before him bowed and those he passed appear to rejoice that he had even spoke to them, I looked at Frank and I could tell he was wondering the same thing, should we bow to him also. But as he stepped pass the last person to bow and calling his dog saying "Come here "Chicken" he asked, "You Gonged."

Frank and I I told him what we would like to do and he answered, "I'm sorry I cannot let you into my Kingdom. Give the Bibles to Peter, who will give them to Paul, who will give them to Matthew, who will give them to John who will pass them out to those that asked for one."

Without another word he turned and left us with Frank and I handed to the rising Peter our Bibles with me ready to run as I notice the families repeated their bowing as the King returned to his Mansion.

We flew to the Truck and Frank was spinning tires as we left.

Frank and I talked on the way home and I'll be darn that after Frank dropped me off at the church went home and he talked to Ellen and the kids and is now joining King Wesley's Clan.

Anyway, I just stop by to say goodbye. Barbara waiting in the car with our clothes and we're supposed to meet Frank at the iron bridge at two. Bye

THE TWISTER

2 liter soda pop bottles with caps
Drill
Silicone caulking
Duct tape
Food coloring or plastic confetti

1. Drill a half inch into the centers of the two bottle caps.
2. Use the caulking to seal the tops of the two caps together without blocking the holes. Allow to dry.
3. Wrap the outsides of the two caps with a strip of duct tape to secure them together.
4. Put the double cap on one the soda pop bottles.
5. Pour water into the other bottle until it is three quarters full. Add confetti or food coloring if desired.
6. Screw the bottle with the double cap onto the bottle filled with water.
7. Grab the cap area or the center of the bottles with one hand, and the bottom of the upright bottle with the other hand. Flip the assembly so that it is upside down. Shake the bottles in a few rapid circles.
8. Observe the spiraling vortex as the water drains from the upper bottle into the lower one. Note how the simulation resembles rain enclosing a tornado's vortex, a phenomenon that gives the tornado its force and destructiveness.

THE GREAT FLY ATTACK

Lorraine took a drink of her ice tea and shooed a fly off the table before she said, "Seeing all these flies, reminds of The Great Fly Attack we had in the late fifties. I think it was in 1960 or 1959. Surely you remember that don't you, Barbara?"

Little Alice was playing with Doc who had its mouth open ready to play bite her hand when she quickly pulled her hand away and asked, "What do you mean Great Fly Attack?"

Barbara answered her and said, "See these flies around us. They have been around as long as I can remember bugging the heck out of us. Well just imaging there or thousands."

"Aw, you are joking right, thousands?" Alice proclaimed as she pushed Doc away who left her flying after a squirrel he saw.

Lorraine stopped her rocking a second and looked closely at Alice and said, "Aunt Barbara is right. We are talking thousands."

Alice's curiosity was peaking and she had to hear this story about these thousand flies so she said, "Grandma, you just got to tell me this story about these flies, a thousand of them you said."

Lorraine lead back in her rocker and took a drink of her tea before she said, "We have had flies every summer and most of the time it is just like now, just enough to bugged us. Well our Mother got to fussing on Daddy how the screen doors needing fixing. They were letting flies get into the house. You remember Barbara what happen when Daddy took those screen doors off don't you?"

"I sure do." Barbara answered. "Alice, those flies must have smelled Mother's cooking and she had gone to take Daddy a hot cup of his Nescafe coffee and while she was gone with no screen door here they come. We were all swatting flies and the more we swat the greater number there was."

"There must have been a thousand for sure." Lorraine added. "Well Mother came back and saw all the flies flying around the house called for Daddy to get those screen doors back on. He replaced them just a fussing until he saw all the flies in the house. You know what he did. He left laughing telling Mother you are on your own, and he went fishing."

Barbara after setting her ice tea on the table said, "I remember Mother was mad and just did not know what to do but good old blind Aunt Flosey save the situation didn't she when she said, "If everyone would get a towel you should be able to shoo them right out of the house." I pretty sure she was the one that came upped with the idea?"

"I believe so, "Lorraine answered Barbara before she looked down at Alice and said, "What we did to removed them was Mother align us in a row across a room and we began swatting at those flies driving them out of that room. We then move to another room and did the same and then to another and there must have been at lease a hundred of them in each room and when we got into the kitchen there was way over a thousand flies. We lined upped again and with the back screen door open we drove the flies toward the door and they were like a cloud in front of us."

"That is right." Barbara said. "They were like a cloud and not many of the flies for some reason separated from the cloud and it appeared we got most of them out the door the first pass. When we did we saw the reason there was so many flies for coming across Canon Mountain was a good summer thunderstorm."

"Yea," Lorraine added, "These thunderstorms sure do move the flies around and that day it move a thousand flies right into our home."

OUT SWAM THE SNAKE

LB looked across at Barbara, smiled as he said, "We only like ten to win," just before he calmly placed the double five upon the table. "Well, we only like ten," Wilber said as he placed the five blank and straighten the dominoes out.

Barbara slowly placed the double blank down and said, "We won."

After Wilber turn his dominoes over, he reached and flipped over the two played dominoes and said, "I saw two big black snakes upon the road this morning. I've been wondering Barbara. Have you ever been chased by a snake?"

LB started to stir the dominoes and asked, "Why you want to know that?"

Wilber answered, "Just wondering is all."

LB started to stir the dominoes as William said, "You all got lucky that game. It will be a different story this time."

The four of them drew and as Wilber placed the double six to start the hand he repeated his question, "Barbara, have you ever been chase by a snake?"

But as Barbara played the six/three and counted, she strongly said, "Yes I have."

"Really," Wilber and the others around the table laughed.

Barbara smiled as she said, "Really I did. When I was a child, Mother took me and my two sisters down to the Bear Creek to let us play in the water in late summer. In my play I wondered across the creek toward some rocks I saw on the other side and out from behind them came a snake. I turned and swam and splash my way like crazy back to the others and that darn snake was right behind me. When I was safe near Mother my heart was beating real hard and I believe I was breathing hard too. That snake really scared me and I refuse to go back into the water."

LB calmly said, "I think I would have been scared also."

"Not me," answered Wilber. "I would have been chasing after that snake."

Barbara looked at Wilber and asked, "Was that before or after you scream "That snake bit me?"

BARBARA AND MILKING COWS

Dakota drop her books and jacket on the couch as she entered before heading for the Computer and caught Barbara telling William, "We had two cows that were so tame we could ride them anytime we wanted too while milking. Shoot I've sat on Terni or Elsie when they let me many a time in the pecking order line and rode them all the way into the Milking barn. What so sad Terni died giving birth to a calf that was coming out wrong? Daddy would not let us go to the barn that day."

William, coffee cup in hand asked, "Just two?"

"Yea, just two and we love them," Barbara answered. "The others were to wild and mean. There were several we had to put kickers on before we could even wash their utter. We did ride on a cow name

Doll and I remember there were six of us sitting on her back one time." Dakota quickly join end in the conversation by asking, "Did you hand milk any of them?"

"There were several we had to do that alright." Barbara answered. "There was Old Red who was always the first into the barn. Daddy had to milk her by hand for any of the milking machines gave her Mastitis. I remember we got in trouble being in a rush one day put the Milking Machine on her and she came down with it and was Daddy ever mad at us. We also hand milk those with calf. I mean the calf would be sucking two tits and we would be milking the other two there in the barn."

Dakota sat down upon the couch beside her stuff and asked, "What did you feed them and what did you do with the Milk when you were done milking?"

"We feed them grain and hay mostly," Barbara answered while lighting the end of a cigarette. "In fact I think we had more than one hay fight in which we had to clean the hay off of us before we went to school. We always started milking at six in the morning and when we were done we had to carry the milk to the house to be chilled. It was there at the porch we clean the cow you know off us before going inside to change clothes if need be, have breakfast and meet the school Bus for school."

Dakota left the couch and as she started to walk by William to play on the Computer in back stopped and asked, "You did that every day?" "I sure did," Barbara answered. "It was a time in my life that I will never forget. I guess you could say I was and still am nothing but a good old country girl."

Dakota left saying, "If you say so?"

"I do," Barbara answered. "I really do."

HOW TO GET OUT OF JURY DUTY?

"Now William, I'm not the one to brag but I've gotten out of Jury Duty every time I've been called but not this time, I want to serve," Sonny said as he took a seat beside me in the court room.

I've known Sonny for over thirty years and he always been up to something. Now it was this call for Jury Duty and here he sat down with the best clothes I have ever seen him wear and he wants to serve on the Jury so I calmly asked, "Now Sonny, you are telling me you want to be on Jury Duty after getting out of so many? What is the catch?"

"Nothing serious," he answered, "In fact I do not even know what this trial is all about. But I'm getting old now and for one time in my life I would like to serve on jury duty if they will let me."

I smile as patted him on the back and said, "Good luck and I hope you fulfill your dream. I really do and if they choose me I'll tell them you're a better man and I'm sure they will just let you waltz right on end and take my place. By the way, how you get out of the other times they called you."

Sonny bent over to me and whispered, "That was easy part, I dressed liked I look like bum."

"That is it?" I asked. "You just wore old and dirty clothes full of holes. That is all you did. It just got to more than that. You must have worn a fake beard or put on rotten teeth are something. I mean no patch over one eye or dark sunglasses to hide the black eye your wife gave you for coming home drunk. You just dress as a bum?"

"There was more to it than that," Sonny answered, "I had to smell."

I laughed as I said, "OH NO, you didn't do that."

He just shook his head yes and said, "I sure did. My best stink came from my gym T-shirt. I remember as a boy in gym class if you hung your sweaty T shirt in your locker over the weekend. The next gym period you would fine good stinky T shirt ready to put on."

"I think that would work." I said leaning back in the chair.

"But," Sonny said still with bent over with his elbows folded across his legs, "If I did not have time to make me a good stinky T shirt I would use the old stinky feet method."

Leaning forward and joining his sitting style I said, "I guess you are going to tell me how you accomplished that act."

"Easy," he answered, "I have pair of sock and old shoes hideaway and if I sprinkle a little water on them out comes that good stinky foot odor and when I take a seat in the court room there not a soul willing to sit around me."

"Stink you say," I asked.

"You bet it did," Sonny laughed as he said, "I've never had to wait long to be dismissed, either. Woe, did it ever stink."

I was about to ask another stupid question when the bailiff call Sonny's name and as I watch him stroll calmly away ever expecting to be place upon a Jury as lease once in his life. But I also did not believe his how to get out of Jury Duty Stories until I heard the Bailiff say, "I see you have clean up and do not stick as bad as the other times you been called?"

"I sure have, Ralf," Sonny answered, "That I have."

STOP, LET ME OFF

Barbara told me this story the other day when she said, "William, It has been 55 years ago. Shoot, I was only six when Daddy took us to the fair. I thought I was older then that but anyway Daddy helped Grandpa raised several Calves and they sold them all but one and that went into our freezer. Daddy had a bunch of money and loaded us three girls upped and off to the Country Fair we went.

Of course I was so excited when we came off that mountain and could see sticking out of the forest a big wheel with baskets hanging off it going round and round and a ride going up and down hills Daddy called a Roller Coaster. After we parked and entered through the gates, I started jumping up and down wanting to be set free from Mother's hand. Eventually as we started passing booths with all kinds of play to win games with flashing lights around them did Mother let me go to run with Elaine and Larraine.

We would peer into the booths Daddy was playing hoping he win us a toy. Eventually we came to a booth where he had to throw a ball at rings and things on the other side. Now Daddy could throw a ball and he won. He won us all a toy and beads which we hung around our neck. Seeing Daddy was a good ball thrower other families were getting him to throw the ball for them. Well, the owner took Daddy aside and asked him to only throw for his family that he was trying to make some money here.

So here we were loaded down with beads and toys we came to the Roller Coaster and Elaine started to beg Daddy to let us ride. Daddy just smiled as he paid the conductor. We climb into that car right into the front seating area and the conductor tied us into the seats. I wanted Mother to come but she only pointed to the babies in her stomach.

That car slowly climbed that hill and before it reached the top I wanted out. Down the hill it flew and I thought I was going to die and scream,

"Stop, let me off." That car went this way and that way. It went up, it went down and I was sure I was going to die. When it finally stopped that conductor let everybody off the car but us and away we went again screaming. Our beads were flying off, our toys who know

where they went and every time we went by that conductor who had the biggest smile on his face as we scream, "Stop." Five times we flew around going that way and this way and up and down screaming the whole time.

When we staggered out of that car we were a mess. Our hair was all tangled, we lost most of the beads and would have lost the toys but several strangers brought them to us. I remember standing beside Mother as her comb my hair hearing Daddy say, "Anybody ready for another ride?"

We all screamed, "No."

I STARTED WITH MUD PIES.

When Mama was a child she told me they would play at making mud pies. They would get pie pans and with their imagination make pies that were somewhat real accept they were made out of mud. They had a play oven and use small twigs as if they were making a fire to cook the pies. It was not long until they had mud from head to toe and would just laugh as they wipe the mud across their face and cloths as they played. Grandma never would complain and even help them at times to clean the mess up.

One-day Grandma and Granddad took us to see our cousins across town. They also played at making mud pies only they had many cans labeled with flour, sugar, apples, cherries, etc. All the ingredients needed to make a great imaginary mud pie. It also helped that their dad filled the cans with mud of different colors. It wasn't long till Mama was joining them. They made several different pies and one looked so real, that she took a bite out of it. Her cousins and sisters just laughed.

Mama smile as she looked over at me and said, "Now you understand why I make the best pies in the country, if not the State of Arkansas. I started with mud pies."

A SIX INCH SNOW

As William learned over the pool table taking aim at the striped ball near the center hole, he said, "Looks like we going to have a six-inch snow by morning and I guess the Center be close tomorrow."

Leonard, as he caulked his pool stick, answered, "I'm sure it will and I'm staying home."

As the striped ball fell into the hole, William said, "Me too. I have enough trouble climbing out of driveway as it is much else trying to do it with six inches of snow on it."

Leonard watched William place another striped into the side pocket and said, "We sure had a lot of snow this year not counting the ice storms that sometimes appears with them. I'm sure not looking for this one either."

"Me either," William answered as he sunk another stripe into the corner pocket.

Leonard laughed as he said, "You know what I did one time when a good six-inch snow fell when I was child."

William learning over to take aim at the fourteen said, "No, what?" Leonard watched William sink the fourteen before he said, "Well my Grandpa was the school teacher at Grandview. Well one night we had a good six inch or more snow fall and the next morning it was cold and sunny and away to school I went thinking we were going to have school. I plowed my way through that snow to the school house and there was not one track leading toward the school. I started to go back home and here came Grandpa just a plowing his way through the snow. He did not let me go home and we had school, just him and me until around two."

William sunk the twelve and as he stood looked at Leonard and said, "Wow, what a great memory your Grandfather gave you that is still with you. A day in your life when for one day, your Grandfather was able to teach his grandson one on one. What a memory."

Leonard laughed and said, "I guess he did at that. But I also learned one thing that day. When there is a six-inch snow covering the ground, do not go running off to school."

DO, DO AJAX

Barbara exited onto the porch carrying two of those large insulator glasses full of ice tea and set one down on the table beside Lorraine who looked upped at her and said, "Thank you Barbara, my throat was sure getting dry sitting here watching Doc chase squirrels up trees."

Barbara returned to her rocker and said, "There sure a lot them around and I think Doc has realized yapping below a tree at them is a waste of time. He just yaps enough to tell them off before returning back here to the house. I tell you one thing squirrels are fast runners. Not as fast Doc but almost. They get a head start Doc hasn't even got a chance of catching one. He did come close couple times."

While swatting at a fly Lorraine said, "You know Barbara, we sure have been blessed. I think back to Mom and Dad and we were so poor yet rich at the same time. As far as I remember we never did without. Do you remember Mom's brown sugar?"

Barbara set her coffee down and picked up her Fly swatter and carefully popped a fly before she answered and said, "I remember alright. She had a special jar she put pennies in and when a holiday came around she would go buy Brown Sugar to made sweets."

"She sure did and I ate many a cookie she made with it." Lorraine added. "If I remember right Ferguson's had a barrel full and Mama would take us with her to buy some and tell us about all the goodies she was going to make."

Barbara swatted at another fly before she laughed as she thought out loud and said, "We were poor alright. I know one thing Mother would not buy any kind of store bought cleaner like Ajax. Do you remember when I asked Mom when we went for brown sugar was she going to buy any "Do, Do Ajax?"

"I don't remember that." Lorraine said with a laugh as she repeated, "Do, Do Ajax," Then while reaching for her ice tea she asked, "And then what happen?"

Barbara had a big smile on her face as she answered, "I guess you don't remember who started to be called, "Do, Do Ajax, either do you?"

JUDY'S FIRST CAKE

Now my sister Judy, when we were children was always begging Mother to let her help her cook breakfast or dinner. Mother always said, "Judy when you're older you can."

Judy did not give up and kept begging until Mother gave in. She would let Judy fix simple things like opening a can and heating corn or peas. At breakfast she would often let her fix the toast and even let her fry the bacon and eggs sometimes. Mother would always tell her how good she was doing.

When Judy was about ten, she started looking through Mother's cook books. She told me one day she would bake a cake. Of course I laughed saying, "Sure you will." That is when she started to ask Mother if she could. Mother would say, "When you're older."

Well one-day Mother was not at home and Judy decided to bake a cake. She had watched Mother make them and she just knew she could think how proud Mother would be when she took a bite of her first cake. Judy gathered all the ingredients for the cake making sure not to make a mess as she mixed it. She had just placed the cake in the oven when Mother came home. Mother's smile turned to sorry as the smell of burnt cake came from the oven. Upon opening the oven, cake was going everywhere. Mother looked at Judy and asked, "How much baking powder did you use?" Judy looking real small by now answered, "Quarter of a cup."

BURNT BEANS

Ulis turned his wagon into the small hardware store saying, "Woo there Cup, Woo there Curly," as they snorted and toss their heads. Quickly Johnny Horton reached and caught the horses and he said, "Now boys, you calm down now. Anyway, what got you two all upset? This is not like you at all?"

"My Fault," Ulis answered as he jumped to the ground. "I had to push them a little to make sure I got here before you close."

"You barely made it," Johnny answered as he left the horses and headed back into the store. "I just going to lock the gate when you came rolling in. Anyway, what do you need that is so important?"

"I need some plumbing supplies and here is a list." Ulis said as he handed it to him.

As Johnny glanced at list he asked, "I see you got a lot of pluming material listed here. Are you remodeling are something?"

"I wish," Ulis answered. "Drain line is all clog up."

"Really," Johnny said as he began walking around the store gathering Ulis' plumbing material.

Ulis just started to laugh as it darn on him really what his beautiful Ray did suddenly became quite funny. As he settled down said, "It is all Mary Ray's doing."

Johnny smiled and almost laughed as he said, "Not your sweet innocence little Ray. She would never have clogged the drain unless she had a very good reason."

"She burnt the beans is what she did," Ulis answered which brought him and Johnny into laughter.

Johnny settled down and said, "She must have really burned them."

"I guess," Ulis answered, "It appeared her Mother told her if she ever burnt the beans she was to pour them down the sink. That is exactly what she did and had to stuff the last the half of the pot into the drain. Did she ever clog it up and it is all because she wanted to hide the fact she had burned the beans from me?"

"How come you just don't wash the lines out with a hose?" Johnny asked as he set the gathered plumbing material upon the counter.

Ulis turned very serious as he said, "I thought of doing that, until I got to thinking, what if I miss some of those beans and they start to gas. It would smell worse than a pig sty as the gas would bubble right out of the drain and fill the whole house with its smell. I don't want that so I'm just going to remove the old and replace it with new."

Johnny could do nothing but laugh as he wondered out back to fetch the pipe sections Ulis wanted thinking what a way to handle burnt beans.

BIG CAT AND THE SMALL HOLE

Lenard stood caulking his clue stick as Rex pulled his favorite clue from the rack asking, "My brake?"

"Sure, go ahead," Lenard answered. "And what has been happening with you."

"Cats is what been happening to me." Rex answered as he caulked his stick and position himself to break. Set the caulk down before he moved the clue ball to the position he liked to break before he continued with, "There been a huge cat that comes begging and wanting into the house and I want it gone."

"Huge cat you say," Lenard asked.

"Yea," Rex answered as he pulls his cue stick back and with a quick forward motion sent the cue ball smashing into the rack with a swap sound and the six ball and ten ball banged around a bit before falling into the left corner and right side pocket.

Lenard move out of Rex's way and said, "I had a cousin that had a big cat that the dogs did not get along with but left him alone most of the time. I mean it was big."

Rex lined himself up and sends the two into the side pocket and left clue ball on the Five for another easy shot and for reason he could not helped it and asked, "The dogs ever try to chase and catch it?"

Lenard watched Rex sink the five before he answered with, "Not that I know of. I was not over ten at the time and one day the cousin and I were left at his house alone. Already knew that the big cat would hide under the sink if one of the dogs ever came into the house. In our play, we came up with the idea we wanted to see what would happen if we placed the cat out of the house and it had no place to hide."

Lenard became quiet as Rex, who just could see the three, hit it down

75

the rail into the corner pocket and broke his other balls out of the pile in the middle and was left with only easy shots.

"I think I got lucky," Rex said as he placed four in the hole and as he stood he asked, "You haven't finish your story, so what happen after you threw the cat out of the house?"

Lenard just held his stick ready to have a turn if Rex missed, answered, "Well, first we had to travel around the house covering any holes that were big enough for the cat to get under the house with. There were no trees around my cousin's house for it to climb. My cousin caught the cat and out the door it went with us two boys yelling and shouting following. Our yelling quickly caught the dog's attention and after that cat we all went shouting and barking. The dogs ran with us not really wanting to catch it for it was almost as big as they were and claws and teeth to go with it. As we followed, it became a chase for the dogs. Usually, when his Mom let the big cat out at night, the dogs don't bother it. But not this time, as the chase was on and around the house the dogs and two ten-year-old boys traveled right behind that big Cat just trying to keep up with it. Three times it went around the house with us shouting and the dogs barking until it spotted a hole we thought was way too small and that big cat hit that small hole and with a little effort went right through it and under the pouch. I mean that hole wasn't any wider than the circle I can make with my hands. But that big cat was able to squeeze through it and escaped."

By now, Rex only had to do make the eight to win the game and as Lenard finished his tell, Rex asked, "How did you get it out from beneath the porch?"

"We didn't, although we did try too," Lenard answered. "And were we ever in trouble with my cousin's Mom with her having to soft talk that big cat out from beneath the porch."

Rex had a smile on his face as he placed the eight into the side pocket. "That the first run I've done in fifty games I bet."

"I bet it has been two hundred games for me," Lenard laughed as he rolled several stripped balls toward Rex who was beginning to rack the balls.

OLD YELLOW

One Thing Daddy did ever sense I was a little girl he would take me fishing with him. My older sisters refused but not me. I drag my old cane pole along behind me and down to the fishing hole below Grandpa's house we go. But we always stopped at the well beside Grandma's kitchen and fill up a jug with what Daddy called the best tasting water in the Ozarks. I can always remember when Daddy and I came back up the hill with our catch you could smell the sweet rolls Grandma had made for us.

Well I guess I was at least six or seven when we arrived at Grandpa's, a solid yellow pup greeted us and he and I instantly became buddies. Down to Lane's hole located just pass Slick Rock we played all the way and of course he helps me with the fish I caught. Daddy did not seem to mind as me and Yellow wrestle and played.

Later, as we ate one of Grandma's sweet rolls, I asked, "Grandpa, what kind of dog is Yellow?

Grandpa answered, "He is what you call a heeler for herding cattle and sheep. They snapped at their heels to move them this way or that."

I guess old yellow and I kind of grew up together and Daddy never fussed on us unless we got to close to his fishing hole. Daddy always fetched him when we would go to pick black barriers and I remember Yellow many a time spotting a copper head and alerting us before it could bite us. I guess that was why Daddy fetched him and he was always ready to go. Hanging his head out the car window barking at any creature he saw beside the road.

As I grew older, we all started to call him Old Yellow. He was known by everyone for lying beside the road, waiting I guess for me to show up and play. But, my interests wonder away into girly things and only visited Grandma and Grandpa now and then. But Old yellow was always very happy to see me when I did. Jumping and barking and running around me wanting to tell me he missed me. I would pet him and I was told he would always travel with Daddy down to the fishing hole with him.

I was married with two boys when Daddy informed me Old Yellow had died. I knew it was not long for he had could barely walk and if he got on the road, he would walk in the middle and would not even attempt to get out of the way of a car or truck.

Grandpa placed him along the trail leading toward the Fishing Hole and I would stop and look at the Grave Marker and remember, telling my boys about the times I played with Old Yellow.

LOST THAT DARN GARDEN SNAKE

One thing I can tell you, Mister, I've never been scared of is snakes. I see them as another of God's creations. There so many of them and they help us out with the little creators like mice. That is what Daddy said. He also told me that their size is basically base on what they can eat and that some even had to convert to poison to eat for they ate big rabbits. I learn this from Uncle Huey and Daddy as a baby when the community would gather together to clear the children's area around the village of snakes and what I saw made me highly respect them but not fear them. I'm telling you.

I remember stumbling around behind my Dad as he would turn rocks over and check in the shadows for snakes. I've seen them come out of their hole so mad and jump at us with their large mouth's open wide. But when it landed Daddy quickly was able to cut its head off. Daddy could wing that axe. And throw it. I mean he could throw it where it stuck in a tree every time. Anyway, they collected all the killed snakes and it was not till later when I was way older did I learn that they fed them to the pigs and they love them and I was told the pigs would even fight over them. Those pigs sure must love snakes is all I got to say.

Now the other day when me and Paul where playing outside with our cars, Paul spotted a Green Racer. Paul wanted to catch it and soon we were snake hunting. I went and fetched us an Ax and Toe Sack and we never caught that Green Racer as we headed for what was left of the rock fences after Daddy sold them. I was so sure we would catch ten or more. But it was not to be. We only caught a little Garden Snake about six inches long and that was after I bet we turned over a hundred rocks. We gave up and went back to the cars all worn out and you know we lost that darn Garden Snake when we were not looking.

Mister, one day I think I'll going to be the best darn snake hunter in the Village. Anyway, I got to go. I see Mother is calling me. Bye now.

A TACK FOR JIMMY GREEN

When I was in the second grade I had a teacher name, "Mrs. Bacon." We would raise our hands and holler, "Mrs. Bacon, can I do this and that." The bathroom of course was just part of our little lives back then.

I sat between Bobbie Berman and Jimmy Green for if I remember right, when school started Mrs. Bacon allowed us to pick our seats and of course we children sat with friends and in some ways it was good and in most ways it was bad. With girls I guess it would work but with boys, add sugar, and I bet it became a problem for Mrs. Bacon. Three boys that played together often slept together at each other houses and always ate together. When one would laugh the other would join in.

I guess Mrs. Bacon after a month or more called our parents and My Mother did it in for us. She had gotten the note I was sent home with and Mother showed up at school the next day. When she walked in, she looked the classroom over and pointed at the three of us and calmly said, "If you would separate them three your teaching life would be a lot easier."

And apart we went but not before we learn to write, "I will not do this and I will not do that," over and over. I mean up to a hundred times." The one I remember might have not been the last time I did that for sure and it happen just before we were separated.

Jimmy sat in front of me and had gotten up for some reason like to write something on the backboard. I could not help myself and I put a tack upon Jimmy Green's seat as he was coming back to his seat, he sat on it. Of course yelled, and there I was writing one hundred times, "I will not put a tack under Jimmy Green's seat."

I think as I started writing I asked Mrs. Bacon, "How come you don't make Jimmy write, "I will not yell when I sit on a tack place in my seat?"

I receive no response from her but laughter did spread across the room.

LOVED AND FUSSED ON

When I was a child, I was the youngest girl and believe me, I was spoiled rotten. Just asked any of my four sisters and two brothers?

They would tell you I was for they did it. Does not mean I wasn't picked on. But for two of my older sisters, I was a big living, walking and learning to talk Doll. They still treat me that way as if I'm still the baby and here I am in my late fifties. But the adventures I would have following every one of them around the house is just way too many to mention. I even had my whole family looking for me one time. That is right. I got lost and it was not my fault either.

I guess I was just turned four and Great Grandpa Horton had just bought the hundred acres where Gramps and Grandma live now. Now Grandpa Horton had many friends and could he play the guitar. When he bought the land, he and Great Grandma Horton were living just outside of town over by Bear Ragland's place. When it came a time to move out to the Cannon every friend he knew showed up with a horse or mule drawn wagon.

You can imagine the looks we got as this caravan of several wagons loaded with furniture and stuff passed by. There were several cows being driven by the older boys. Our milk cow was being pulled along behind one of the wagons. Chickens squawking and I know Grandpa Horton had at least ten pigs. We look like an old time wagon train moving down the road.

I remember the going was slow enough us girls could jump off the wagons and play. I being the littlest I had to be help on and off the wagon sometimes. Well down near Hold some's corner is where it happens they first missed me. I had gotten tired and had hid myself in one of the wagons where they could not see me and Grandma panicked. She brought the whole caravan to a standstill as they hunted for me. I think that is when I awoke from all the commotion and asked what was happening. Mother got hold of me and I never knew I could ever be loved and fussed on at the same time.

THEY DID FIST FIGHT, TOO.

As Elaine was pulling away from the house, Barbara took the fly swatter and caught two of the flies Elaine had let in upon open the screen door while leaving, Barbara said, "William, did you know Elaine and Woody been married since Elaine was eighteen and did they ever fight."

I was just reaching for the screen door to exit the house and Barbara's word "fight" caught my attention and turned to her and asked, "Did you say fight?"

Barbara reached for a smoke as she said, "Oh yea, I mean a knock down drag out fight."

"From the look of her I would never taught that." I said turning to regain a seat in my rocker I like to rock in for I knew I was about to hear a story.

Barbara took a drink of her coke before she began her story by saying, "I mean it William. They would have a downright good old fist fight. In every one of them Woody ended up running for Elaine always got the best of him. They would separate but it never last long.

I was visiting them one Christmas and I found out Woody was taken Karate lessons. I asked him why was he taking Karate lessons and he said so Elaine could not beat him up anymore.

But they fought in other ways. A good example is the time Woody had decided to take his lunch to work. He bought a lunch box with bottle and mug and gotten Elaine to fix it for him. How he was able to get her to fix it I'll never know but Woody did.

Well Monday morning, just after I exited my car out the back door came Woody almost at a run with Elaine and that lunch box in her right hand right behind him yelling, "You forgot your lunch?"

Woody yelled back, "NO" just as he reached his truck. "I don't want it."

Elaine puffed up and wide eye said, "Yes you are going to take this Lunch box for it is not staying in this house." Then she threw it at Woody where it landed by his feet and there it stayed as Woody drove away. Elaine, still mad rushed while grabbing a nearby stick and for several seconds just beat that lunch box to pieces.

I follow Elaine back entered the house and as I sat across from her drinking a coke, she said, "He got me all work up on making his lunch for him and all he was after was to see if I would do it."

I had to put my mouth in her story and had to asked, "With all that fighting you would never think they would still be together fifty years later."

Barbara answer with, "You would think that. They actually love each other. I remember Elaine had won or been given a weekend stay at one of Branson's fancy hotel and shows. Well something happen and Woody could not go or they had a fight over what to take and stopping at Mother's did not help either. In the end, Elaine went by herself and I asked her later did you have fun but her answer was, "I had possible the worst time in my life I have ever had."

NO BROTHERS WITH ME

When I was a young woman, I needed to go to town. I had something real important I had to do that day like get my hair fix for my hot date that night and wanted to look my best for the guy who was gonna coming pick me up.

Mother and Dad were pretty free with me and my dating at 16. Anyway, that night Don was coming to pick me up at 7 and I just had to my hair done. I told them what I wanted to do and pleaded with them to let me borrow the car. My problem with them was that I haven't been driving for very long. But, in my eyes I was a good driver.

They talk about it between themselves and came back with, "The only way we will let you have the car you must take your brothers with you."

I died right there thinking, "Oh, My. What will I do with my brothers?"

But I said, "You want my brothers to come with me?" "Yes," they both replied. "They need a haircut."

As I drove down the dirt road and by the time I got to the big curve. I had it with their fussing or whatever. I stopped the car and looking at my two twin brothers said, "Ok, Russell, Reynold, I'm not taking you to town with me. So get out and walk back to the house and wait for me to return on the back porch."

They morn and complain as they always do. So, I left them thinking they would do as I say and of course those little rascals didn't.

It appears they did as I told them and waited on the back porch for me. But, Daddy must have saw or heard them. Then where they could hear him plainly he said, "I bet Barbara pulled a good one and left the boys somewhere on the way to town. I just bet she did?"

Now when Daddy said that, they just walk their little selves into the house and said, "Yes she put us out over at the big curve and we been waiting out on the back porch for her to get back."

Barbara just laughed as she said, "So, when I got home, I was in deep trouble."

WHAT ARE THEY THINKING?

"Johnny, I love our children but some days I want to pull my hair out." Mother said as she slipped into her side of the bed. "And I mean it. Sometimes I just do not know where their mind is and what they are thinking."

Daddy laughed as he sat upon the edge of the bed to remove his slippers and pants before he said, "Ok, what they do today?"

Mother adjusted her pillow as she said, "It all started this morning when Lorraine told Russell he was hatched from a chicken egg and he believed her and started to cry. I tried to tell him different and I scolded Lorraine for saying that but for some reason Russell would start crying for no reason but Lorraine was not far from him when he did. I knew something was amiss but her play did not show she had done anything to him."

Daddy stood and as he pulled back the covers to get into bed, "She is sneaky alright and always seems to be picking on Russell that is for sure and mostly to get him to cry."

Mother stretched and with her eyes closed said, "Well I found out at the lunch table what she was doing to cause him to cry and you will not believe this. She very sneakily laid her hand flat on the table and out of the corner of her eye would lift one finger and point it at Russell and when she did Russell would holler or cry. I would never have caught it if I had not been watching Russell. He was staring directly at her hand with his eyes wide open and all she did was barely point at him and that was enough for him to take off."

"I guess you got that fixed." Daddy said as he pulled the covers over him.

"Yea, but that is not all." Mother rolled over and placed her hand on Daddy's chest.

Daddy with a snicker said, "Really."

"Barbara decided to give the kittens a bath." Mother said as she rolled her pillow to a cool side. "She put them in the minnow bucket and took them to the creek and tosses the bucket into the water. These little kittens were just a hollering and when she took them out they were almost drowning. Then all the children pushed and shoved on their little chests and luckily revived all of them. Sometimes I just do not know what they or thinking."

Daddy rolled over and held Mama before lightly kissing her on the forehead before he said, "I did not know you were having so much fun with the children. It almost wants me to stay home tomorrow. Then slowly he said, "But not quit."

As he rolled back over, they both laughed.

BLACK WING GRASSHOPPERS

I was just starting to put the roast in the oven when Billy came and sat down at the kitchen table searching for something to drink. He looked frustrated and I asked, "You sure seem down in the dumps today. What's wrong?"

"It's this darn rain." He answered. "It has been raining for a week now and being cooped upped in the house is bad enough but at school today it is the fifth day we had no recess either. I sure wish it would quit."

As I closed the oven door I said, "I know what you mean. I have not been able to hang a wash on the close line either and the clothes is sure piling upped."

Billy, as he watched me fix him a glass of the ice tea asked, "Mom, when you were my age what did you do when it rain?"

I sat the tea before him and laugh as I said, "Remember Billy, I had two sisters and two brothers to play with and you only have Wesley."

Billy took the glass of tea from me and asked, "But what did you do at school when it rained?"

"Same as you," I answered. "I think we had to place our heads on our desk and close our eyes. I bet you'll never guess what we did this time of year just before school let out for the summer."

After Billy took a drink of his tea, he said, "No what?" "We chased the Black Wing Grasshoppers." I answered.

"Aw, you didn't?" Billy said with a laughed almost spilling his tea.

I sat down at the table and as I stated to peel the potatoes that I was going to have with the roast, I said, "Have you ever tried to catch one of them. It is not easy. This time of the year they would show up by the hundreds and the school yard was full of them. We had a game we would play to see who could catch the most and I can tell you I never won. Those buggers, just when you thought you had one it would fly off and away I would run after it. I was lucky if I caught two. Then when recess was over we always let them go and try to catch them the next recess."

"That sounds like fun." Billy said as he stood to leave. "But we do not have many of them as you did."

"That only means you will have a lot harder time catching one." I said with a laugh as I placed a peeled potato in the bowl.

As Billy left the room he said, "I'll just do that if it ever stops raining."

"It will." I called after him. "It will stop eventually."

"I sure hope so." He replied as he disappeared from my view.

DADDY'S THREE FRIENDS

My Dad had three friends that would come by the house quit often, Tommy Gray, Jack and Billy Battleshell. Sometime alone, but most of the time all three would show up. When they did, they would drink and get drunk and end up sleeping on the mattress in the hay loft.

Jack and Billy had a sister who married Virgil Wells and I remember Lorraine and Elaine would tell me where Mom would not hear they were going sell me to The Well's Buy, Sell or Trade Store that use to be where the Manor Housing is now. I think I would run and tell Mommy and she would fuss on them but sometimes I thought she wanted to agree with them.

But many times Tommy, Jack, and Billy would pick Daddy up and they would go fishing and always ended up drunk out on the Buffalo River or somewhere else. One such time Daddy came home hurt with broken ribs. Mama told us they had tried to throw Daddy out of the boat by turning the boat shapely with Daddy being drunk had landed on the boats railing and gotten hurt. They said it didn't happen that way. Daddy had a big fish on his line and when the line broke he fell backwards and hit the boat railing.

They may have gotten drunk out fishing or around the house but when they went hunting that was another story especially when they went squirrel hunting with Old Red or their own dogs. They mostly would hunt the woods around the Canon area. When they did, Daddy always came home with a number of squirrels for supper. Then the three friends would either stay and get drunk with Daddy are leave with their squirrels in hand.

Daddy didn't always go fishing with them. I remember one fishing trip Daddy went fishing with Thomas McDaniel down below a dam somewhere and over the spillway came a man and his boat. He hit his head

92

on some rocks and Daddy rescue and save him. A few days later the local paper came to the house to interview Daddy, take his picture and get a statement for saving the man. But when they came by, Tommy, Jack and Billy were there and by that time it was late in the day and all four were quit drunk and Daddy refuse to be interviewed or have his picture taken.

Daddy's three friends were our friends also but as time passes they quit coming over and I guess move on with their lives as we move on with ours. They are all gone now and I still see many of their children around now and then. If we meet, we would talk about the times our dads would do this or that with us but we never talked about the many a times our Dads would sit at each other's house with whomever had enough extra money to get a bottle or two and invite the others to join them. To me, it always appeared to be at ours.

ALWAYS LATE

Elaine, my sister, is always late for everything and of course her children were to. She was late to church, to work, people's funerals, and the worst was beauty parlors appointments. Now her children were always late because they had to travel with her causing them to be late and soon acted just like her. I think she got it from Mama. Mama was always late and she would even sleep during preaching. Roxie sitting behind Mama would punch her awake. Mama, Elaine, and now her kids being late, everybody thought they would be late for their own funeral.

I remember many times Stacy and Bryan her boys would miss the bus and had to fetch a ride. Even in school they were known to be late. Sometimes they would call me for a ride. They would not call Elaine, just me or they stayed home. Of course Elaine knew and was mad at them especially if they stayed home

Well one day they missed the bus and noticing Uncle Doug had left his big Honda there, they decided to take it to school instead of calling me. Anyway, they got as far as to the bottom of Still Springs Hill and the darn thing ran out of gas. Being a short distance from home, they took turns pushing the big Honda back. Wore out, they decided to stay home and just watched TV. Elaine was so mad but glad at the same times as she told me, "I'm glad they ran out gas. They could have gotten hurt or something worst."

They are still that way today, always late.

COWS IN THE WILD ONIONS

I sat the coke beside Barbara and looked at Loraine and asked, "You sure you don't want something. We have tea, coffee and even milk if you want some."

Loraine smile as she said, "You can bring me a glass of milk I guess. I don't want a coke. It sometimes gives me heart burn."

As I started to open the fridge I heard Barbara say, "Isn't it too hot to drink Milk right now."

"No," Loraine answered. "I still drink milk three times a day just like Mother made us do when we were young. I really never stopped.

I've been drinking milk morning, noon, and night for years."

Barbara lean farther back in her recliner, laughed as she said, "We had milk alright. Daddy would milk those cows and we drink their milk and churn our own butter."

I handed Loraine her milk and asked, "Anything else. We have donuts."

Loraine looked at me and said, "I'm good."

I started to leave them alone and go back to my writing when Loraine said, "William, you didn't know Aunt Flosey but she helps around the house a lot even though she was blind."

"Barbara already told me a lot about her" I answered.

Loraine looked at Barbara and said, "Did Barbara tell you Aunt Flosey churned the milk every morning and gave us fresh butter. Put a little salt on it and Mom skim the cream off the milk. I mean we had fresh milk, butter and cream every morning."

I politely said, "No."

Barbara laughed as she added, "Unless the cows been in the wild onions or garlic."

Loraine laughed with her and said, "I forgot about that. William, we still drank the milk after we learned if we held our noses, we did not smell the onion or garlic in it."

Barbara after taking a drink of her coke added, "You remember when we taught Russell and Reynold to do that and Daddy was so mad at us."

Loraine answered, "I sure do and poor Daddy had to send the milk to the cheese factory."

I left them as I heard Barbara say, "Mom still could cook with the milk and she always said that her food always tasted better after the cows been in the wild onions or garlic."

The last words I heard as I left them was Loraine adding, "I think Aunt Flosey said so also."

DOG FOOD FOR FISHING

"Hello Bill or should I say good morning," Wilber said as he sat down at the Domino table and began to flip the dominos over to shuffle them. As he finished, Bill flipped a 5/3 over followed by LB with a 2/2 and Billy Joe with a 3/2.

"I guess it you and me Bill," Wilber said as he flipped over a 5/6 and smiled as he added, "I get first down."

Soon the Domino Game was on with Wilber lying the Double Five on the table followed by the Five Blank from LB. Wilber non gallantry said, "Never fails. Down the Double Five without the Five Blank and the next player always has it."

LB laughed as he said, "It seems that way."

As the game continued Wilber said, "That big puppy at the house, besides having all teeth, seems to be hungry all the time and I'm going have to get some dog food today."

As Bill played the Double Three, he said, "Did you know dog food is good for fishing?"

Billy Joe answered, "I don't think the dog food would stay on the hook very long."

"You don't put it a hook, Bill Joe." Bill answer, "You throw it in the water where you want to fish. In my thinking, the best fishing is along the bank of the lakes and even gets better if you cast a hand full dog food into the water where you want to fish. Just wait a bit and will soon be catching a fish almost every time you cast."

As Wilber counted off the Five he said, "I guess all you catch out in the middle is catfish off the bottom if threw the dog food out there." Bill answered and said, "That may be true. But I prefer the edge of the bank, myself."

LB after studying a bit before playing said, "I heard Don Horton telling someone he doesn't need to throw a line into water to catch fish using dog food."

Billy Joe looked over at LB and said, "It is one of your jokes isn't it LB?"

As Bill placed a Double Four on LB's play which was his only play said, "LB never jokes do you LB."

LB watch Billy Joe count off the spinner with the Five Two before he said, "Don told me whenever he gets the notice for some fish to eat, he would just before he goes to bed at night walk down to his lake and throws two or three hand full of dog food into it. Then in the morning in the grass around the lake he hunts down any large fish out chasing after the rabbits."

Billy Joe said, "I knew it was one of your jokes."

Wilber placed his last domino, the Double Two, on Billy Joe's play said, "How much you got."

As Bill counted the points LB and Billy Joe had in their hands, Wilber asked, "LB, what kind of fish did Don catch out running the rabbits anyway?"

LB, out the corner of his eye he answered saying, "I think he said he only caught those that were out of school."

AUNT RUTH

"Now my Aunt Ruth was something else. I'm telling you." Barbara said as she stood looking over the other house members seated around her. It was her turn at telling a story of your past and she smile at she brought back the wonderful memories of her.

Suddenly Sam said, "You're not going to tell us another Aunt Ruth story are ya?"

"Sam, this is my first time at telling stories." Barbara popped back at him thinking, "He always causing trouble. Darn his hide anyway."

"Well don't let me interrupt you." Sam said taping his cane on the floor before him.

Barbara looked upped toward the ceiling asking the Lord for patience before she said, "Aunt Ruth was my Dads sister and loved to wear her hair long and I mean long. I've seen it down to her knees until she cut it back to her bottom. It was a golden brown and we girls just loved to brad it for her when she came a visiting. Now my two sisters and I would sometimes go home with her where we played games."

"What kind of games." Sam uttered at her as he tapped his cane afterwards.

Barbara looked down at Sam and said, "Girly games. Ones only us girls know about and you boys don't."

"I was just wondering." Sam replied with a smile.

Barbara looked upped, again asking the Lord for patience, before she said, "Now and again Aunt Ruth would take us home with her. But every time she would, she would get scared. Then half asleep we would get back into her car and spend the rest of the night back home with her sleeping with one of us. She got married and moved away. My last good memory of her was when Daddy went to fixing his soup. Not just any old soup either. It was his special soup he made when the family would get together to celibate Grandpa's birthday. They always did it our house and Daddy always fixes his soup and Grandpa like it filled with peppers. That is just what Daddy did.

Now us girls had just finished braiding Aunt Ruth's long hair and were entering the kitchen, when Aunt Ruth noticed Daddy pouring a

big bowl of peppers into his soup. Aunt Ruth yelled, "Not more of that Gull Dang Hot Soup again."

Now we kids did not get any but Aunt Ruth got herself two bowls full and even took home some. I had fond memories of her funny ways. I got more but I'll tell you later after I get my story straight.

As Barbara started back to her seat Sam said, "That is it. I thought you tell how wild and loose she was or something."

Barbara stopped and looked hard at Sam before she said, "Not this time, Sam." I just wanted to introduce you to her. I'll get to the juicy part of her later."

Then to teased Sam she said, "If I'm not mistaken she about your age. I'm sure she is single and just could be looking." "Hump," Sam answered tapping his cane.

HOW YOUNG MEN

It is strange how young men become friends. I had a few but I only really did not gather friends but as I sit here I begun really thinking of John Wilson who died from Agent Orange couple years ago. He was a short stocky type of guy and was from up in Northern Pennsylvania area. I first met him in the barracks at Fort Deveins, Mass. He would holler right after the barracks lights went out and yelled "Ellis, say "Oil" for us." I would say in my best Texas accent, "Aw-il wells," He would just laugh. So very childlike in many ways.

We went to school together learning how to fix Radios and such. But it was war games we played before going to Vietnam called TTC we really became friends. It was the last day of TTC which was the escape and evasion night and together we scouted the area for our escape. John had chosen to follow me after Bill Waid got out of that night by getting his eyes hurt with gases when one of the blanks from a M1 Rifle went off in his face. Bill Waid really had become my best friend by living in the bunk above me. We hit it off and had many adventures together. But not this one, it was me and John Wilson.

My friendship with John peaked while sneaking down the highway edge. I had missed my turn and stopped by a house I could see lights on and asked where the TTC was. As I returned to the right path, I heard someone in front of me sneaking also. I hide but suddenly here came John Wilson a yelling "Friend" over and over.

We met on the side of the road and I hugged him and he hugged me for I was sure he had been capture and he thought I was also. There we were just off the road telling our narrow escape to each other before we moved on trying to reach our safe area within the TTC

Training grounds. Where earlier, they had thrown close to twenty or thirty large fire crackers with smoke into the mock Vietnam village we had just capture.

After I left the military I no longer had anything to do with John even after he stopped by Houston for his wife was having some physical problems and John had gain a little weight. He became a Telephone line man up at Collage Station and his wife left him. But a

few years before he died of Agent Orange but after twenty years or so of being single he met another and they were married.

But meeting him upon the side of that road during TTC Training before actually going to Vietnam I will cherish till the day I am too called by the Lord.

I THOUGHT A SMALL COKE BOTTLE WAS BIG

During my early childhood years we live in a two story white house that had four large columns station in front of the house. Around the house, Daddy planted a field of at least forty Pecan Trees. I was free to wonder the yard and visit the chicken yard. We had a dog that lived outside. If you open the top floor windows, the Gulf breezed would blow through the house while on the ground level there were none.

Daddy had to return to sea and I remember while parked by his ship waiting for him, I noticed a man floating in the water below. I told Mother there a dead man in the water and she had the guard called the police. For many years after that, I thought when you die you turned black.

Living by the Galveston Bay, Mother and Daddy also loved to fish and crab. They often took us to a small bayou where they could fish and crab from the bank. I remember once when Daddy had caught a big blue crab and thrown it upon the bank, I took a small coke bottle tried to stop it from going back into the water. The darn thing reached up and pinched me on the hand. I cried and held my hand out for them to look at. Yep, those were the days when I thought a small coke bottle was big.

THEY ARE PRECIOUS IN OUR SIGHT

Years ago Barbara Jean and I started singing at nursing homes around the area. I went to all the junk stores and thrift stores and bought every gospel record I could find. I copied any song I thought would make them happy on tape. Bought sound equipment and would stand before the nursing home members and sing along with the gospels artists I had recorded on cassettes.

Of course we fell in love with many of them. One home we went to had many in the last feeble state of life. Barbara could not take it as

I sung to the many beds the nurses rolled out for me to sing to. It got so I was singing eight hours a week in five or six homes.

My story is really about a lady name Sue. She would always sit with Barbara and bum cigarettes off her. We've been going there close to two years and the members just love us. It seemed every member of the home would gather and listen to me sing and preach to them. To show how precious they all were, one day as I was setting my system up, here came Sue. We greeted her as we normally did and she smiled at us and said, "Hi, this is my first day here."

THE SCARY MOVIE

William heard his older brother was going to see a double feature at the local theater that night and after must begging, his mother gave in and let him go. She was concern with William being just over nine years old but he wanted to go with Huey so bad even if was to see two movies with the names such as, "Not of this Earth, and Crab Monster."

William followed Huey into the Village Theater, got a Slow Poke candy bar and was quickly sitting beside his brother talking his head off about seeing a scary movie. Huey just smile and told him to be quiet the movie about to start. William calmly settled himself into a seat on the left side of Huey and opened his Slow Poke. Glancing up at his brother he gave him a smile as the thought of what was in the movies was beginning to fill him with fear especially with his brother adding words to it.

The first Movie, "Not of this Earth," had men and women that wore sun glasses and if they took them off their eyes were all white and when they look at somebody they died. Their death sent visions into his young mind. For though it was scary, it has no reflection of real life as he saw it. Although there several times William had to duck behind the seats as some guy's eyes was melting some pretty girl.

Then came the "Crab Monster," and this was to a close to real life for him. William knew all about crabs having one of them grab his finger and hold on to it with their massive claws not too long in the pass. Fear just grew in him for by this time he had no Slow Poke left to release his fear upon. But when the Giant Crab began to use the voices of those whose head it had chopped off and ate was too just too much for him and fear was now screaming within his head and body.

Now alone through the dark streets he walked. His hands buried within his pockets as visions of the movie dashed through his mind. At times the fear was so great he had to shake his head to clear the vision. He soon arrived home and in the darkness of the house he crawled into bed. Visions of the Movie still racing across his mind and in the darkness of the house fear grew in him such he cried out for help. "Mom, I'm scared can I come and sleep with you, Please, I'm scared."

"No," came back the answer, "You wanted to go to the scary movie now live with it."

William tried several times to change his Mom's mind but to no avail and soon, as eyes closed, his troubled mind was eventually overcome by sleep.

THE RAG WEED PATCH

Lorraine and I had to go fetch the cows and there it was growing between them and us just waiting for us to pass through them was a patch of Rag Weed full of seed ticks. I looked over at Lorraine and could see she was thinking the same thing, "Seed Ticks." As I look back at the Rag Weed I weakly said, "What are we going to do?"

Lorraine walking in front of me said, "We got to get the cows somehow. It is our job today. Besides Daddy will be mad if we don't."

I looked passed her and there just past the Rag Weed patch and I could see the cows were all watching us and I said, "You know what I think, Loraine."

Lorraine stopped and turned toward me. I could see she was frustrated and said, "What?"

I answered and said, "I think those cows are grazing over there to see what we will do. Look, they are all watching us."

I raised my arm and pointed across the Rag Weed and added, "Look?"

Lorraine followed my finger and upon seeing all the cows just standing there watching them, just could not help it but laughed saying, "I think they did at that."

I got beside her and said, "Race you across." Lorraine smile said, "One, two three go."

Across the Rag Weed we flew hoping none of them seed ticks get on us but it was not to be. Grabbing whatever we could find we quickly brush the tiny ticks off us and each other while several cows would mow at us knowing we had come for them to be milked or saying well done girls you made it across and still alive.

As we walked toward the now grazing cows was when we began to holler, "Snook Cows, Snook."

Soon we had them herded toward the Rag Weed patch only they did not walk through it. They ran as we did and again as we exited it had to stop and brush the seed ticks off of us. We now only had to follow the cows. For as I watched they already had begun it line up in some type of pecking order with Old Red always out in front.

MY ONLY SQUIRREL HUNT

I guess it was late fall the only time I went with Daddy Squirrel Hunting. I was at least six or seven. That was before he found himself a good Squirrel dog he named Nixie. But, before that, it was which one of children he could get to walk the woods with him.

I guess he thought I was old enough and he said, "How would you like to go squirrel hunting with Daddy. It would be just like fishing."

I believe him and as we were about to leave here came Aunt Bee all upset with a crying Jason. She hollered for Mother as she carried Jason into the house and Mother slowly calm Jason down to find out what happen. All he said, "Pincer tried to get me."

Suddenly Aunt Bee stood and said, "I guess old Wilber's Doberman Pincher must have gotten loose and it being friendly must had gotten close to Jason. I did not know what had happened when I heard him scream. I mean one out of pure fear and I ran out of the house thinking something had happen to him. There was nothing around him and seeing him so upset I thought it best he be brought here. You see Jason here believes having the name Pincher meant the dog would pinch you into at the belly."

We left them calming little Jason when Daddy said, "Come on, Barbara. Let us go Hunting."

I following him as best I could and Daddy and I looked up into the trees for a squirrel. Daddy spotted one sunning itself along the top of a tree and shot it. I ran and really not wanting to collected the squirrel for him. Eventually we came to the squirrel tree as Daddy it. I looked up into that very large tree and I saw nothing.

Then Daddy motion for me to walk around the tree and I kept looking upped and in doing so tripped on the brush several times and even fell down once. I saw nothing until Daddy fire his gun and there must have been ten squirrels in that tree that took off through the tree tops as Daddy shot. He was able to shoot a couple of them before they were gone.

That was the last time I went squirrel hunting for Daddy hollered for me to fetch the squirrels and one them was still alive. When I reach to pick it upped it swirled around and bite me. I bet Mother heard me.

For I know I scream as loud as Jason when he thought he was going to be pinched into by that Doberman Pincher.

NOT A WOMAN'S HAT

Grandma was 72 and all Cajun when I was born and I was the apple of her eye. She often came and picked me up to go shopping with her and show me off. She was a great cook and showed Mother how to prepare many types of Cajun dishes. My favorite was her Gumbo. She was a tall woman and was very aristocratic. Always in charge and demanded the best wherever she went.

Now Grandma would not let Mother cut my curly hair. One day Grandma left with me and when she returned all my hair was gone. It appeared someone said, "Oh what a cute little girl."

I was such a believable child. Whatever Grandma told me I believed. There were these blue things I could see floating on the water and washed upon the beach when we went into Galveston. Grandma told me they were women's hats. One day I saw one close to the bank I could reached. I got loose when she was not looking to fetch that women's hat. To my shock my hands became inflamed as I reached under it to pick it up. I learned right then a Portuguese Man of War is not a women's hat as I came running and crying back to Grandma holding my stinging hands.

Grandma was born in 1872 and lived to be 99 and supposedly the oldest person drawing social security at that time. I know one thing; she was something else.

OUT FISH US

When I was in my early teens, Daddy and Uncle Johnny would eventually give in to my begging and take me fishing with them. It did not happen often though and when it did it was always to the fishing hole they called, the Pier on the Buffalo where we caught White Bass, Sluggers or Catfish.

I remember one trip on a cool day in October we settled upon the pier early. Now Uncle Johnny like to fish for catfish using cut bait. I was looking down the pier for a good place to fish from, when a catfish hit Uncle Johnny's rod and jerk it off the pier into the shallow water at the edge of the bank. Daddy quickly threw his line over the pole and snagged it before the big Catfish pulled it into deep water.

I soon left them and wondered farther down the pier fishing here and there using worms until I discovered a White Bass Hole as Daddy called it where I caught one after another. Some I even snagged. Both Daddy and Uncle Johnny tried hard to let them fish the hole and I would not let them. They would huff and puff but left me alone and after about four hours I finally wore out and took the many fish I had caught for Daddy to clean. There was a couple of old men that had been fishing on the bank nearby began packing to leave. I asked you leaving so soon and one said, "If a small teenage girl can out fish us, we're going home." I just laughed.

When we got ready to leave Daddy check the catch and we were over the Limit. He smiled at me as he wrapped several Catfish and hide them within his jacket. The Game Warden checked the fish and never did notice Daddy holding the fish under his coat with his left hand. Sometimes as I look back I sure do miss them specially the love they gave to me when I was a little girl when they let me go fishing with them.

SHAVE AND A HAIRCUT

Barbara set the glass of ice tea before Loraine just before grabbing the fly swatter and saying, "I guess it is my turn to catch the next fly that come end. I think we tied at forty or you maybe one fly ahead."

"I think we are tied." Loraine answered as she rocked back and forth in her favorite rocker with the large arm rests she liked to sit in while visiting Barbara.

Barbara took a seat, took a drink of her ice tea before asking, "Sure glad to see ya Loraine. It has been over a week since you last stop by. Been busy?"

Lorraine reach for her tea and as did she said, "Not really, I drop the boys off at the Barber Shop and instead of waiting at the Barber Shop thought I wait here. They will call me when done."

"Do you remember when you and I gave Daddy a shave and a haircut?" Barbara asked with a big grin on her face as she settled back into her rocker looking at Loraine.

Loraine laughed as she said, "I sure do and I was not even ten-year-old when Daddy offer us six bits to give him a shave and a haircut and he was so drunk."

"Was he ever," Barbara added before they both busted into laughter.

As they settled down from their laugh, Loraine said, "Barbara, when Daddy offered us that six bits for a shave and haircut all I could think of was what I was going to buy when I went after his razor and soap dish."

Barbara was wiping her eyes as she said, "What got me Loraine, Daddy just sat there while we put that soap suds all over his beard and face. He even sat there quietly as we hack off his beard and he even said nothing as we nick him with that razor several times trying to shave off his tough beard."

"We did a good job, I thought," Loraine said as she rocked backwards.

"If I remember right, Mama and Uncle Ernest thought so too and said the pieces of paper across his face gave his face quit a unique appearance."

"I think the hair cut was by far our best job." Barbara said.

Loraine set her tea glass down as she rocked forward and said, "I think so too. We each fetched a pair of sizzlers from Mom's sowing box and you took one side and I took the other and was ever Daddy mad when he saw what we had done and would not pay us our six bits either for that fine shave and haircut we gave him."

Barbara just could not help herself but laughed as she said, "He did have a few gaps in his hair that went all the way to the scalp. I still think we did a good job."

Loraine said, "Yea, we did at that. But poor Daddy had to catch a ride into town and have his head shaved anyway."

"He sure did," Barbara said, "And he never offered to give us six bits again for a Shave and a Haircut that was for sure."

"I know one thing," Loraine said as she took hold of her tea glass. "Daddy sure fussed on us whenever we got hold of his razor to shave our legs."

"That he did," Barbara added as she pop a fly before handing the fly swatter to Loraine and saying, "Your turn."

SISTER ELM

Sister Elm was Mom's best friend. Grew up together you might say. But, Sister Elm had not married even by the time Mom was pregnant with Barbara. She was always showing up at our house showing off a new dress or shoes. "Trying to impress the boys, I am," she would say to us girls as she spun around and around just a laughing showing off her new outfit she was wearing to go dancing down at the rolling rink.

And boyfriend's she had, always stopping by with one in hand, holding onto his arm showing him off to Mother. Mom would smile and when she could get Sister Elm's arm out of his, she would drag her off to the side and I heard her say, "Where the hack did you dig this guy up?" or say "That your second cousin you can't date him."

Sister Elm would always answer, "But I just love him. Isn't he just the cutis creature you ever saw?" Then she would spin away from Mama and rush back to his side and take hold of his arm. To me, I was not too sure who had who for the guy often times had this, "Lord help me," look as they went out the door.

Then one day she brought Larry to see Mother. I remember Mother got Sister Elm away and said, "If you don't marry this guy I will." To Sister Elm, Mom's words just perked her up and I'm sure she was singing as they went out the door.

Well, the Wedding was on and was to take place in Mountain View and I remember Mama putting on her Sunday Morning dress and us leaving for I was to be the ring bearer. But when we arrive, there was a tear face Sister Elm, packed and standing outside of the small church ready to leave. As she entered the car I remember her tear stain face saying, "I'm not ready for marriage."

Well, one week later here came Sister Elm with her arm through

Larry's flashing a wedding ring at us. Larry just stood and smiled as she got him to show us his ring also.

"We decided to elope. So we got married at the Courthouse." Sister Elm proclaimed. But the sad thing is Sister Elm was soon bringing new guys by for Mother's approval.

I tell this story a little heavy in heart to visualize this wonderful character whom had so much love to give but could not pined it on one man was change in an instance when she broke her back in a car wreck and we never saw her again.

STUCK TO THE ICE

Barbara opened the screen door to let Doc out to chase out after the neighbor's black cat and watched as it stood its ground to Doc. She thought he has done that a hundred times and the results are always the same. Then Barbara said, "I guess he just goes over and say hi."

From behind her, Lorraine said, "Shut the door. You are letting those flies in."

"Sorry," Barbara said as she slowly returned to her rocker.

Lorraine popped one the flies that had entered and said, "It sure was good to see Rita again. She has not changed a bit, just getting old like us."

"I was thinking back to the time she got stuck to the ice." Barbara said as she shooed a fly away from her ice tea.

Lorraine laughed as she popped another fly and said, "I remember that. That was the first time we all got drunk and it all because of Phil who we met running around on that cold night with a bottle of Rum and bucket of cokes."

Barbara reached for her fly swatter and said, "It sure was cold that night and we thought that Rum and Coke would warm us upped and Rita drank way too much of it that was for sure."

"She sure did." Lorraine answered. "We did build a fire and as we passed the glass and Rita not knowing had sat down on some ice. I guess the snow had melted into her plants and when she went to get upped found herself froze to the ground."

"Was she ever?" Barbara laughed. "She hollered and all of us being drunk did not help any while trying to get her remove from the ice. She did not want to take her pants off and we push and pull on her and eventually pried her loose. Then she could barely walk."

Lorraine popped another fly and she leaned back into her rocker she said, "I remember she got to talking on the way to take her home and when we got her there, we had a hard time getting her to be quiet as we tried to sneak her into the house."

As Barbara left her rocker to let Doc back in said, "We got in trouble that night that was for sure."

Doc entered and went straight to Lorraine to get petted. Lorraine petted him as if to say hello and said, "Did we ever. I remember we got her quiet and as quiet as we could half have dragged her to her room. Then as we settled her on her bed out the closet came her Mother and said "Rita, your drunk."

"She sure scared the hack out of us when she popped out of that closet." Barbara said as she took aim on a fly. "But I do remember Rita's answer."

"What was that?" Lorraine asked as she continued to pet Doc. Barbara laughed as she began to rock back and forth just before she said, "She sat right upped in that bed and looked right at her Mother and said, "I'm drunk and I'm proud of it." "She did?" Lorraine asked.

"She sure did." Barbara answered as she rocked ever the harder thinking what a great fiend Rita was when they were young and the fun and trouble they had together.

THAT IS A GOOD DOG SPOT

Barbara and Lorraine were sitting out on the front porch just a rocking away when Barbara looking off in the distance said, "You know Lorraine, I was thinking back to my childhood and the way we lived back then compared to now. Families just lived together. Our old would come and live with a family member and we children would watch them die before us. It is just not that way anymore. I guess that is why so many of the young have no fear of God. Death is something you watch on TV and pop in at the Church to say good bye to a great Uncle or Aunt they knew nothing about."

Lorraine stopped her rocking and reaching for her coffee said, "I think your right there. I sure do remember Aunt Flosey when she lived with us, Old blind Aunt Flosey, Grandpa's sister."

"She was something." Barbara said as she swatted a fly that got to close. "She moved around the house as if she could see and I remember we better not move the furniture. She would give us a thing or two for doing so."

"Do remember Spot, her dog?" Lorraine said as she reached for the fly swatter.

Barbara laughed as she said, "Oh, I forgot about that. Yea, I remember and to this day, I do not know if she knew we were not her dog."

Lorraine swatted at a fly as she began to rock and said, "That was just before she died when we played Spot. I remember she would hollered, "Spot, Spot, bring me a cup of water or tea and she like cookies."

Barbara swatted at the fly Lorraine had missed and started to laugh before she said, "Those peanut butter cookies Mom made were her favorite. I do remember we would put one of those cookies in our mouths and crawl on all fours into her room just a barking. She would take the cookie from our mouth and pet us on the head while saying, "That's a good dog, Spot."

Then both laughed, rocking all the harder.

THE BEAR

It was one of those cool lazy afternoons after a big Thanksgiving dinner and everybody was sitting around the front porch when Barbara asked, "Elaine, do you remember when Daddy after being outside awhile would come in and scare us telling us a bear was outside."

"Yea," Elaine said as nodded her head as if she was thinking. "He did that to us until Uncle Harrell shot the car window out."

Now always sitting near Elaine was Alice and she quickly asked, "Grandma, tell us the story how come he shot the car window out, please."

"It will be short." Elaine answered.

Alice stood and yelled, "Grandma going to tell a story. If you want to hear it better come on."

It was not long everybody was gathered around Elaine with her just a rocking thinking how to tell them about Daddy without making him out to be a drunk. Then she thought, "Well he was."

Alice interrupted her thinking when she said, "Grandma, we are ready."

Elaine looked over the faces of her family and friends before she began with, "My Daddy liked to drink. Not all the time mine you but only when he had the extra money to buy a bottle or two. My Mother called it, "His Booze."

Now when I was around ten, Barbara here was five or so, our Dad started to tease us by telling us a bear was outside and could get us. We would jump out of bed and into Mother's lap we would go. We did not know he was drinking. He hid his boozed bottle or bottles outside out of our reach and sometime when someone came to visit they would sit outside and drink until late. Sometimes Uncle Harrell or Uncle Wesley would come and go squirrel or rabbit hunting with Daddy. Then upon returning, Daddy would go fetch his hidden bottle and they would get

120

drunk out on the front porch. Mother never would allow them into house when they were drinking.

But us girls would sit and listen to their wild stories of bears and cougars and snakes. When we went to bed our heads were full of animal stories and Daddy would come and scare us by telling there was a big brown Bear outside wanting to get us. We just scream and to Mother's lap we would go.

Well it was one of those dark Moonless nights, one of those hard to see the hand in front of your face nights. Daddy and Uncle Harrell were drinking sitting out on the porch. It was late and Daddy had a new bottle and it was over half gone.

When Daddy was refilling the glasses, Uncle Harrell heard a noise and he told Daddy. Daddy just said, "It that old bear that shows up every time I get drunk."

Now Uncle Harrell was peering into the darkness, when suddenly said, "I see that old bear. In fact, I think there are two of them." He then reached for his squirrel gun and took aim and as gun wobbled around and around in front of him he said, "I'll get rid of that old bear for you." And he pulled the trigger.

Well it was not the roar of a bear they heard it was the shattering of glass. Daddy got a flashlight and they found the big bear had been nothing more than Daddy's old black Studebaker which now had a bullet hole through the windshield.

THE CRAWDAD HOLE

During the warm summer month when it had not rain for a while and dried the creeks, me, my sister and my two cousins would go down to the spring and Crawdad fish. Mother or Daddy would cut us off a hunk of salt pork from the smoke house and help us prepare several crawdad lines. Then we would head for the creek bank we would go and once there, fight over a location to throw our lines for we could see those darn crawdads moving alone the bottom in the clear spring water.

My cousins would throw rocks out into the water trying to drive some of the bigger crawdads they could see toward their bait and when one finally took hold of the bait, those crawdads hang onto it so hard allowing one of us bring it out of the water to catch it. It was mostly done by my two older cousins. Those darn things would throw out their claws as they try to crawl back into the spring and the big ones, only the boys caught. I would not go near one.

I think it was third day of my cousin's visit that summer when they came up with the idea of cooking some instead of returning them back into the creek along with the bait. We gather some limbs while Fred had gone back to the house and fetched a kettle. When the water finally got hot, my cousins drop four of the biggest crawdads we had into it. Having no salt or seasoning their tasted awful and those awful smelly guts, ooh. I tried to eat but just couldn't. I just couldn't.

I was not always happy to see my cousins come and visit but they did provide a lot of entertainment for us girls specially the picking which I just loved for they always seem to pick on me. It is too bad they both have gone to meet Jesus. I hope I'll see them again where can we can sit and talk of the many joyful days of our youth when we fished for crawdads.

UNCLE BUCK

I'm not the smartest man in the world but I have sense enough to get out the way of a falling tree when I cut it with a chain saw but not Uncle Buck. We've been out getting wood and he would stand right beside a falling tree daring it to hit him. I've seen it come close that was for sure, more than once. Then we cut and split it and we got ten-dollars a rick. Shoot we will make easily thirty dollars in a day and back then that was a lot of money.

I mean we would get calls from all around the county for one to two ricks. We furnish only white oak and for fifteen we furnish red oak. We delivered, stack it were they wanted, and often times get a five-dollar tip. Especially from old man Ragland out on back bone. Rough old ride to his place I'm telling you.

Well one day a tree got Uncle Buck. Got him good I'm telling you. It was not one of the big ones either. He was cutting a small dead oak tree in his backyard that had died. It had a large limb sticking out on one side and the Oak was located right in the middle of Aunt Bee's flower bed which was also outlined by big old rocks. She had the prettiest flowers blooming in that flowerbed all summer.

Anyway, Uncle Buck went to cutting that oak and he chose the wrong angle to cut and as it was falling, the trump slip off the stump onto the ground and began to fall upon poor Uncle Buck. He still had the chainsaw in his hand as he was trying to get out of its way, tripped on Aunt Bee's rocks. Down on his back he went and at the same time, the big limb hit and the trunk kind of rolled onto Uncle Buck catching him just below the groin on one leg with that hot chain saw caught between him and the tree.

Aunt Bee answered his call for help and because they had no phone or car she ran out onto the road and flagged the first car that came. It was AJ

Reed. He took his truck and flew across the field to Uncle Buck and using it able to roll the Trunk off of Him. When it did you could smell burnt flesh were the penned chainsaw had burned him.

Uncle Buck moved slowly for a while but he never again stood close to a falling tree that he had just cut that was for sure. I'm telling you he never did, really. Well almost never.

WHERE MY SADNESS FALLS

I guess there a lot of things in this world that is sad. I mean really sad. Like the sadness of death that comes to those we made friends with. I still remember the day of my Mother's funeral. I do not believe I ever been that sad as I was then. She was the only family member I truly love. Don't get me wrong I loved my father, brother and sister. But if they were to pass away I would not feel the pain I had when Mother died.

She was sick a long time with a bad heart and the Doctor's fix her heart but back then they could not handle the blood as they do today and she had a stroke. I remember visiting her in the hospital and she told us she heard her dead brother and others auguring outside her door. I guess that was when God was getting ready to take her. After she had the stroke, each of us would take turns sitting with her. Lucky for me she died while Daddy was with her.

Those times of sadness all of us have faced at some time in our lives. I am no different than you and I have to bury many a friend, living and dead. The old saying the best Goodbye is to leave and when they look for you, they just find you gone. No hassle, no argument, and no tears. Don't have to promise that would you call or whatever. It is like picking up a hitchhiker. You become friends as you travel. You let him out and he is gone. I met some smelling ones that I had a hard time getting their stink out of the seat later.

Today my sadness is not for the living but for all them that chose to not fear God. Remember God has chosen to be our judge. It is something I believe he never intended to be. But Satan forced him to be. The story is one third of the Angles were also. It is obvious on judging them, God made sure there would be a difference between let us say the Good and

Bad Angles. Then Satan, with a couple words from God, became a snake forever when he tricked Eve into eating the forbidden fruit.

Right now my sadness is for those I see, not knowing the word of God, and not knowing we have already been judged for there a difference between the judge and the ones that been set free. Just like the Angles, we that have been saved, have been transformed into a new creature. I am sad for all those that chose not to become such.

I remember when Barbara Jean, before her transformation, was taken and shown Hell and Heaven. For while she held Jesus' hand a man came to them within the fire and asked for one drop of water. Jesus with any remorse looked upon him and said, "You made the choice."

LAMAR TOOT

"Hi Mom, William," Billy said as he sat down in the lounge chair across from Barbara, "Just came by to tell you we got ourselves fifteen laying hens and if you like, I'll bring some fresh eggs every time when I can?"

"That will be great Billy," Barbara answered.

I had to throw my two cents in by saying, "I raised chickens twice in my life."

Billy laughed before he said, "William, when was that?"

I was going to answered when Barbara said, "When you finish I have a story to tell also."

Billy just looked at us as he opens his hands and said, "Well?" "Let me go first," I asked.

Barbara answered, "OK, only if you go get me a coke?"

I did and as I handed the coke to her, I said, "The first time was when I was a teenager. I was in charge of feeding and caring for around 20 white leggings and my mother usually gathered the eggs always checking on me to see if I fed them right."

"And the second time," Billy asked as he took the coke I held out to him.

I took a drink of my coffee before I said, "The second time was when I lived in Tennessee and rented a three story farm house, hay barn and all. Got a bunch of mixed chickens and among them were four Roosters and the hens split upped among three of the Roosters and the small Bandy Booster was left out. I can only remember the name of one of them we called, "Fog Horn." A big long next neck Rooster with red and black feathers and in the morning could he ever crow. And that poor Bandy Rooster, he was always chasing after a hen that had strayed little bit too far from the Rooster watching over them. What I really remember was the time a Hen came out of the barn and she had twenty-three baby chicks with her."

Billy lean back after opening his coke and said, "That is a lot for one hen?"

Then turning toward Barbara asked, "Well Mom, what was it you were going to say?"

She rocked a second in her chair before she said, "What I was going to say was when I was a young girl, we had two roosters that chase after us. I mean lower their head and get after us if we to get close to their hens feeding. I learned real quit to stay away from them but not Dewey or his brother Lamar. They would play and see if they could outrun the roosters and I'm telling you those roosters caught them many times before they could reach the fence."

We laughed and as we settle down from our laughter, Billy asked, "Didn't Lamar Horton have a nick name or something?"

Barbara was quiet for a second thinking before she answered, "Yes he did. Brenda and her brothers called him "Lamar Toot." I don't remember why but I can imagine."

"Me too," both Billy and I added.

A PASSING THOUGHT

I think back across my life and I've had four animals I loved and now are gone. I had a dog name Beauty as a teen while living in Waller. I needed a friend and she was it unless I was not running around with Milton at the time. He was a dear friend whom I could had make something of myself with while living in Waller.

I was beginning to notice girls. Anyway, I still had my bikes back then and I wanted to see if I could ride to town back in August or June. Hot time of the year and Beauty followed me and just Vanished. I search and search for her, had a crying fix with Mom and Dad and I guess someone stole her for she still could have pups and did. We raised Rabbits and the wild ones she would never chase and they learned she would protect them. Look out the window and there she was on guard on the ground and not five feet away could be two or more rabbits eating grass.

Beauty's death or whatever freed me to travel alone and I did until I was sent to the Military School called Allen Academy. It was a school of over 300 boys. It was not that I really wanted to get away from Mom and Dad, it was a new adventure and I just had to experience it.

Milton was hurt and thought he was the cause. I think my Dad was really concern because the Blacks were moving into the white schools. I had a lot of fun at the Academy. As I grew older and at nineteen join the Army as the Vietnam War called. I was becoming or being made into a Military man until I rebelled when I realize in many ways it was a prison when I could not leave school to go to Mother when she was not expected to live from a heart attack.

I could have gone the route into being an Officer but I did not want to lead men. I wanted to gain some knowledge, to excite my curiosity. For example, I wanted to Box at Allen's Academy. So while doing nothing I played and Boxing was one of my games I played at the Academy. I did well until I boxed a trained boxer and had a headache for three days afterward. I never boxed again. I was in it for the fun and others wanted it to be serious. That is just the start of all the Adventures I travel. The problem I had many of them I could have ended up playing the same game every day for my whole life. So instead I ran.

I guess my main problem I have had all my life is George.

MY FIRST GOOSE HUNT

It was the first winter after we had move to Waller and did my life ever change moving to from the city to the country. I had just turned fourteen and my life had just been turned upside down but not my "I want to play outside" never change. I was an outdoor boy and that is what I did.

This time of year, across the field in front of the house was a very large corn field and now thinking back, I am thankful Mr. Smith for leaving a pasture between us and his huge corn field because when the Geese came, there are thousands of them, mostly Snow Geese. At times the corn field was just covered with them and I as a fourteen-year-old was itching to bring one home for Mother to cook.

The only weapon I had at that time was my bow and arrow set and my play overcame my common sense and across the pasture I went with my bow and arrows in hand. They had dung a drainage ditch across Smith's land and as I near the pile up dirt along it, I was hoping to hide myself. I heard a car stopped upon the road and couple men came out of the car yelled but I could not understand so I ignored them. As I was about to enter into the huge ditch I heard a gunshot and over my head rung a bullet as it passed by me overhead. I quickly removed myself from their vision as another shot was fired and again I heard the rung of the bullet as it passed by and thinking were they shooting at me?

But my mind was upon the geese by then and I worked myself down the ditch to a bend that brought me a little closer to the feeding Snow Geese. I peeked out of the ditch and their sharp eyes caught me and their heads stood straight up. I poked my head back down and thinking, "What am I to do. They have already spotted me."

Thinking back, I should have charge them and as they lifted themselves into the air shot my arrow at them. But that is not what I did. Instead I shoot the arrow way into the sky above them and hoping as it would come down upon one. They must have been wise to that move, for as all three arrows came down the geese seem to see it coming and moved out the way. Frustrated, I retrieved my arrows watching the Geese scattered skyward before me and I could see they were not happy with me being there. So I quickly returned to the ditch and just shot my arrows at objects in the ditch pretending they were the geese.

As I walked across the pasture for home, I wondered if those guys in the white car were actually shooting at me. That ringing bullet was not far above my head as it passed by and I think I will never forget the sound it made either as it whined by over my head.

My first Goose hurt was not a success. But the adventure of crawling close to the ground as I tried to sneak upon those Snow Geese while I tried to get a shot at one of them with my bow and arrow still lives within me. I guess for a little bit I was a true Indian almost.

THE PICTURE SHOW

My Mother allowed me to be quit free on most outside activities as long I did cross certain line of thought which to this day I do not know what it was. She allowed me to ride my bike to Bobby's but to go there I had to travel through the Rice Village beside Rice University. Even allow me to work at the Rice University Stadium selling Cokes.

But on Saturday morning was the day of the Picture Show at the Village Theater and with my 25 cents allowance in hand I would meet Bobby at the door. Get a slowpoke and to the very front row we would go.

We were not alone for if the show was good the Village would fill up with kids, girls sitting with girls, Boys sitting with boys and to me it was not noisy but it just had to be. When the room would go dark the "Woo's" and the "O's" come forth until the movie would start and only a giggle or two could heard.

There I sat beside my friend Bobby Berman. Slow Poke in my mouth, on the front row in the middle if I could where when I looked upon the screen it filled my whole vision. As a child, it was the way I entered into a movie, get right into it. Laugh at the funny jokes, cringed at the scary parts and always sucking on that Slow Poke.

WANT HURT ME?

When I was a young boy, the only toys I had were mostly those I played with in the yard. In the summer time was what I could make from around the yard. At birthdays and Christmas time, it was cloths and a shared game and every three to four years I got a new bike. Mostly I hung around with Carl and Paul Skipper next door. But when I was by myself, my outside cars and army men is what I played with I had bought using money from mowing lawns and racking leaves or whatever I could fine to make a quarter or more.

If I remember right, it was just after school had closed for the summer, Carl or Paul came up with the idea that we could make rubber bands out of old inner tubes and stretch them over a homemade wooden gun. That is just what we did. Down to the local gas station looking for the real rubber enter tubes. They had reddest decorations within them. We also looked around the neighborhood for any thrown away lumber. Sense we were always left alone to do the boy thing as long we did not disturb the neighbors; we made ourselves some war toys.

We cut out some gun shapes long enough to just be able get that rubber band we cut out the inner tube over the end of it. On the handle we would clamp a cloths pin on it using one of the rubber bands. Then we stretched that cut out rubber band over her and after a bit and with several knots tied in the rubber band we were blasting away at each other. The rubber band only traveled about ten feet straight before quickly falling to the ground. It was more like a glob of rubber flying at you. We played enough together to not aim at our faces but to other places it was fair game. I'm sure I got shot more while trying to reload then not.

About the end of the summer I found a junk board that was over six feet long and I made a giant gun out it. It took four Rubber bands to stretch down that baby and did it ever gather knots as I shot that beauty around the yard. It was way too big to run around with so I mostly shot it to see how far it would shoot and the more knots it got the farther it went.

Well Carl, being two years older than Paul and I, did a very brave thing as I think back on it. He wanted to be shot with that darn thing right in the chest. I do not remember what I was thinking as I aimed that big bugger at him. I'm pretty sure I was thinking this is gonna hurt. I remember he stood about twenty feet away and puff out his chest as I took a bead on it and let that blob of rubber fly.

I was expecting him to fold up with pain but instead he just smiles at me and said, "That did not hurt one bit."

Some years later, Carl and I got to talking about those homemade rubber guns we had so much fun with when he said, "Remember the time you shot me with that six-foot rubber gun of yours and I told you, "It want hurt me?" I'm telling you I hurt for three days. It even put a bruised on my chest. But, not for a million dollars would I've told it hurt when you expected it to after that blob of rubber flew into me."

GOD NEEDED AN ARMY

When 9/11 occurred a neighbor brought this to me. She told me while she was weeping for those that had died Angels began to sing this song. She wrote it down and brought it to me saying I would know what to do with it. I sent it to a New York News Paper. "United We Stand" was the only outcome I believed came out of it. You make your own opinion.

God Needed an Army

God needed an army of Angles looking down from afar
Some standing right beside you, others sitting on a star
They want to tell you God needed them up above
That they are okay and they send their love

So, say your goodbyes and morn and do it your way
But remember God will bring us together one day
Don't think for a moment that they are lost
For they died for our country and God as the cost

So how much more proud of these souls could we be
More than words could say, they are hero's to be
So as they stand one by one getting their wings
Another Angle stands and sings

America, America we will not fear
For as we stand together remember our Father is near

Bonnie Coppersmith is no longer with us. I believed her myself.

GOBLE WARMING CAUSE BY WHAT

Professor Parkman lifted his head from the test papers scattered across his desk and looked into the blues eyes of a very beautiful young women. He leaned back in his chair and as he did, he asked, "May I help you?"

A smile greeted him as the young women said, "I'm Susan Haywood, your new volunteer student. I was sent from Volunteer Department located on the third floor of the Rainbow Education center."

Professor Parkman quickly leaned forward, stood and as he did he said, "About time. I asked for someone two weeks ago."

Susan laughed before she answered, "Your request was odd and it appears most of the volunteers avoided it. I been always interested in Space Science and when a friend told me you were looking for a volunteer to help you in your research for the outer space temperature Earth encounters as it travels around the Sun intrigued me none the less. So here I am ready to help you if I can?"

Professor Parkman smile as he walked around his desk holding his hand out saying, "Well Sandy, I hope you find your volunteer job here rewarding and a challenge. I guess I should say, Welcome Aboard."

After they shook hands Professor Parkman led her to a desk just outside of his office. A nice computer system was upon the desk and a large file cabinet beside it. As he pulled the nice office chair away from the desk he said, "This will be your office so to speak. I have several programs already install on the computer you should find useful in organizing the data we will be collecting."

"I can use this find computer anytime?" Susan happily asked as she sat down in the office chair.

"Yes you can." Professor Parkman said as he gently pushed her before the computer. "Now I have test papers to grade and must leave you. The password for the computer is Huey which is my first name. We'll start tomorrow at three thirty after I teach my last class. I got to leave you now and let you acquaint yourself with the programs you will be using."

"What if I have any questions about them?" Susan asked as she turned the computer on.

As Professor Parkman left her, he said, "Ask me tomorrow."

Susan quickly became his right arm in gathering the research data. She was not the first volunteer he recruited to help him in his quest to answer some of the unknowns within the unusual characteristics between the Earth and Outer Space. He liked her and found her to be one of the brightest students he has had and was diffidently the prettiest. He gave her names and places to ask for data and finally after three weeks of searching she stood before him and said, "Professor Parkman, the requisition to NASA for their Outer Space Temperature Data from the many Shuttle Flights has been granted. Here is the letter telling you it will be delivered within four weeks. It also says that they will also be sending the Space Station Data along with it."

As Professor Parkman took the letter from Susan he said, "About time. I've been trying to get this data for months and you send one letter and they just gave it to you. I wonder if ending the Space Shuttle Flights has anything to do with it."

"I don't know about that." She replied. "I believe the data is coming from a former volunteer. I think you remember him, Wilber Waid."

Professor Parkman leaned back in his chair and laugh before he said, "I remember him alright. He was the volunteer in my research in how many meteorite craters where located on the Moon's surface. Did you know, he wrote several programs that did just that? Very smart programmer he was. Anyway, we found using his programs that the number of craters to be way in the millions. We also discovered that at least 60% of the craters impacts cover many older craters impacts. In the end, we could only estimate the number. Still it was quite large."

Susan left the Professor and returned to the computer station located to the left of his door. She loaded one of the programs she was using to analyze the many different temperature inputs and began to enter some of the temperature data she had already obtained. She first entered the day, the time and the location that the temperature measurement was taken which including the distance from the Earth's surface and if it also measured the upper ionosphere temperature. The data came from every source she could find on the internet as well as the library and any source across the world she could contact. But the main source of data would be coming from NASA. How much she did not know.

Susan thought as she typed, "I hope it is enough to fill in the many gaps."

The next few weeks, before NASA's Data would arrive, she continued to search for data on the internet. That was when she found an interesting article by Gaillard JR speculating that the rise in Earth's Temperature could be directly related to two natural reasons and had nothing to do with man. It defined natural occurrences, as events that occur naturally that affects the whole world's temperature and not just local areas.

It described the first Natural Theory for Goble Warming as the result of our Solar System wondering into a region of Outer Space that has been warmed by one of the exploding Nova Suns million years ago. The article determined these large heated regions of outer space once formed drift away from the original exploded material area and float through outer space slowly cooling off. The article surmised when our Solar System enters into one of these drifting hot regions, the warmer outer space temperature causes a rise in Earth's temperature resulting in the Global Warming as seen today. The article almost as an afterthought asked the reader to think what would happen if the orbit of the planets were slowly rotating within the direction the Sun was traveling would this not also do the same?

The article then generalized that the other natural cause for Goble Warning to be results of a large concentration of carbon dioxide gas escaping from the world's oceans. It summarizes that carbon dioxide is collected by the water vapor in the atmosphere which eventually falls back to Earth within the rain droplets as carbonate acid and eventually migrates into the oceans. It also pointed out that there were lots and lots of data collected from analyzing pass volcano eruptions that the masses amount of carbon dioxide emitted during those eruptions must have been removed by some natural cause and only the water vapor in the atmosphere could do that. Otherwise it stated, the large amount of carbon dioxide emitted by the volcanoes would have maintained its presence within the atmosphere and melted the icecaps long ago. The article determined that

Earth has a self-cleaning atmosphere using the elemental properties within water vapor allowing it to collect anything that enters the atmosphere and eventually sends it back to Earth in the form of rain. It asked the reader to consider how much water vapor is above the oceans and how hurricanes are formed and how strong they can become. Consider how much carbon dioxide was removed from the atmosphere by just one of them. It clarified its analysis by proclaiming that this was the natural way for cleaning Earth's atmosphere of any unwanted elements or gasses that has surpassed its normal saturation level in the atmosphere.

The article then summarized that if the reports are true that the carbon dioxide level in the atmosphere is rising, it could only mean carbon dioxide is entering the atmosphere faster than the system can remove it. The most promising Natural Theory for Goble Warming and the most likely reason heat waves appears in seasons had to do with carbon dioxide in large amounts dissipating from out of the oceans at one time. It explains this theory by referring the reader to a time of intense volcanic activity some billion years ago. The tremendous amount of carbon dioxide emitted by this activity was collected by the water droplets and through natural events eventually finds itself within the world's oceans. Then after a few hundred years this high concentration of carbon dioxide that is now totally mixed within the world's oceans eventually rises to the ocean's surface an escapes causing a sudden rise in carbon dioxide the cleaning system of Earth cannot remove except over time. This cycle is repeated over and over while many new carbon dioxide cycles being added until now Earth experiences this event one or two times a century. The article seriously determined that each time this sudden rise in carbon dioxide appears there is also a slight global warming. Still it stated there must be times when these carbon dioxide events do not appear for a time causing a global cooling cycle resulting in colder winters and such. These cycles have been going on forever the article claimed. The rise in carbon dioxide in the atmosphere today the article surmised must have been provided by volcanic activity somewhere in the distance pass when enough carbon dioxide was emitted to warm the atmosphere enough to melt the icecaps.

Susan presented the article to Professor Parkman to receive his input. He started to laugh until he thought what if the guy was right. Can the temperature data he is collecting for the study prove this fellow right in his first theory on Goble Warming? That our solar system is traveling through a heated region in space? He presented his view to Susan. In the end their only conclusion would be to wait and let the data determined if this article was right or not.

Every time Susan sat down at Professor Parkman's computer she had a new purpose. To find out if the cause for the rise in the temperature in Earth's Atmosphere was or was not the result of a heated region in outer space.

She got to thinking, "What if we have just entered this heated region of Outer Space and the closer we get to the middle of this heated zone the hotter we become. If so then all is lost for Greenland's ice will surely melt resulting in flooding the shores lines of the whole world. I hope he is wrong."

Almost four weeks to the day after receiving the earlier letter from NASA, the outer space temperature data arrived. Susan showed it to Professor Parkman for there were over a thousand pages and on each page the temperature data, when and where it was collected, was listed randomly.

Susan said, "I would think NASA had better records than this random listing."

Professor Parkman examined the data for a few minutes looking through the many pages and said, "That because it comes from many sources and departments over time. I guess no one has ever organized the data or needed to. From what I can see, the data was only reported when it was required."

He looked at Susan's worried face and said, "If you like, I can get others to help you. I know you only volunteer six hours a week."

Susan smiled and a sign of relieved followed as she said, "That would be great."

For the next few weeks, NASA's Temperature Data was inputted into the many different programs and a picture was slowly appearing in the data. Susan said nothing about it as page after page was entered filling the many gaps she had with her earlier data. The other volunteers came and went. Some worked for a week. Some worked for a day. They all asked questions concerning the data. Professor Parkman or Susan gave the same answer that they were just trying to establish the temperature of outer space around Earth as she orbits around the sun. Does it vary or does it remain the same?

When the last page was entered, Susan and Professor Parkman began to work the data into a usable form. They created a listing from the earliest recording to the latest. They work carefully to sketched charts and established a well-defined temperature pattern located within the data. They also created a summation of what the temperature of Outer Space was throughout Earth's orbit. The results shock both of them none the least. The data diffidently showed that the temperature of Outer Space around Earth has been heating up ever so slightly over the pass forty years. But the analysis of the outer space temperature Earth encounters on any given year as it travels around the Sun only changes slightly when Earth's orbit is at its closest and farthest from the Sun.

Friday before the conference, Susan entered Professor Parkman's office with a copy of the data he had asked her to leave on his desk and she thought as she looked around the room at the Outer Space Pictures hanging on the wall, "I bet the Outer Space temperature has been rising like this for over a long time. Maybe sense the last ice age even."

Susan placed the data with a note attached to it upon his desk where he would surly find it and left for the weekend. She was pleased with herself. She had helped Professor Parkman prepare for the Environment Conference that was meeting that weekend in Little Rock and the data and graphs showed clearly that the Outer Space temperature around Earth has been heating up.

But as Susan stood outside his office she thought, "Have I forgotten anything? I've left a note with the data he wanted copied telling him I have the original data and paper work. I have copied all the computer programs and Data on several of those removal storage devices. I just hope I haven't forgotten something. For some reason, I feel deep down in my women's instinct Professor Parkman's data is going come up missing. I just know it is."

The next Monday afternoon as Susan was about to knock upon Professor Parkman's office door she noticed her computer system was gone. She quickly walked over and examined her work area. All the paper data was also missing from the cabinet. Susan smiled and said, "I was right. Professor Parkman's data and report was in danger. I wonder how the person that took the computer and data even knew about Professors Parkman's research. I bet from the conference. He must have surely made an impact there."

Susan turned and quickly entered Professor Parkman's office and there tied to his chair and gagged was Professor Parkman. She could tell he was real happy to see her as she entered.

Susan quickly rushed over and asked, "What Happen?" as she nervously started to untie the gagged from around his mouth.

Professor Parkman took a deep breath before he said, "I am sure glad to see you. I thought I might be like this forever. About noon I was organizing the data to put in the research paper when three large men in gray suits entered. One of them told me our research was unlawful. Then they tied me up, gagged me and left with all our data and programs. I also heard them take the computer outside arguing over who was going to carry it."

Susan eventually got Professor Parkman's hands untied and as she straightens upped said, "But all is not lost, Professor Parkman. I felt in my heart all last week as we were finishing organizing the data that your study was in danger. So, I have made a copy of all the data papers including the work I left on your desk. I took the original data and left the copies in the cabinet. I know from watching Judge Judy if you do not have your original research data it would be difficult to prove you did or did not do it."

Professor Parkman, as he untied his legs from the chair said, "That is great."

Susan left his side and said, "Who do you think wanted to destroy your research anyway."

Professor Parkman stood rubbing his wrists, smiled as he said, "I bet it was that group of specialist blaming carbon dioxide emissions for Earth's atmosphere problems. I listened to them at the Environment Conference Saturday. It appears that they are about to make millions, if not billions off the tax payers with their many gadgets to stop carbon dioxide emissions."

Professor Parkman looked at Susan as she gathered the rope from off the floor before he said, "At the conference, I presented our research and explained the data we collected. That our Solar System was traveling through a hot zone in Outer Space. I displayed the graphs and proved the theory with all the Outer Space temperature data. I was asked many questions about this new theory. I answered them as best I could. I also told them I would have our results published within a month or two. I been thinking I must have scared the carbon dioxide people enough to believe our research was about to prove them wrong and they would lose all their governments contracts. Particularly, if any research from other professors also proves us right. I talked with Professor Green from Northern Flicker and several more professors in private. They were all excited about this new theory. I told them where we got our research data and that I would be happy to help them if I could. They only asked for the Outer Space temperature data and I told them I would send a copy to them to analysis. That way they could determine for themselves if our research is right or not."

Susan placed the rope in the trash can and asked, "If you have a list of these Professors, I could send them a copy of the Outer Space Temperature and research data."

Professor Parkman walked over to the coffee pot and poured a cup full before he said, "Yes, I have it. But there something I have not told you."

"What is that?" Susan asked worriedly.

Professor Parkman turned, set his coffee cup down and seriously said, "Susan, those men told me that if I publish the research, they will come and hurt everyone I love. That also includes you. I am sorry. I mentioned your name several times at the conference and reported that without you I could not have found this new theory for the global warming."

Susan walked over, pushed Professor Parkman aside and began pouring herself a cup of coffee saying, "I think I need a cup after what you just told me."

Professor Parkman retrieved his coffee quickly moved away from Susan seeing she was very upset and nervous over his words and said seriously, "Susan, I'm sorry to say, I just cannot publish. As I sat tied to my chair I had time to think and I have determined that neither you nor I can change what is going to happen to this world. We can tell them and shout it loudly from the roof top. I am almost certain our cry will go unnoticed. And another thing, I do not want to live in fear the rest of my life and that is just what I would be doing if I publish the search data we have worked so hard to obtain."

Susan took a good drink of her coffee which seemed to calm her, looked sadly into the Professor's Eyes and even more sadly asked, "What do you want me to do?"

Professor Parkman thought for a second before he said, "I found your note Saturday morning before I went to the conference. I guess you better bring back the research data and programs you have. Your foresight last Friday to save our research Data and programs is greatly appreciated."

"Thank you," Susan embarrassing answered as she looked away while taking a drink of her hot coffee again feeling its calming effect.

Professor Parkman looked seriously at her and said, "Susan, after you leave the data and programs, I want you to go about your school work and forget about me. I will send out the copies of the data to the professors myself leaving you out of the ring of fire if trouble occurs. I do not want you hurt and another thing, I believe it would be best you never come back here at all. I do want to tell you it has been a great honor to have such a bright and very beautiful volunteer student around the office. I'm just sorry things have worked out as they did."

Susan sat her coffee down beside the coffee maker and took a deep breathed before she said, "It will be late this afternoon before I can fetch it from home. If you're not here, I'll just leave everything on your desk."

She turned to leave the office Professor Parkman said very graciously, "That will be fine and I will miss you."

Susan stopped at the door, returned a small smiled and sadly said, "I'll miss you also, Professor Parkman."

Professor Parkman sat back down at his desk after Susan left the room and opened the top drawer. Calmly and slowly he picked the cashier's check out of the drawer and looked closely at the colorful designs on its surface. A nice smile filled his face as under his breath he said, "Five zeros you have written on you and I'll be getting nine more just like you for not publishing my research data. It's too bad I had to fool beautiful Susan. I knew she would never understand and I had to get back the data she saved."

Professor Parkman leaned farther back in his chair and held the cashier's check up above his head examining the amount written upon it. Slowly he brought the cashier's check to his face and ran it under his nose imagining the sweet smell of its money in his hand. Lowered it to his lips, kissed it and as he again lifted the check into the air he proudly said, smacking his lips, "Five zero's you got and I'll be getting nine more just like you."

THE ISO 10,000

Professor Joey Williams placed the ISO 10,000 within in the photographic compartment of the Fan Telescope located near the perimeter of Huey's Multi-Telescope System and closed the door. It had taken him almost ten years of waiting to get his turned here at the research Telescope Center located on the far outer banks of the Solar System. It wasn't because there was a lot of Professors. It was because it took a little over two months of space travel to get here and due to excessive bone lost, you were only allowed to stay one year when the next shuttle arrives with replacements. Of course he was not the only Professor to make the trip with him but he was the only one researching the outer most reaches of the Universe at this time. He had been sent by The Department of Astrology at The University of Freeport in Texas to gather as much information he could using the newly developed photographic plate able to catch the faintness of light. It was believed could catch and image from the far reaches of the Universe, The ISO 10,000.

Joey pushed himself from the Telescope and floated toward the controls thinking. "I hope this works as well as it does on paper."

He was just positioning himself before the computer when Professor Carl Boren floated in and said, "Good Morning Joey, just stopped by to tell you breakfast is ready below."

Joey looked at Carl who had become his good friend and said, "Just starting to expose my first ISO 10,000 Plate. Did you know it took Fred Newton and me all day yesterday to position the Fan upon the outer reaches of space where earlier research indicated there was nothing but empty space?"

Carl floated over beside him and said, "It did and where is Fred?" "Sleeping I guess." Joey answered and smiled at Carl.

Carl drifted over to the computer image and examined Joey's telescope positioning and said, "It does look like empty space."

He then drifted over to the ISO 10,000 Plates and said, "So that is what an ISO 10,000 Plate looks like. I thought it would be bigger from all the hyped about them."

Joey set the computer controls to open the Photograph Chamber to the vacuum of outer space and said, "Their design to fit into a Photographic Chamber of these telescopes and still work."

Carl drifted back toward the door and asked, "You never told us you had ISO 10,000 plates to work with. I've read up on them and my department is thinking of using them in the future to see if we are able to obtain photographs of the insides of many of the far out Galaxies."

Joey laughed and said, "I guess I didn't. Just did not want to be question all the way here and you know their construction is really not a secret? I really only know the fundamentals myself."

Carl asked, "The fundamentals are all you know? Well tell me something to ease my curiosity."

Suddenly a beep was heard from the control panel indicating the photographic chamber had reach space vacuum and Joey could open the ISO 10,000 Plates to the telescope input. As he answered the Yes on the computer screen, Joey said, "Here goes ten thousand bucks."

Joey looked back toward Carl and said, "I was told the ISO 10,000 Plates were developed by the corroboration of many research facilities over the last ten years after the discovery there were many liquefied solutions when placed within a perfect vacuum could be manipulated by an electrical field."

Carl, as he took a closer view of one of the plates, asked, "You mean these are really vacuum chambers."

Joey laugh as he said, "I guess you could say that."

"But they look like any of the other photographic plates we use," Car asked with a puzzle sound to his voice.

"Let me tell what I know about them and isn't very much," Joey said as he check the computer read outs.

"Well make it short. I'm hungry and I'm late for work already." Carl said as he pushed himself closer to the door.

Joey double checked the computer readings and wrote down the time before pushing himself away from the computer to follow Carl who was now waiting outside in the hall smiling. Joey exited, locked the room's door and listened for a second of the door sealing itself before turning toward a smiling Carl and asked, "So you want to know more about the ISO 10,000 plates do you?

Carl laughed as he started down the hallway saying, "Yea."

Joey, following closely behind Carl, said, "Now inside one of the ISO 10,000 Plates is a liquefied compound of some type caught within a very low charged circular electrical field. I was told the electrical field could be adjusted to capture the compound in layers as thin as several thousand angstroms to several millimeters depending upon the mutagenesis atom structure used. Anyway, once caught and establish within this electrical field the compound becomes very stable until a single light electron enters and collides with one of the elemental mutagenesis atom structure freeing the Phosphorus Atom attached within it. The Phosphorus Atom remains fairly stationary while the incoming light electrons freed more and more Phosphorous Atoms recording the existence of distance Galaxy formations which we otherwise are unable to see."

Carl, while reaching for another push along rod, asked, "How do you analyze the results?"

"That is the easy part?" Joey answered. "We exposed the plate to very low power Ion field which locks the Phosphorus within the untouched elemental mutagenesis allowing us to view the results, make pictures or whatever."

Carl said, "That is very interesting. But what kind of image would you get if you expose it to let us say Galaxy X792 or one of the closer Galaxies."

Joey answered, "Way too much light unless you could expose it for a Nano Second or less."

Carl stopped himself at the stair leading downward and said, "Just an idea. Anyway, let's catch breakfast before it gets cold."

Joey followed and said, "It is always cold."

Twenty-four hours later Fred and Joey removed the first ISO 10,000 Plate, expose it to the Ion field, waited the required time for Ion Stabilization before they carefully removed the vacuum chamber hardware from around it.

Joey lifted the ISO 10,000 negative toward a light source and examined the negative within. Then while he handed the plate to Fred he said, "I guess we should make an enlarged print of the negative." Fred took the plate and floated toward the door asking, "Ten times ought to do. Don't you think?"

Joey nodded as he said, "Yea," and as an afterthought, yelled at the disappearing Fred and said, "And make sure you use the photographic materials we brought with us."

Joey floated over to the Fan's photograph chamber and placed another ISO 10,000 Plate into it and closed the chamber's door. Floated to the control computer and entered the start sequence to expose the ISO 10,000 to the vacuum of space. Floated toward the only window in the room and looked out across the telescopes pointing toward the stars.

When Fred returned he said, "Charley told me the print should be ready within two hours."

Joey still looking out the window said, "You know Fred. It is hard to believe they were able to build this research center with sixteen high power telescopes evenly spaced around and along its pill shape body. Then place it in an obit beyond Pluto where you could focus on one star, leave for twenty years and when you come back it would still be focus on that star."

"It is a wonder I do say." Fred said as he floated over to the computer which indicated the photographic chamber had reached the vacuum in space.

Joey left the window and said, "Start her up and let us exposed this one for three hundred hours. If the first one won't show us anything maybe this one will."

Fred opened the ISO 10,000 Plate to the telescope's input and said, "I hope so."

Fred and Joey fool around the room until a phone call indicated their print was ready. Left and as were the rules, locked the door which also sealed the lab if a vacuum breach should occur.

After retrieving the print along with the ISO 10,000 negative, they floated to the special viewing room with its fancy equipment for analyzing prints and negatives. The viewing room was empty when they entered and Fred quickly set the print within the quick view which was basically a real fancy microscope allowing one to magnify the prints surface several times.

The print itself indicated the same image as the telescope image back at the lab except for one very faint area near the left side of the print. Fred placed it in the higher power system and the image showed at times a where it collected many pin points of light and one larger. What they indicated at this time was unknown and even the larger pin light area did the same.

As they left the viewing room, Joey said, "Fred, I am really pleased with the results so far. I believe the next ISO 10,000 Plate will unquestionably give us a better understanding of what we notice here today."

"I believe it will." Fred said as they floated toward the lunch room.

The next few days Fred and Joey randomly checked the computer readouts finding all was well with their telescope set up. After three hundred hours and as with the first plate, they ran it through the Ion field, acquired a large print and traveled to the viewing room. Under close examination their finding was nothing what they expected. There were many more very faint pin points of light on the print and the largest one appeared to be a ball of light. It confused them until Professor Boren and Professor Ming entered the picture.

Joey was in the dining room discussing his findings with Professor Boren over coffee the next day when he said, "Those are not Galaxies you are seeing. From what you have described they appear to be far off Universes like ours."

Joey looked at Carl as he took a drink of his coffee analyzing Carl's words. Then as he sat his coffee container into the drink holder he said, "Why do you say that?"

"It is really very simple." Carl answered. "Our Universe appears to have a diffident size while space itself is boundless. Doesn't it seem right that our Universe is not the only Universe in space but just one among trillions?"

Joey lean back in his chair and asked, "That could be true. But what if they turn out to be Galaxies?"

"It is the same scenario." Carl answered. "If space is boundless then the Galaxies must be boundless also. I for one think it will be Universes."

"Carl, you know you just shot the Big Bang Theory to pieces." Joey said as he picked his coffee from out of the holder and took a sip on the straw.

"Not really." Carl said, "Remember our Universe has its own identity and it could expand and collapse just as the Big Bang Theory theorize."

Suddenly from the other eating table beside them came, "I hate to interrupt you. I've been listening to you theorizing over your research findings and I have another theory."

Joey looked at Professor Ming from China and said, "Let's hear it. Can't be any crazier then Carl's."

Ming seemed very serious as he said, "We at the Zong research Center and several other Centers across the world have been calculating the shape of the Universe not by trying to locate and plot every Galaxy but are doing it by groups of a hundred thousand or more Galaxies. You could say we are doing it in sections. Right now the research in inconclusive but what we have is showing our Universe to have a very slight spiral shape somewhat like a giant Galaxy."

Carl raised his hand and said, "Woo there, Professor Ming. Are you saying our Universe is actually a Galaxy of Galaxies?"

"That is what the research is showing." Ming answered. "But that is not my theory."

Joey said, "Well continue please."

Ming pushed himself away from his table and settle at theirs. Set his tea in the cup holder and started to say something when he noticed the other professors in the dining room settling themselves around their table to listen. Ming's hand with one finger slightly out was before him emphasizes his words with it as he said, "As I said, the research is showing the Universe has a very faint spiral shape somewhat like a giant Galaxy. I saying that loosely for the Universe is still a ball only there is a higher concentration of Galaxies position such if you could view our Universe from afar I believe it would appear to have a faint spiral shape like one of the Galaxies."

Ming stopped and looked at both Carl and Joey and asked, "Understand so far?"

Both Carl and Joey nodded their head and said, "Yes."

"Good," Ming said as he lifted his tea and took a draw on the straw before continuing. "I agree with Professor Boren, that Professor William's research data is indicating the presents of other Universes located outside of our Universe. I believe when Professor Williams is done and has a clear image of a far off Universe he will find they will also be a spiral shape located inside. I can only add to Carl's theory if you find just one Universe it could mean there is no limit to them. I mean we could even have a

Universe of Universes having a Galaxy shape and so on. Because Space is boundless, this scenario would repeat itself over and over again forever."

Joey, when Ming finish said, "I hope my data proves your theory Professor Ming. It's a good one."

Carl agreed.

Joey looked around at the professors gathered around and said, "I have calculated it will take at least five thousand hours of exposure to obtain any kind of clear image. It would be best if I could have other Telescopes doing the same in other directions. Help to prove Professor Ming's theory. My problem is my school can only afford one Telescope."

For the next hour the Professors within the Dining Room discuss Ming's theory and the need to add more Telescopes in proving it. As those in the Dining Room continued to discuss Joey's need for more Telescopes, word spread throughout the facility. Soon the room was filled with Professors wanting to add their opinion.

Finally, Professor Harris, the Director, received word concerning the meeting in the Dining Room and just what was being discussed there. When he entered he yelled real loud, "Quiet."

The room quickly quieted down as he floated across and settled before Joey. Look around the room before he turned to Joey and said, "Professor Williams, I have heard about the results you are finding with the new ISO 10,000 Plates. Right now we have six Telescopes not being used and I see no use of letting them sit."

Then turning towards the other professors he said, "You all know we are actually a team working together to provide knowledge of the cosmos to world back home. I want twelve volunteers to aid Professor Newton and Professor Williams in their work by setting the six unused Telescopes onto six areas along the border of the Universe where there is empty Space."

After the meeting, it wasn't long till six more ISO 10,000 Plates were in operation, gathering the faint light from the regions of empty Space the twelve Professors located. The whole Station was in anticipation of what the ISO 10,000 Plates will show after the exposed time is reach. Over the next few months, besides checking each Telescope System daily, Fred and Joey worked with many of the other Professors who needed help.

Finally, just two weeks before the shuttle arrived, they removed the seven exposed ISO 10,000 Plates, ran them through the Ion field and placed them into the Print Center. Several hours later, Fred and Joey carried the finish prints into the Viewing Room. Carl was waiting for them just inside the door and said, "I'll be outside making sure no one interrupts your examination. The word spreading and I'm sure many curious Professors will be by if I don't"

Joey said, "Thanks, but that won't be necessary. I have a sign for the door. But you can spread the word I will report our findings in the Dining Room at seven. That's six hours away and should give us plenty of time to have some kind of results by then."

Carl did spread the word and at quarter to seven, Fred and Joey entered into a packed Dining Room. Joey waited till all was quiet before he said, "Professors, I want to Thank you all for the support and help. The ISO 10,000 Plates worked like a charmed and has giving the world a better understanding of the Cosmos we live in. Now for the first time we have a clear view of what is beyond our Universe borders. Fred."

Fred smile as he placed a very large print upon the display board before them. There was a grasped as the Professors looked upon a beautiful image of a Universe in all its glory. It had an almost perfect ball like shape with a brightly well-lit center and there within it was a faint spiral shape somewhat like a Galaxy could be seen.

Joey pointed to areas outside the Universe image and said, "I also want to point out to you the many faint stars located around the Universe. I believed they indicate the existence of many more Universes."

Suddenly, the Professors began to applaud Fred and Joey's results with several yelling, "Way to go."

As the Professors settle down, Fred placed the image of three more Universes upon the display board which seem to excite the Professors even more. No longer was the room quiet as the Professors began discussing Fred and Joey's results among themselves for all three Universes had a very similar ball shape with a bright center with one of the Universes having a greater image of a Galaxy shape within it.

But when Fred place the other three ISO 10,000 Plate images upon the display board, the Professors really grasped for there before them where three images of thousands of pin lights like one would see in the night sky upon Earth and one even showing the star lights in a slight Milky Way alignment.

The Dining Room had become very quiet as each Professor was really beginning to grasp just what Professor Fred and Joey had accomplished. It remained that way even as Joey placed himself before them and said, "I believe our research has shown to all here that our wonderful Universe is not alone in the Cosmos. That beyond our Universe borders, they are as many Universes as there are Galaxies in our Universe. But Space has no limit. I have a feeling there is really no limit to the number of Universes in the Cosmos, that they go on forever. I know there have been several theories floating around. They all could be right for all I know. In a couple weeks we will be taking our Data Home and releasing it to the Astrological Science Community to study and report their findings to the World. I say our, for there is not one Professor here that has not had some input or has not supported us in one way or another. Now if you will forgive us, we must have organized and prepare to return home. Again I want to thank you and I will leave the prints on the display board for you to study at your pleasure."

Two months later Fred and Joey exited the Space Shuttle and as they entered the lobby, there to meet them were many reporters yelling questions. Joey looked at Fred and said, "We in for it now."

Fred answered as the two of them entered the group of reporters and said, "I agree."

SORROW

In my early forties, I was in a battle with myself and I needed a rest away from all the problems I had generated around me. So I bought a three-wheel bicycle and a small covered wagon, placed my camping gear in the wagon and down the road I went leaving everything behind. I was seeking a time alone and of course seeking a little adventure at the same time as I walk away pulling that bike and wagon out into the unknown and pulled it I did. It was also something I wanted to do ever since I was a child.

I would pull that bicycle and wagon up a hill and could hit 35 mph going downhill from the speedometer I mounted across the front tire. I did it just to see how fast I could get. Just like a kid would do. It Is not to say, I didn't get worried a few times thinking I was going to crash now you. Then as night came, I always was able to fine an out the way place to sleep just off the road. Made a little fire and rested under the star light after I had given prayer of thanks for good day of traveling.

Nobody bothered me I as I travel along the country roads of Tennessee and as I neared the Louisiana border about an hour before Sundown I met my first road traveler not long after I had exiting a small town called "Paradise." He was sitting on one of those cement walls across a small bridge all hunch over and as drew closer, I asked, "Hello friend, you walking the road also?"

He looked at me and I quickly notice in his breaded face there just seem to be sadness about him. He was not old yet not young either and looked like a traveling prophet with his long beard and his all white robe. He stood as I drew closer asking me, "Mine if I walk with you a ways?"

"Sure," I answered noticing he had no backpack or gear at all.

As I continued walking across the small bridge, he followed me and looking back at him thinking, "There walks a man that has an image of someone that in agony and pure sadness with his body all hunch over, head down and at times, was not sure he wasn't crying. He just followed me as I traveled and at times he would walk near me whenever I slow down pulling my bike and wagon up a hill. Not a word did he speak just stared down the road as we walked in his sadness and as the rule of the open road there is no past so I asked no questions. But his hunched back walk with head bent down gave him such a sad appearance that even reflected all the way into his wrinkled breaded face.

As night fell, I found a place for us to camp well off the road in the woods and using my small barbeque pit I carried, I made a fire in it from dry wood I found. A few mosquitoes were buzzing and I was hoping the fire would keep them away. As I prepared my bed, my traveling companion took a seat beside a tree sitting cross legged watching me. The sound of the cicadas filled the woods. Fire flies were flicking their light around us probably complaining of the smoke from my fire.

Satisfied, I sat down and closing my eyes, I thank God for nice day and I sought the Lord on behalf of my new traveling friend. But before I could ask the Lord for a good tomorrow there came a very strong Spirit of Peace in me as I have never felt before. I looked at this sad man feeling the Holy Ghost's great love and wonder did he feel it also.

So I broke the silence asking, "You have an image of someone in great sorrow my friend."

"That I am," he answered before lowering his head shaking it in sadness.

"Why do you say that," I asked taking my shoes off massaging my aching feet after they had worked so hard to get me where I was at this moment and it felt good too when his words made me stopped, "I discovered my little girl and boy dying. When it happened, I was resting and awoke to the knowledge of what they had done."

"Wow, that is sad," I answered before going back to massaging my feet and using the hand cream, I added that to my massage and as I looked upon the sad man, his sorry reached way into my Soul and somehow in the Spirit I felt his pain while trying to imagine what could have happened to the children. As I continued massaging my feet and lower legs, I just could not help myself and asked, "What did they do" and after that came out of my mouth, I thought, "I should not have asked that, darn my hide."

He seemed to study me for a second before from within that sad bearded face he said, "Would you like to listen to my story."

"Sure," I answered as left my feet and filled my cup full of hot tea from the pot I had placed upon the small fire and as I did ask, "I would like to hear it and would you like some hot tea."

He did not answer me only said, "I should never had planted that poison fruit tree in the Garden. I did and now they are both dead."

As he took a minute in his sadness, I settled back against the tree with my cup of hot tea watching him and his sorrow was feeding my soul, mine you. As I took my first taste of the hot tea and as its nice favor filled my mouth, I was thinking he was just going to sit all cross legged like that all night. But I opened my mouth when I should have kept it shut again and politely said, "Wow, I feel for you."

Suddenly he stood to his feet looking down at me saying, "You cannot even imagine how I felt as I held my beautiful little girl in my arms and watch her die. Her eyes looking upon me for help that I could not give. I place her upon the ground and reached and picked up my lifeless morning little boy and held him in my arms wanting so much to bring him back to me."

Tears felled his eyes as he folded his arms into a position as if he was holding the boy's body. Then he began to rock back and forth weeping while lowering himself till he was on his knees. His rocking and his tears was a display of sorry, as I have never seen. I could not help it as his action and words brought tears to my eyes watching this man in a white robe reenact to the time he held his morning son in his arms giving me an understanding of his sorrow and his image even became ever more sorrowful as slowly he unfolded his arms and lower his head all the way to the ground and out of his sorrow and within the weeping came, "I told them to stay away from that tree and do not eat any of its fruit for within its fruit was a great poison that I could not remove from their body and if they even took a nibble of its fruit the poison in it will kill them."

As he lay weeping before me, I had a hard time taking a sip of my hot tea thinking on how much pain he must have had to enter his garden to fine his Son and daughter dying and also thinking at the same time that I might feel the same as he does if they were my son and daughter."

As I took a drink the last of my hot tea, I watch him rolled over and settle again into a cross legged position facing me, he wiped the tears from his eyes saying, "You probably wondering why I planted such a tree in my garden?"

"I was wondering that very same question," I answered watching him again wipe his face with his robe's white sleeve before asking him, "Would you like some tea."

"Thanks, but no," he answered me as he leans back glancing up at the Stars saying, "I've worked a long time creating my Garden. I place everything in order making sure the land beneath it did not erupt and destroy my work. I put life in it and I was pleased with what I accomplish and had one fruit tree that was the most beautiful tree in the world. When it blooms it had flowers that sparkled with beauty and the air was filled with their sweet smelling fragrance. Even the fruit hung was a delight to see but within its fruit was a great poison. I enjoy its great beauty and placed my Daughter and Son nearby such that when I visited the garden to let them name the many beautiful creatures living in the Garden I could look and admire its beauty."

He glanced back at me before he continued saying, "I explained to them they could eat the fruit from any fruit tree in the garden but the fruit from this tree was a great and powerful poison. That if they did, they would die just knowing they would obey me. They did not."

Again he bent over and lowered his head shaking it while repeating sadly, "They did not. They did not."

He became quiet before he looked upped at me and with tears in his eyes said, "With my beautiful fruit tree's poison in them I had to place them out of my Garden. I'll never forget having to pick up their poisoned bodies and carry them toward the Garden's gate and all around me every Angel in Heaven was weeping along with me causing the heavens to shake under their morning. Many of my wonderful creations gathered around me as I slowly traveled toward the Garden's gate also feeling my great sadness.

Suddenly his nature changes as anger filled him as he stood and throwing his white robe back of him and speaking with a loud voice said, "I look at that fruit tree and I strip it of its beauty and cut the life it lives on from it. But I could not kill it and now, it sits waiting to be awaken and it beauty bloom again. Then I holler out, "Satan, come here."

As he spoke his last words, the Holy Ghost seem to explode within me and as he looked down upon me, I'm thinking there is way more to this sad breaded man than meets the eye as he postured seem to change as he suddenly turns and walked out into the darkness leaving the campsite. But at the edge of the flickering light from the small camp fire and within the flickering and flashing of the fire flies, turned and glanced back at me and within that shaggy bearded face, I could just barely make out a smile as he said, "Goodbye my child and thanks for listening to my story."

The vision of him walking away leaving me all alone within the dying embers of my fire never left me as I added more wood to get the fire going again. Then as I adjusted myself into my covers for night, I keep glancing out into the darkness around me wondering was he really God.

ROBERT'S MONEY

Let me tell you a little story about how Robert a good friend of mind views money. I always wondered why he was so generous with his money. He was going on seventy like me and was one of the pool players at the Senior Center. He was a tall man and strong, but like me, falling apart for to work brings pain. So we sit and play games and the men had their own room with dominoes and pool and we had our but Robert sometimes would play cards with us but not today far I saw Lenard drive up outside.

But before Lenard enter and as Robert was getting himself a cup coffee, one of his sister kids, a grandchild to be exact and said, "Uncle Robert, Wesley done got himself in a fix and was wondering if he could borrow couple hundred off you."

As Robert picked up his coffee cup and took a taste he asked, "What has happened now? Has Wesley truck broken down again?"

She gave him a glance in a way I knew she was lying as she answered, saying, "Not his truck, Edward's. Wesley working on it and needs a part and I'm fetching it. It cost three hundred and twenty and his hoping you will help him out getting the part he needs."

As Robert reached to pull out his checkbook, he started to look for a pen when Paula held one out to him saying, "Here Uncle Robert, I've got a pen."

He took the pen and looking down at her, gave her a smile saying, "Expensive part but everything cost more today it seems."

He wrote the check and as he handed the check and the pen back to her said, "Paula, I added a ten to get Wesley and you something to eat."

"Thanks, Uncle Robert," Paula answered as she turns and left him.

I watched her go saying, "You just gave her the money no questions asked."

Taking a drink of his coffee Robert glance at me and said, "They don't come seeking unless it is really needed. So I help them."

"I'm not sure I would," I answered.

Robert turned and refreshed his coffee saying, "Most people want give to strangers I agree. But I have different view of Government's money than most. You see I trust our government will send my Social Security and Disability VA check every month. So the way I see it, I have way more then I need to live on, so I help people that need it and if I give, I don't seek a repayment. If you had a need I give to you if you asked."

"But you earn that money," I returned.

"That is true for Social Security but the VA disability check I did not ask for," he answered.

"How did you get that," I asked as I walked around him to refill my almost empty coffee cup.

Robert move out of my way saying, "I had a heart attack ten years ago in 2006 and they put several stents in me and then out of the blue called me in to see some women doctor from Washington DC and she listened to my heart and next thing I knew VA claimed I was 70% disable and I began to receive a check in the mail from the VA and way I see it, that money is the people's money."

"It is still your money," I added.

As he sat down at the nearest table before he answered saying, "That also may be true but I also owe God ties that I have never paid. I feel I owe him a fortune and giving to the need of others is my way to paying my ties."

As I sat down in one of the opposite chairs asked, "Where did you get this idea?"

As he took a drink of his coffee, I could tell Robert was thinking. Then after another drink he said, "I guess it was twenty-five years ago when I really got this view from a painter that was painting Rita Henry's house before she died. It needed painting real bad and she did not really have the Money but this painter had an Ad in the local paper he would paint a house for two hundred and fifty dollars. She called him up and this painter upon seeing the house told her that she must buy the paint and she told him she did not have the money that she only had enough to pay him to paint the house for her two kids has moved away and when she married George they had disown her and his care after his stroke takes up all their money."

"I guess he didn't paint the house then," I asked interrupting him. "He painted it alright but I bought the paint." Robert answered with a laugh.

"You bought the paint," I asked not surprise he would do that after seeing him just give away two hundred.

"I sure did," Robert answered rubbing his breaded face. "You see, this painter upon hearing her words saw me checking him out. He left her and walked right up to me saying, "I see you seem to watch over her and Mrs. Henry has a need and do you think you could help her out?"

Now I was shocked at his words, but I answered saying, "Depends on what it is."

"She can't afford the paint," he returned. "I want to know do you fear God and would like to tie to him and buy the paint she needs."

"Now his words did shock me and I stuttered but before I could say, "No," this Painter said as he pointed toward the house, "Just look at her house and for me to make it look like a new house it will take me a week of hard work. I charge her really nothing to paint it for I believe I owe God and this is how I pay him back for saving my soul by painting the homes of the old but the paint is their responsibility to buy. You're her neighbor and I was wondering do you love her and right now she has a need so how you going to show God you love your neighbor?"

"I looked at him and realized what he was asking and without a word I left him walking over to Rita Henry and told Rita not to worry I would buy the paint the Painter needs to make her house look new asking her what color would she like. This Painter told me what he needed and did he ever make her house look new by the time he was done. I mean he protected everything with sheets and left the extra paint with me and was gone. But I still remember his words about owing God and I have keep that vision he gave me so when someone comes to me seeking help I will not turn them down for I feel I can never repay God for writing my name in the Lamb's Book of Life and giving to the need of others using my extra money I figured it is a small way to telling God I love my neighbor."

As he finished, Lenard came walking in from outside to fetch himself some coffee saying, "Come on Robert let's play some pool."

Robert ignores me as he stood saying, "The way you have been shooting lately, I think you have beaten me every game we played this month."

"I've been hot alright," Lenard answered back. "But it is another day and this could be your day."

"Yea, right," Robert answered as he also refilled his coffee cup and as he followed Lenard back toward the pool and domino hall added, "Only if you spot me five balls?"

PENNY GUM

Grandma watched Barbara and Elaine fighting over the last stick of Gum they found in their Mother's purse and laughed remembering how she use to get gum when she was a child so she called out to them reaching for her purse saying, "Hey Barbara, if you fetch my purse for me, I think I have a pack of gum you and Elaine can have."

Barbara, instantly let go of the gum letting Elaine have it saying, "I'll fetch it Grandma."

As Barbara handing the leather purse to her grandma said, "Did you know how much bubble gun cost when I was your age. Your five aren't ya?"

"No Grandma, I'll be seven in a week," Barbara quickly returned as she helped Grandma dig around in her purse asking, "How much did it cost Grandma?"

"One penny," Grandma answered as she placed the gun pack in Barbara's little hand.

"Only one penny is all it cost," Elaine asked as she scooted over to sit before Grandma, quickly join by Barbara who was opening one of the gum pieces.

"That is right, one penny," Grandma answered before leaning back in her rocker saying, "You know us girls have a hard time getting money to buy gum and unless we find a penny or dime someone dropped we never have any money."

Only Elaine agreed for Barbara was too busy stuffing the gum piece into her mouth.

Grandma then said, "Let me tell you a story how I got gum when I was your age and it was not easy either. Back then it was a lot harder to find a penny then it is today. We live with your Great Grandpa in a two story house over on west Main Street near where it enters 65 and down on the corner where the school bus picked us up set old Frank's Dime store. I would go into the store to wait and he had the gum place right where I could reach it. So I devised a plan, it was simple enough and it worked."

Then Grandma gave them a smiling before she said, "But not the first time, I stole myself one of the double bubble pieces and quickly left the store."

Suddenly from behind them came Grandpa's voice saying, "That the only thing she stole. She stole my heart."

"That I did," Grandma answered before returning her attention back to the girls saying, "Girls, I did not open it but stuck that gum in my pocket and all day I kept it hid there and I remember as I left the bus wondering and worried if my plan will work as I walked toward home or will I get into deep trouble."

Then giving the girls her smile asked, "Think I'll get a whipping?"

"No," both Elaine and Barbara answered.

Almost laughing she said, "That is right, no whipping. I went straight to Grandpa and pulling the gum from my pocket, I told him I owe Old Man Franks a penny. Grandpa almost laughing gave a penny and I went to The Dime Store just a chewing that gum to pay for it."

Barbara quickly asked, "Did you try that again?"

Still feeling she wanted to laugh answered saying, "I did until Mom found out."

Her answer only brought on more laughter.

GUARD DUTY

Bill Waid looked over at Frank Adams who was now leaning against their truck's tail gate in the shade of a one of big local trees that lined the road way. He was holding his M-1 loosely across his body suddenly Bill asked him, "Who do you think will be the first in line when they finally show up."

"I say the Generals will," Frank quickly answered back while shaking his head. "Yes"

Bill looking toward the sound of marching men that still was miles away said, "I wonder how many unarmed Germen troops do you think there are, I heard maybe as high as fifty thousand?"

"I hope it is not that many," Frank quickly replied, "We'll be here a week or more and I'm ready to go home, I tired of this war, sleeping on the hard ground, eating C-Rations and no toilet paper."

"I could not have said it better," Bill added as he sat down on the tail gate next to Frank saying, "What I'm worried about is I will be out of cigs, no women and no beer."

Frank took his Hemet off and as he rugged his blond head asked, "Whose idea was it that had us place all these signs we placed along the road and I have no idea what they say, they're in German. At least they made it easy on us saying place the red dot signs fives from this food center, the blue dot four miles and so on and the two big signs on each side of the entrance here at the Gate to enter this huge feeding place."

Bill, after lighting his cig said, "And here we are now guarding the food the local Germans going to hand out and I hope there is not a mad rush when they get here. I say let them fight for I'm not interested in getting in the way of hungry men myself."

THE HOUSE PAINTERS WIFE

There was once in the Galveston community a house painter. A middle age man, who was starting to need himself some money, he was a very smart man but like have adventures. He been working as a Failure Analyzes, found himself a good woman, who was willing to walk an adventure with him. Now he was driving down the road in his red 1986 Chevy Sprint with his extension ladder tied to the side of the car, back seat folded down with a six-foot ladder leaning against five-gallon paint buckets full of paint brushes and laying across a mound of sheets he uses to cover the plants and surfaces around the house he was painting. He was wearing clean paint splatter clothes and a hat that most would has toss out that also was covered with paint.

As he turned off the freeway, he was hoping the house wasn't like the last one that had a huge eve located around the house and made him spend two weeks on it. In some ways painting gave him peace with his wondering mind and he liked to paint for gave him beside just the peace but a feeling a job well done as he reminds himself what the house look like before he started and he always added a touch of his own art to the house. Make them happy for most of the houses had a retire couples or a retired women living alone inside of them.

Most needed a lot of work and he never will forget the last house he painted was an old lady's house who wanted white with black trim. The house was one of the worst he had come across but he works hard and was able to change the looks of the house to a vision of beauty. The neighbors all bragged on him for doing such a great job. He just thanked them and left the house just as happy as those who had their house painted.

Mostly he painted and Barbara waited at home are running around having her own Chevy Sprint. When he first started to paint houses he talked her into coming and watched him paint. But that went over like a limp rag. He always thought she married for his looks but decided it because she found someone crazier than she was. Only problem he was having with her was she was dying slowly with sugar diabetics. He had reached out for God's for help many, many times and her problem slowly became worst. He loved her and besides being a Black foot Indian, she could see into the Spirit world around them.

He did not know she had such a gift when he first met her and she did not fear them that she saw. To her the Grave Yard is not hunted but a field of homes.

PRACTICING BEING A HOUSE WIFE

I've been friends with many girls over the years but this Dakota is another creature and I just love her dearly. She has shared her life with me and her feelings about life and body and we are friends. Calls me up every day and tells me what things girls do, feel, hate and love. She has been moving into boys at the age of fifteen and falls in love and out of love as fast as the cat comes in and out of the house.

But her life is full of emotions and has many beds for in her whole life I bet she has never slept in the same bed for a month. Her Mom does not bother our relationship with me and her Dad lets her be. But she met a boy few months ago name Chris that had just move into a house across the street and he wants to marry her.

Dakota now older and a phone plays with boys' emotions and has gain couple boyfriends in Oklahoma but too young and really was not to girl happy and Dakota did have an attitude to deal with. But she latched upon me and being someone that she can love as she really enters the real love life and outgrow me. Not every minute thing but just short time where can she relieve her emotions and go back to her crazy life.

When she would stay with her dad, she would call me upped hungry getting me to buy her something to eat. I go pick her up and give her a twenty and let her buy what she wanted and her dad always would ask for cigs having no money. It got so I would just give her a twenty and let her find a way to buy her food and I know her dad us it to buy cigs and knowing her that what she was after in the first place with her dad pushing. I should just buy some food and take to them for Dakota was a typical girl, having no way to get money would get some somehow.

One day she called me for food and when I went by to see really what their need was I found her washing dishes and was shock to find her doing

169

that which was way out of the Dakota's personality that I had come to know. The last time I saw Dakota a week earlier, her new boyfriend asked her to marry him so as I entered the kitchen, I made some joke about it and she said, "I'm practicing to be a house wife."

MY HOT ROD

I like cars ever since I was a child. Shoot, I still remember the first cars I ever played with. I guess I was around age of five when I

Grandma bought me a set of little cars. I think there was like a hundred of these small, one or two-inch-long cars and trucks in all kinds of shapes and sizes and I think made out of plastic. The last I saw of them was around the edge of the Mon's fancy living room carpet. I had place then end to end along a black strip that ran around the edge of the carpet and I left them. Never saw them again. If my Mother did not like one of my toys, as I slept on garbage day, it was gone.

But as I grew older into the back yard I flew and quickly became my playground and for hours on end, I made roads through the Saint Augustine grass under the big Pecan tree with an old red brick. Build forts and push my cars I wreaked as lease a thousand times. I mean I blew them up, smash them, buried them and threw them. They were well made and really would take a licking. So there I was pushing those cars I bought with money I had earned mowing lawns around the neighborhood until one day my Mother chewed me out and saying I was way too old to play with cars. I quite them and I just move onto bigger cars.

The very first car I ever own was and 1940 Studebaker I got free from Mr. Cresdarn when I was about 17 just before school started. Pulled it over to the ranch and parked it out of the way to work on next summer when I was out of school. Came home for Christmas and Daddy had it haul away. I said nothing but was a little piss out. But I grew up with a home life where only thing that was mine was what was in my room, barely.

After coming home from Vietnam I bought a 1969 Chevelle SS and women ran a red and smashed it. I took the blamed for she got hurt and let my insurance help her. I still was fishing so I bought a Rambler Station

Wagon. When I Graduated, I bought a Vega which was a piece of junk. Got a job in Tennessee and left the Vega for a 1980 pickup with a cover that got 8 miles a gallon and 30 miles a quart of oil. After returning from being trained by IBM in Pennsylvania I bought a 1969 Dodge Charger.

One time had 14 of them around the house trailer. But best car was a small Chevy Sprint that got 56 mpg. It got so it was too dangerous to drive and my hot rod now, is a1998 Infinity. That is will be the last Hot Rod I'll ever own and already got the front end fixed. It needs a good hot paint job and seat covers and floor coverage. The window got crack during a big Ice storm so that needs to be fix also. I really got more money than sense, so I'm going to get the place looking good.

MR. TRIPLET XX

I have a proposal for you to possible make you a bit of money on your many different items you have in your store for sale. It is simple enough. I place the items on the internet for sale. Our cost to ship them would two ways by either offering some for sale with free shipping and others we do not. It is just a name, picture, place on internet, and respond to the buyer using only PayPal as payment, send out item to them we listed.

Mr. X, you are the collector of these items and will make all the money off the sale but 5% for us retailing it on the market. If you already have credit card setup can use that method selling on Amazon.com for it has no PayPal only cash or check. I feel most will sale but not all for some will not sale for months to where they never sale. We must live and learn what and will sale and over a few months come have quite a fun time collecting things that will easily sale around the state.

There many out of work around and I was thinking it would be away for them to make money. The internet system is sitting open saying come and play and Marshall could be a center to it. Way to advertise your store that travelers stop and check you out.

Time has mostly cleared the many ways for crooks like to use it to steal. It is not to say they do not try it now and then. For the common man to use the internet and when it comes to money it better be safe for many have millions put into it or you are out of business.

I hope you are visualizing my concept of what can happen. There could be a lot of money made as you reach and fine different produce of the same type to sale that will sale on the internet by the ton.

They have even Develop a way to ship it cheaper in packing and such for we only want a very satisfied customer as they will come back to us and tell others if we did good or bad. I myself want to get back reports we did good, fast, product is as we say it is, packed for protection during shipping for you are going to have many a fragile piece to ship. We live and ship like we are the one receiving it. What better way to show the world what kind of person we are?

As you consider my proposal remember, this will revolve around you and your book keeping and the product you want to sale on the internet. The going will be rough at first as this business of selling on the internet starts. If you think it want, I assure you it will happen but I believe in the end you will be glad -you did as this could grow into a good business being that Marshall is located in the center of this country. Cost to ship is the same in all directions. Shipping always takes a week or more and our mail system does not often hurt things we ship and if that happens we gladly replace it if we can.

What the percentage we receive on the sale as part of this business venture we will discuss person to person and more of what could happen in the future. Marshall your home as well as many others and if we can organize this venture right and others join, Marshal could be become a center of internet selling and once known and known to be trusted what can happen is just a guess on my part for I know in the beginning we will first have a great challenge as we learned this internet way of doing business and with our experience we can help others join us.

There will be the need of a good paper work trail on all produce we sale. EBay helps with PayPal records. I'm sure the government will want a good report and good paper work, darn their hides especially if a lot of money comes into play and the possibility of this happening is very possible.

JESUS SHOES

My brother and loved to fish around Hall's Lake and West Galveston Bay. Brought me with him and I learned how to fish for the different salt water fish. Got myself and nice Flat Bottom plywood boat that was built by my brother's wife cousin. Ran the bays with till I got me better open bay boat for the flat bottom perfect for shallow water but the open bay was not its best partner. Those waves saw the flat bottom boat as if it was nothing but a stick upon the surface. About sunk her several times and the open West Bay area was just calling for me.

When I was out by myself fishing I found a peace that I needed during my early twenties after having been in the military since I was sixteen. Now in my latter years at times I would love to do that again. For my Father had a small aluminum Boat and a 10HP outboard motor and I never borrowed the boat or even fishing with him for it was a something was his thing and no one was invited to come alone and that included me.

My brother was just the opposite; he like to fish but not alone. Help him build a floating camp at the mouth of Halls Bayou and from it go fishing and he like to fish the Intracoastal Canal for those big Gafftop and Flounder at night with Colman lanterns with a reflector mounted with came with handles, we would Flounder the West Bay along the sand banks formed when they dug out the Intracoastal Canal. But the wind had to die down and that was only a few times a year. If not there it was Halls Lake and was it had a mud bottom that was soft and ever step was need deep into the mud. The flat bottom boat came into play then. But that was way after my Brother's Jesus Shoes came into play.

I guess I was around seventeen or eighteen when Huey presented Jesus shoes to me as we arrived at the houseboat. He never tried them floundering yet.

Now if it has not rain for a while, Halls Lake becomes quite clear and the all along the grassy backs the Flounder would settle in. How they set along the banks depended on the tide. They were pointed in at incoming tide, pointed out on the outgoing tide, and settle at different angles along the banks edge at other times.

As night fell, we loaded into the boat and on the far side of the Lake we slowly came to rest not to made any wake and dirty the water. I help start the lanterns and as I climbed overboard I instantly found myself knee deep into the muddy bottom. I complain as Huey brag on this Jesus Shoes that was not going to happen to him as he put then on and when he settles overboard on the mud sure enough he did not sink into the mud.

We laugh and joke on how I had to travel in the mud, sinking to my knees every struggling step while he just slowly moved along on top of the mud able to stay in front of me and of course gig any flounders we came across while I pulled the boat along behind us where Huey threw the caught flounders he gigged. We got six are seven large ones before Huey gave up for I learn later it did take a fairly amount of strength to walk in his Jesus Shoes because of the size and far as I know he never used them again.

THOSE THAT ARE FILLED

I was writing on a short story about visiting a church that needed help and I got to thinking I could get myself in trouble and open my mouth when I should keep it shut. Dakota pointed that out to me several times in many different ways saying, "Shut up."

While I was thinking this an understanding of gift of tongues means chosen. I've know many Spirit fill men and women that do not but those that do speak for God through Tongues and translation of tongues. I've seen as many as five translations come forth. Mostly it was a message of love giving hope.

Today we have many churches that have the movement of the Holy Ghost in them and those that do not. This is where the Holy Ghost filled chosen speaking in tongues for they are to go forth and feed the flock. They are to sit in churches and let God bless them through the power and movement of the Holy Ghost.

But human nature tells us to stay in the Spirit filled Church and be comfortable. I love to feel the Holy Ghost moving through me and out my belly and watch and hear the Spirit filled Church drink and get drunk. But the Spirit wants me water elsewhere and filling like a sinner that I am just grasping this understanding he has giving me that I need only go to the Holy Ghost filled Church's when I need a freshening if I feel down that I need to only walk among the weak and bring the joy of our loving God to them by the Spirit of God that is within me.

I reach out toward you Lord and to see and know who I am. I always end up loving the wrong way, always giving when I should run, forgiving when I should punish. Take my old red pickup that was used in a runaway attempt and the old trunk got smashed in a creek trying to hide but wreaked instead. Now I should punish but I got to thinking about that old truck and the great adventure and excitement it gave Matt Armstrong. Why should I destroy that adventure Matt had trying to outrun the cops and enter myself into it. The truck is gone and I am not paying to bring it back it is hard to turn the other cheek now and then.

Father, I am sorry I have misunderstood the path you set my feet upon. Please forgive me as my sinning nature seems to be in overdrive lately and let love and friendship is what it is. I seek no wrong yet I yield to temptation so easily as my flesh over powers me and I give into what should not. Eat sugar and it is such a No, No. I do it anyway.

Help me Father to allow me to yield to the Holy Spirit so that the needs of others are met. That many Prayers will be answered, especially now that I'm in the last years of my life. I felt you pull me away from giving to those that already have. I did not understand and wondered way off the path you have chosen for me. I have walk in darkness yet thy light I cannot hide as you expose my many sins yet when I look I only see you. Now in my later years I feel as if I'm a lamb getting ready to be slaughtered. Each Temptation placed before my eyes, I yield too. Yet the path I followed has been so muddy and when Barbara Jean left me to go home to die I have been lost ever since. She was the one that held my hand and when she let go I have wondered lost having my flesh pulling one way and the Spirit is pulling me another and I having my wild imagination in-between. I do not claim that following one's heart for another I am perfect at for I have yield to temptations and must force myself to run.

GORILLA'S APPLE

As Uncle Fred sat down in Grandpa's old rocking chair, leaned forward placing his elbows on his knees given us a sad look as he glances over at Grandpa saying, "I saw in the news yesterday that Zomba had died."

Grandpa seem shocked as he answered saying, "Zomba died, shoot Fred, I haven't thought about him in a while."

"Who is Zomba Grandpa," Billy John asked as he lifted his very sweaty tea glass from off the table.

Grandpa looked over at Uncle Fred asking, "You want to answer him or shall I?"

Uncle Fred smiled as he leaned back into the rocker and as he began to rock, motion with his hands for Grandpa to stay seated saying, "I'll do it, Milton."

Grandpa seemed relieved saying, "Good."

Grandpa's actions seem funny to Billy John and his laughter fill the air for a second.

Uncle Fred waited for Billy John to become quiet before saying, "Billy John, Zomba was a large male Gorilla that lived in the Rainbow's Zoo Gorilla habitat. We were not over twelve when they first began building the Gorilla Habitat and Zomba was the first Gorilla they obtain for it."

Billy John seen shocked as he asked, "Zomba was a Gorilla?"

"Yes a Gorilla," Uncle Fred answered. "We first met him when we were running around the Rainbow Zoo. With our bikes we could get there in fifteen minutes or less rain or shine. Now at this time, the Gorilla exhibit was just being built and the first Gorilla they brought in for it was Zomba. He was young like us and just a boy in a cage. We would play hand motions with him, stick out our tongue or whatever came to our mind and Zomba would copy it and we kind of became friends and whenever Grandpa and

I could get loose from home, we would travel to the Zoo and play with Zomba."

Uncle Fred stopped his rocking and leaning forward while lifting a finger upward saying, "Now Billy John, one time Grandpa and me took our lunch with us and Grandma had packed an apple for each of us for a treat. When we finally found Zomba he seemed so sad and I still had not eaten my apple. I yell at Zomba would he like my apple and I as I held it out for him to see, Zomba responded by holding out both arms out for me to throw it to him which I did. It seemed to cheer him up as he ate the whole apple core and all."

Billy John seemed to laugh as Uncle Buck lean back in the rocker letting what he just said sink into Billy John's thinking and notice the other family members were gathering to listen.

"You know what we stated to do," Uncle Fred asked with his head slightly tilted while he rocked, waiting.

Billy John seemed to think for a second before looking up saying, "You stated to bring him apples."

"We sure did," he answered. "We also took pears and bananas but I always believe Zomba liked the apples the best."

Billy John move his chair closer taking his ice tea glass with him as he asked, "Did you ever touch him?"

Before Uncle Fred could answer him, Grandpa said, "We sure did. You see Billy John, Zomba was our friend and when was with him, we did not see him as a Gorilla."

"Did you know he save our lives," Uncle Fred spoke clearly perking Billy John's and the other family members attention. But they remain mostly quiet waiting as Billy John asked, "How did he do that Grandpa" with a few of the other family members agreeing.

That is when Grandma coming out of the kitchen carrying two cups of hot coffee and while setting the cups beside Grandpa and Uncle Fred, she promptly said, "Huey, why don't you tell them just how he did that and I want to know how come I never heard about this Gorilla saving event?"

Grandpa gave her a smile saying, "Because Dr. Sheer ask us not to is the main reason for he told us if the world knew what had happened, they would shut the Habitat down and Zomba would be taken to another Zoo and both Fred and I sure did not want that to happen. Even had Fred and

I to sign several papers saying we would not and you know I always have lived by my word which I was taught to do by my Dad and a belt when I was a child."

"That is right, Dr. Sheer had us sign some papers and promise we would tell no one what had happened," Fred added before asking, "Huey, why don't you tell them since you love to tell stories."

Grandpa seems to think a second, before he answered saying, "I guess it want hurt the Habitat to tell the story that we have keep to ourselves most of our lives." He ended with a giggle almost spilling his coffee and even laughed a little louder as he added, "But where should I start my story."

"Beginning of course and keep it simple," Uncle Fred answered.

Huey stood and looking around at his family, gave Bobbie a smile before saying, "I want to thank my family for coming to this Birthday Party Bobbie created for my 69th birthday. Now there is plenty of goodies still left and you feel hungry just help yourself."

He then walked over to Bobbie, gave her a hug before saying, "And I know Bobbie wants to hear the story of how Zomba save our lives. Isn't that right dear?"

Laughter was his answer as she returned, "I sure do want to hear this story how a gorilla name Zomba save your hide."

Huey waited for the room to become quiet, took a drink of his coffee before he gave a good look over his family before turning his attention to Billy John saying, "Uncle Fred and I first met Zomba the day I turn twelve and was given ten dollars to spend on whatever I wanted. So with my birthday money in hand, Fred and I rode our bikes for the Rainbow Zoo. We had heard the Zoo had obtained for their new habitat a Gorilla and believe me I was itching to get a view of this gorilla first hand.

Fred added, "Me too."

"Now on the way to the Zoo, Fred and I joked with each other about how much each of us looked like a Gorilla. Then after we locked our bikes within the bike racks located at the Zoo's entrance, paid our 10 cents and followed the signs leading to Zomba, Fred and I both played acted like a Gorilla, beating our chests or walking like one. The path led us to the many large cages for the many different animals they were going to place within the habitat and there all alone was Zomba and seeing him for the first time Fred and I was shock to fine Zomba was a young gorilla sitting on a large tree limb across one corner of the cage with many ropes strung across the ceiling and hanging down.

We were alone as we came to a stop before his large cage. But when Zomba saw us, he left his large limb grabbing hold of several ropes and swung himself down landing right before us with both his hands grabbing hold of metal bars that separating us.

His actions shock me and I took a step backwards just catching Fred's arm to steady myself when I heard from behind us, "Hello Zomba."

Turning I found a middle age man dressed in a nice suit and now I understand why Zomba came flying as the man reached into pocket saying, "My name is Dr. Sheer and Zomba and I have known each other for a long time and he likes sweets. I was wondering if you two boys would like to give Zomba a treat for me."

Both I and Fred stumbled over our words as we became excited at the thought of what he is asking saying, "Would we."

He then handed each of us half of a Tootsie roll and looking at Zomba said, "Zomba, like you to meet two new friends, Huey and Fred."

Zomba look at us and appear to be mostly looking at the goodies in hands as we drew close. I was not sure what was going to happen but behind us Dr. Sheer kept pushing us. As I drew closer to Zomba's extended hand, he had a look about him that cause my fears to disappeared and pushing Fred aside I gently laid my half of the Tootsie Roll in his hand and right then and there I and Fred became Zomba's friend.

With school out, every change we got we would take Zomba something and that became apples as Uncle Fred describe. We began calling all the fruit we took to Zomba, Gorilla Apple, Gorilla Pear, Gorilla peach and bananas we called Ape banana. Well one day as we were tossing our Gorilla Apple into the air when Dr. Sheer after exiting the entrance into Habitat's interior called to us and had a big smile on his face upon seeing us with two apples.

He told us Zomba was no longer in his cage but has been released into the habitat display and needed us to enter the habitat and give Zomba our apples. Not quit realizing what we got ourselves into Dr. Sheer lead us to the entrance into the habitat and said for us to enter and when we meet

Zomba give him our apples. He needs cheering up he added, as he opens the habitat for us to enter.

Now Fred and I looked at one another and I could see he was thinking like me and had to fight him to go through the door first. Now both of us have been all around the habitat walking around the visual area and there was not a place in it that a creature could hide we thought and the viewing area was such one could see those inside but the viewer could not be seen except at several locations.

As we walked out into the jungle, I guess Fred began to toss his Gorilla apple into the air calling out for Zomba asking" Did he want an apple" and here I was wondering should I be in here or not when off to the left, I heard the rustle of limbs springing back in shape. Neither Fred nor I could see anything when after it had become quiet I just caught a shadow before Zomba appeared really out of nowhere and came swigging down toward us on a large fake vine and landed with a stomp before us and after catching himself I saw really how big Zomba was and I mean he was huge as he stood upright before us after he landed.

Fred tossed him his apple which Zomba easily caught before he just sat down before us and bit into the apple and I could see he was eying the one in my hand. So when he finishes Fred's apple, I toss him mine and as he caught it I glance back to the entrance and DR. Sheer was gone leaving us all alone with him.

I was a little worried being alone with Zomba but your Uncle Fred here. He just walks over to Zomba and sat down beside him motioning for me to join him and as I was about to take a seat beside him, Fred pointed to the other side of Zomba who was watching me closely and I swear Zomba suddenly laughed as I sat down beside him just before he gave me a gentle push and then he did the same to Fred.

So there we were three friends touching each other laughing and you not going to believe this but Zomba were ticklish. I guess we been in there an hour or more when Dr. Sheer came and fetch us and Zomba sure wanted to walk out with us.

Dr. Sheer upon exiting asked us if we would come and interact with Zomba after school and he would provide the fruit. He also said that in a few weeks they will be bringing in the other Gorillas they have for the Habitat and when that happen we will no longer able to play with Him.

Well that is what Fred and I did for a couple hours after school. Mother and Dad were concern about us playing with an ape but Dad said it was Ok for we were part Ape anyway. But that Habitat was a big place with all the trees and vegetation and the fake Vines running this way and that and believe me Fred and I wondered all over that Habitat playing with Zomba. Chase after him and he would chase after us swinging on one of the vines.

I guess it was about a week before the other Gorillas were to show up. Another Zoo gave the zoo a young big Jaguar and they place it in Zomba's old cage which had a door leading into the Habitat and it appear close but was not and that Jaguar got loose in the Habitat unknowing to Dr. Sheer or any of the other keepers.

That afternoon after school here we came but school had let out early and Fred here wanted to sneak up to him so instead of hitting the bong Dr. Sheer had placed telling Zomba we were here. We took off into the jungle knowing were Zomba like to sit. We assume it was a good place for him to watch the lookers that came to see him. Which at times would watch Fred and I play with him so several had stopped us telling us how brave we were to do that.

So off into the Habitat we flew running down the trail leading through the foliage made with large flat rocks and I guess we were about halfway to Zomba when that large Jaguar Leaped out of the jungle and landed before us and I swear his eyes were glowing and gave us a vicious growl to boot. Fred and I were caught by surprise and while coming to a halt, both of us ended up on our butts. I wanted to shout as I saw the giant Jaguar take two steps and leap to land on top of us and never made it as Zomba swinging caught that Jaguar in the side with his feet sending it on passed us to land rolling across the rocky trail. Fred and I quickly stood to face the Jaguar when Zomba landed between us and the growling Jaguar and began to beat his chest while giving his yell as if saying I've bad and it was loud enough that I had to cover my ears.

That Jaguar suddenly had a quick change in attitude as it turned and left giving Zomba a snarl several times as it disappeared into the Habitat's foliage and with its disappearance Fred and I ran for the exit with Zomba swinging overhead.

But the keepers didn't believe our story for when they checked the Jaguar, it was back in its cage and the door leading into the Habitat was closed. But Dr. Sheer did and had us sign some papers we would not tell anyone what had happen.

We still visited Zomba until the day more Gorillas entered the Habitat it not to say that we didn't try to anyway but Dr. Sheer only thanks us saying we could not. Eventually Fred and I wonder into our teen years and only visited the Zoo now and then. But I will always be thankful for the time Zomba became our friend and save our lives."

Grandpa looked over at Uncle Fred saying, "You want to add anything."

"Yes," Uncle Fred answered and he left his seat to stand beside Grandpa and while placing his hand on Grandpa's shoulders said, "I and Grandpa have always thank him, for as I look around this room if it wasn't for Zomba saving our lives I and Grandpa here would not be looking at a family he has also given both of us."

Then Grandpa stood and raising his drink with Uncle Fred said with all the family agreeing, "Thanks Zomba."

AUNT IRMA'S NEW CAR WAS TRUCK

I was almost half asleep beside Mother when Betty came running shouting, "Its coming, Aunt Irma's new car is almost here." I ran with the others to the end of the driveway as it entered the dirt road taking hold onto Mother's hand as I settled to watch Aunt Irma's pass by and hoping she would stop and give me a ride in it.

It was the first car anybody here in the Ozarks Mountains ever seen. Especially I, since me was just now going on five. I have seen them in some of the magazines over at Aunt Irma's when we visited and I always dream of riding in one. But now to see one for real just gave me such a trill that I felt all the way to my toes causing me to jump up and down in my excitement. I was so excited to see a car for real and I could see it moving slowly toward us barely disturbing the dust as it rocked back and forth on the rough dirt road that was filled with pot holes. Daddy and Mother was always complaining about them pot holes. To me, it made riding the wagon fun rocking back and forth.

As Aunt Irma's new car drew closer, I saw it was not like any of the cars in the magazine. It had a wagon bed on back and I could see Uncle George was driving and the noised it made as it drew closer, cause me to cover my ears. It was so loud and when they stopped before us I could see it was nothing but a wagon with a covered front end some kind of motor I could make out under a fold out cover that bang as he halted and it was not new for there were a many dents across the top of the carts barrier and when Uncle George turned the motor off it made a loud Bang which cause me to jump behind Mother for sure.

Uncle George left the cab and standing by the wagon railing, patted it saying, "What do you think of the truck? Isn't she a beauty?" As Daddy started to walk around the truck, give us the "OK" for Elaine and I to leave Mother and running and jumping we follow him as he examined Uncle George's truck.

When we got to Uncle George I asked, "I thought you were getting a new car?"

He looked at me a second before saying as he patted the truck, "Barbara, to me, this is my new wagon. Only it is pulled by a gasoline motor and not bunch of mules."

Then Daddy asked, "Do you still think it will be cheaper to feed than your mules?"

Uncle George seem to look off into the distance before answering Daddy with, "I don't know about cheaper, but when Aunt Irma toll me to buy her a truck to ride in for she was tired of getting dirty riding in the wagon to town. I jumped and this old truck over at the Carl's Used Cars in Pig Hollow found something we could afford and Aunt Irma is happy now."

Daddy laughed before bending over and looking inside a second before saying, "How can you tell she's happy, she still in the truck." "Simple," Uncle George answered. "She still is in truck. If she was not happy, she would have told me and once home, she would not get in it again."

Uncle George said goodbye and while we hug Mother. He tried to start the truck several times with a big pop as it motors stopped causing me to hug Mother even harder. When it started I had to cover my ears as Uncle George drove that noisy truck away and Aunt Irma hanging out the window yelling "Isn't this truck wonderful?"

DID THE EPOXY EVER CRACK?

I was working for Teledyne as a Failure Analysis of Electronic Components when a special rush job came in concerning a resister pack that were cracking into while the finish Potted Units was being shocked tested. As they left them with me, I asked for several unspotted samples for comparison.

Now what the resistor packed consisted basically of a thin section of ceramic glass which a resistor material in placed upon and then covered with a thin epoxy glass covering.

It is really a simple constructed component. I took pictures and such. Cross section several of them and examined the cross sections using the Scanning Electron Microscope. Compare the good and the bad and quickly determined there no specific answer to the problem before me as I examined the results.

The only specific thing I notice, the surface of the glass covering on the fail resister packs had several cracks that did not split the resister pack into. I got to thinking and I remember years earlier, I was working part time operating the Scanning Electron Microscope for Texas Instruments. At that time the semiconductor industry used evaporated glass to cover the surface of the chips. It did not perform well and the glass coverage would crack if it became thicker than three thousand angstroms.

I took pictures of the good and bad and to support my theory and found that the epoxy glass was indeed far thicker than the good samples furnish for comparison and was the only reason I felt to be the cause for the cracking. I finest my report and because of its importance discuss my findings with the Boss which approved my answer.

About six months later, I learn they took my theory and some government department or the resistor producer itself, tested to prove if my theory was right. Which they did and I heard it cost over a million dollars to perform.

I have done thousands of failure analysis over the years and I hope that many of my answers I gave helped to make the electronic Industry as good as it is today.

JUMP UPPED AND SCREAM

I entered into the lounge area of the Center and just caught the words Rabbit. As I entered, Lenard looked at me and asked, "William, ever been rabbit hunting?"

Without thinking I answered, "Sure have." "When was that?" Lenard then asked.

I looked at Lenard wondering why the questions I asked, "Why you want to know anyway?"

Lenard said, "I've asked Bill and Wilber here and they both said, "They couldn't do it." I need someone to go hunting with me this weekend and I can't unless I get someone to go with me."

"I've been hunting." I said as I sat down upon the couch. "I remember when I was around sixteen I had a friend name Tom and one time we camped out in the woods to go night hunting Rabbits. We had spot lights and walk around looking for rabbits.

Well in early morning I got hungry and I knew where a rabbit was near the briar thicket. Well, I left our camp to fetch that rabbit for breakfast. I sneaked over toward to the briar thicket and sure enough there sat a nice pulped rabbit. I adjust the light to the 4/10 and blasted away.

Now that rabbit fell right over and I could just barely reach him among the briars and just as I was going to grab the rabbit, I'll be darn if that rabbit did not jump upped and screamed. It startled me I assure you none the lease in the dark and alone. But the rabbit only went a little farther into the briars. I reach for that rabbit again thinking he dead for sure now and I'll be darn if that rabbit jump up and scream again.

By now he was way into the briars and I just left him. My heart was still pounding over the fright he gave me.

Lenard set his coffee cup down and asked, "You'll go hunting with me then."

"Nope," I answered, "That was my first and last rabbit hunt I went on. Now every time a see a dead rabbit, I think back to time when a rabbit scream at me in pure fear."

OUR ONE AND ONLY RABBIT HUNT

It was one of those cold Northerners that come through over the night and as Daddy was getting out his shotgun, Loraine and I began to beg him to let us go rabbit hunting with him. We knew he always went hunting over onto A D Horton's pasture after a good Northern had come through and that morning Loraine and I wanted to go with him and were quite surprised when he said, "Yes."

Mama help us put on our warm cloths and out the front door we went. It had rain the day before and now the ground was quit frozen with ice everywhere. Still Loraine and I ran to fetch Old Red. He was Daddy's hunting dog at the time that was known to be the best Rabbit and Squirrel Dog around. Even Uncle Johnny and others would come fetch him and he was always eager to go. Of course Daddy had to come along with them and always left with a small liquor bottle in his back pocket.

Not that morning as out across the frozen ground we followed Daddy trying to be as quiet as we could. Old Red was off to the right sniffing away and just after we entered A D Horton's land he caught a sniff and away he went. We quickly followed and when we reach the small creek we had to cross it appeared to be frozen over. Daddy quickly jumped over it but not us and as we tried to cross upon the ice covered water, the thin ice broke beneath us soaking our already cold feet. We yelled and cried and Daddy gave in to our shivering state and quickly took us back home.

Now Loraine and I upon entering the house wanted hot water to soak our feet in but not Mother. She said our feet must be in cold water first to make sure there was no Frost Bite. If she were to use Hot Water, she said it could damage our toes.

We stuck our feet in that cold water she brought and it felt colder than the snow and ice that was outside. We cried and hollered and morn until she appeared to give in and removed the cold water and place our feet in some good old hot water and it is hard to described how good that felt.

Needless to say, "We never begged to go rabbit hunting with Daddy again. That is for sure."

SWAMP MOSQUITOES

While working for the Philology Department at the University of Houston, a new undergraduate from San Antonio was bragging one day that mosquitoes never bother him. While others were being attacked he wasn't. I looked at him and said, "I Know a place where they will eat you alive." He said, "You're on."

That next Friday we headed for Hall's Bayou. We arrived at the boat ramp just before sunset and after placing the boat in the water, I drove her the ten miles to my brother's houseboat located at the edge of Hall's lake. The boat ride is a great experience and I always enjoy the boat ride and the cool ocean breeze hitting my face.

When the houseboat came into view, I slowed the boat down and right off I could see those mosquitoes waiting on the houseboat's white walls. I usually pull up on the windy side of the houseboat. For Dave's pleasure, I pull to the leeward side and asked him to tie the back end to the catwalk and I would tie the front. Right off those swamp mosquitoes attacked and I was struggling just to tie the bow line for my hands and face was being covered with them. All of sudden I heard Dave yell and I heard a plash as into the Bayou he dove. I ran to the end of the boat and yell, "Dave, you OK." Dave yells back at me and said, "Those are not Ma-quitoes. Those are Man-quitoes.

HOW CAN ANYBODY BE SO DUMB?

Huey, my brother was ten years old when I was born. As a small child he put up with me and if I could I would go anywhere he went. Yet by six he was no longer around and by the time I was nine he was married. Now my school work was the pits. I think I was failing everything mostly because I had ear problems and could not hear all the syllables in spoken words. What I heard, it reflexes in my speech and my spelling. I eventually grew out of it a little.

Now Huey got involved in a Chess Club at collage. I was taught the game by a couple neighborhood boys when I was around ten and by twelve become a very good player. Now one day my brother wanted to play me and of course I won. At that time, I could play a game and if they wanted, could replay the whole game over for them. Not now.

That was the last and only Chess Game my brother ever played with me. I had work out a plan and it worked like a charmed. I checkmated him with only five pieces on the board and he had only lost three are four. He stood up and said, "How can anybody be so dumb play chess so well." He quick the Chess Cub and never played again thinking if his dumb little brother could beat him he was not a very good chess player.

THE METEOR IN THE DREAM

To begin this, I must return to the dream as I visualize the meteor if I can call it that for it was nothing like the cold rocks that float throughout our solar system. As I watch it in the vision it was hot and appeared to be very round. I could see what looks like dark red fire rippling across its surface. I then looked in the direction it was traveling and I come see the white dots of the planets with the sun to my left. I realized it was the doomsday. It will be coming from the west if I'm right.

The meteor I feel comes from way in space possible from an exploding sun or planet. Maybe a solid ball of the enter material which is all radioactive. A small sun so to speak which is slowly moving closer and closer toward our solar system.

Is Earth in its path are will it pass close or will it miss us. Coming from the west means it will enter moving in the same direction as the planets. Maybe it is moving faster or maybe it is moving slower. Our Sun's gravity will effect it slinging it around it and possible cause it to hit us from the east. Whatever happens it want be good.

To spread the word what good will it do. Who will hear and there be no place to hide. It does not even have to hit us. Just pass us by to bring us death as the mass of radioactive alpha and beta rays destroys all life on Earth. I guess only a solid lead shell could save some of us from this kind of death. Where could we find one? Make it ourselves out of used batteries laying around at the gas stations. Will that even be enough?

Then there is the fire rippling over its surface. The dark red fire with it canvas like image, rolling like the waves of the ocean hitting nothing just flowing and flowing. Why is it there? Does it still represent the center of a sun's power? Will the flames streak across the sky covering the whole earth with its dark red flame? Burning the surface of all life, melting everything man has made and turning the oceans to steam sending clouds of it across the sky to meet it.

As the Earth travels along with it with it slowly enter the atmosphere sinking ever closer and closer to the surface. The rotating Earth slowly scraping away at it until the ball and Earth become one leaving only a massive scare. The molting material of it never cooling as it melts its way toward the Earth's core taking the flames with it, leaving only scattered pockets that were cooled on the ocean's floor as the salt water tries to return to its former self.

That may not happen. But what would happen if it hit our beautiful Earth traveling just a little faster than us. A different picture occurs as it sinks slowly into our atmosphere. I can see the dark red flames streak leaping out toward the surface burning and melting the whole surface of the Earth as she rotates beneath the slowing sinking round ball of death. Oceans turn to steam, mountains tops flow like water as they melt under the extreme heat. The radioactive radiation from the core sending its killing rays in every direction. They even travel toward the north and south poles killing everything along the way. This dark red heat following after the killing radiation and burning everything in its path. Instantly, this dark red heat turns the ice into water and into steam.

But it was just a dream that I hope was only a dream.

BETSY MAY'S FIRST KISS

"Hey Frank, what's been going on," Thomas asked as he entered almost hitting the sign not watching where he was going which Read "Dominoes being played tonight at The Card Garden."

"Same oh, same oh," Frank answered as he pulled a set of dominoes and set them on the table to use and glancing over at the Winners Circle displaying the pictures of pass winners said, "Tomas, I've been thinking of closing this place down. I look over at the winner's circle and many of those winners have gone on to be with the Lord and I feel I'll be there soon. Going on eighty now and my bones feel it.

Tomas slipped himself between the box of Dominos sets and Frank saying, "Let me passed them out for you."

"I was doing just fine, mine you," Frank returned with a sneaker. "I'm not saying you are not doing great," Tomas answered as took hole of the box of domino sets and when he started to place a set on next table said, "But still being on table #1 for ten minutes is not moving at all. You've been waiting for me haven't you?"

"Now why would I just do that," Frank returned as he found himself a seat in one of the covered lounge chairs and was just getting comfortable when Thomas return with the empty box asking, "Isn't this the last night of the Domino competition?"

"Last night, that it is," he answered before adding, "And the house is going to be packed for the two couples paying tonight are both good players."

"Better than you and me," Thomas asked as he placed a coffee cut under the automatic coffee maker and press "Mild."

"Get me a cup also," Frank commanded before saying, "Frank looking back if I remember right, you and I lost every game we play as partners.

198

I mean we tried Pinochle, Hearts and Dominos and not one game have we ever won."

"Oh but we did against Charlie and Bill," Tomas returned as he set Frank's coffee on the table beside him.

"That don't count," Frank answered after he took a drink of his hot coffee and as he held the cup close to him added, "They were only ten are eleven years old at the time."

Tomas took a seat having a question running through his mine, "I've had known Frank going on four years after he retired here in Marshall and although Frank never stops talking I have never had the chance to get him to talk about how the Garden of Games began." Then Tomas glancing over at the clock and seeing it read 8:25 began thinking, "It will be hours before the many gamers begin to show up and since Dwain and Charlie was not here yet," so Thomas asked Frank saying, "Frank, when did you open this place?"

Frank took a drink of his coffee and after he set his cup down, he rubbed hands across his face adjusting his glasses and feeling better Frank said, "It wasn't me, it was Betsy May that really started the place, I was just along for the ride."

Thomas still digging asked. "Betsy May, and how she do that and where has she and Judy gone off too?"

"Yard sales," Frank answered, "It is Saturday and Judy always drags Betsy May off to go with her and they always come home with more junk. I mean just look around at the windows and all the crazy looking glass and pottery figures displayed and it is always changing. They would come back from yard sales and replace one thing with another and fight over where to place the item for an hour wanting everything just right."

Thomas added saying, "What I like is the item of the day on displayed at the far end. They place an item in the lighted display and write what it was and who made it and how old it was. It amazes me they can find out that much info on the items?"

"You don't know them two as good as I do," Frank said almost laughing. "If Betsy May or Judy do not have any info on what they are going to display as the item of the week, they would make it up. Dates, who made it, who own it on and on most of the items the age was always a guess."

"Still, what they say about the item are interesting," Then standing and picking up his coffee cup asked, "I think I'll get a refill before Dwain and Charlie show up. Want a refill?"

"I'm Ok," Frank returned and while watching Thomas pour his cup full of coffee he said, "Thomas, I was going on 19 when Betsy May entered my life she was like a savior and I fell in love with her and back then her Mother and Dad own this here building."

Thomas was laughing as he refilled Frank cup with coffee and just had to say, "Are you sure it wasn't a three story building you fell in love with and it came with a Betsy May."

Frank look at him cockeye before his said, "No, it was all Betsy May. I met her working here making donuts at Mama's Donuts and we just hit it off. I asked her out and I took her dancing and would still be dancing but our heath became such we can't."

Then Frank pointed toward the picture by the door waving goodbye to the players as they leave saying, "That's Betsy May and what she looks liked when we first met."

Thomas walked over to the picture he has seen a thousand times but never really gave it much thought. He notices right off that Betsy May had not change and still a heavy set women wearing a nice white and blue flowered blouse, dark blue pants and light blue sandals. Her face was round and smiling and wore her hair somewhat like she does today and as the other women around her age do, easy to take care of.

As he returned to his seat he said, "Your right Frank, she was and still a knock out. I think I would have falling in love in a heartbeat. You say she was a good dancer and I know she can cook; I do believe when you found Betsy May you found a winner."

But Frank returned, "I found way more than a winner for we are two friends who are now spending their last years of their lives together."

Thomas was laughing as he said, "And now where does this building come into play."

Frank thought a second trying to remember and even took a drink of his coffee before he said, "I found out about the building her dad had given her while doing Betsy May taxes after we got married. It appears her dad had been running a big poker gaming hall and law came and shut him down so he willed the building to Betsy May free of any debt and taxes paid up for fifty years."

"So this place was a Poker hall," Thomas asked looking around thinking it would have made a good one at that.

"Still is," Frank answered before adding, "But Tomas, when we first walk into this building Betsy May and I walked around and using flashlights went upstairs and check each room out and of course I tagged along checking them out also and did the place ever needed cleaning."

Thomas now more curious then ever asked, "Whose idea was it to start this Garden of Games anyway, yours or Betsy May's?"

Frank stood to fetch a refill of his coffee saying, "It was all Betsy May's idea and I think she came up with the Idea but in the startup it was touch and go for awhile."

As he finished filling his cup he asked, "Like a refill?"

"I'm OK," Thomas returned before asking, "I bet this place must have wild life at one time from the stories I've heard."

"It has a History alright," Frank answered causing him to laugh as he took his seat. "You know the sound proof Stage Room where the camera system is set up for those want to perform on Face Book. Did you know it was a striptease stage during Betsy May's Dad days of running this place? Same set up as now but the pay to view web site is gone and Betsy May made me put the Camera on one of those Story Time Websites and today it's on Face Book."

"You are talking about that Red Door where one must place couple poker chips in a slot to enter," Thomas asked before saying, "I never been inside in the four years I've been playing games here. But I heard they get their money back if they leave the place clean."

"It was a trick," Frank answered and feeling cocky added. "I left a sign saying, "They could not take the money without cleaning the place up before they leave for the eyes of Face book is upon them. It worked like a charm and I never did have to clean that room. There even been young men and women will come and actually clean the place to show how good they could work seeking a Job using face book."

"What's it like inside," Thomas asked catching Frank thinking back to the day Betsy May and him walked into the Stage Room and the mess it was in.

So after he took a drink of his coffee Frank answered saying, "The room is nothing more than a large stage before a wall full of cameras, lighting and now thanks to some organization from the better tomorrow groups, my small computer screen was replaced by a giant TV screen and they upgraded the camera system and using the latest thing going using the Cell Phone to control what image they want to display upon the giant screen calling up songs, scripts or even their X hoping she still loves them."

"But what was it like when it was used by Betsy's Dad for the striptease act," Thomas asked.

"When Betsy May and I first entered the Stage Room we found was on the left side of the room was a large camera mounted halfway up a wall surrounded by stage lighting and before the stage what was called at that time the teasing couches just out of camera view where a guy could come and really be tease. There were curtains dividing the room and a change room on each side of the stage for the strippers to change clothes or put some on."

Still digging Thomas asked, "Is that why they close him down."

Frank took another drink of hot coffee thinking before he said, "No, it wasn't just the strippers. It was the whole operation. I think her Dad had his hand in every illegal operation in town and opening a Gambling Hall in the middle of town brought in some rough looking characters and a shooting now and then. But not the stripper show. I heard the Mayor at the time was one of Betsy's Dad best customers on the Tease Chairs which Betsy May said her dad had them steamed cleaned every week."

"Ooh, I can imagine why," Thomas spoke trying not to visualize what action could be going on happily on one of those Tease chairs so he asked, "Speaking of Betsy May and Judy, where are they?"

"Out running the yard sales," but as Frank answered he notices Dwain entering the game room so he called out, "Where's Charlie?" "Coming," Dwain answer stopping by the coffee pot and began filling the white coffee cup he brought with him.

Frank looked over at Thomas saying, "If you want to know about Betsy May's dad, Dwain and Charlie can tell you, they worked for him." "Charlie and I did that alright," Dwain answered as he took his coffee and headed for the Domino table with the only yellow painted chair in the place. It was Frank's Chair and whatever table it sat at would be the game table that day. But after playing every table in the Game room Frank settled for a table near the coffee pot saying "I've played them all and not one lucky table among them" and Dwain was glad he did for as he took his seat and gently scattered the dominos out across the table he said, "Sure makes getting Coffee refills easier."

Dwain was shuffling the dominoes as Frank and Thomas join him each turning over a domino and Charlie was high and Dwain was his partner then as everybody was seated Frank began shuffling for Charlie to start the game being high man.

After drawing their seven dominoes, Charlie started the hand playing the double five and Thomas followed playing five blank with Dwain following with a double blank. Then as Frank was thinking Thomas asked, "Charlie, did you and Dwain really work for Betsy May's dad?"

"We sure did and right here in this building," Charlie answered. Dwain added, "We were young men back then and we made money off of tips fetching drinks or smokes or Mama's donuts." "Mama's Donuts," Charlie said as he places the double six for twenty. "I forgot all about her and those great donuts she made."

Thomas passed and as Dwain counted again with the six one he said, "You didn't know them but Betsy May's Mom and Dad ran this place like a business and Betsy May was always off to some girls' school and never set foot in the Club unless her Mom needed help making donuts because some worker quit."

Frank play the five one which was the only rock he could play and Dwain made another twenty with the six Five finishing the hand by domino-ing. After counting the losers' rocks, Dwain began to shuffle saying, "Thomas, it is not what you're thinking. To work in the Poker club, you had to pay to get in the door to get a job and if you played it right and dress well and being good looking young man helps, one could make over fifty dollars in tips and of course that could include a good tip for some after hour play. But to work in Mama's Donuts, you were paid to make and deliver donuts at several of the local stores with a sign over the boxes saying, "Mama's Donuts always fresh"

As they drew their seven dominoes Charlie said, "But donuts were not the only thing we delivered out into the poker rooms. There were peanuts, beer, liquor and cigarettes and anything that was use in and around the poker and slot machines and we had to keep the place clean and often I remember getting a big tip by some winner saying thanks."

Thomas played the six four to start the new hand saying, "Sounds like Mama was the supplier and Dad had to pay her for the things he used in the poker hall making his money stay at home and I bet Mama Donut's was making a good profit too."

"Hard to say," Dwain answered but as he played the six one making five points added, "But they sold out every day and night."

After Frank played the double four, Charlie played the double one making ten asked, "Have you and Betsy May talked about reopening the poker hall."

Frank turning one domino over and over answered saying, "Not really, the slot machines are gone and the same thing that close her down has not moved and now the church has double in size and with Betsy May and I being a member, I don't think it will not go over well. This place is almost a type of Senior Center. The money we make is just enough to pay the utilities. But Betsy May has been talking about reopening Mama's donuts but the startup cost is beyond our income."

After Thomas played one two making ten he added, "But I check the equipment and Mama must have had the equipment clean after they closed down for I'm pretty sure I can get it up and running again."

Charlie, while looking over what he should play looked at Frank asking, "Does Betsy May have Mama's recipe book of the icing she used."

"I'm sure she does, "Frank answered.

Deciding on cut the four with the four three making a nickel before looking at Thomas saying, "Thomas, Mama had many donut coatings. She always had us make plain and chocolate cover donuts and then she had her special of the day coating that could be anything and everything you can eat with chocolate. I always like the coconut and chocolate one myself she named them "Mama's Coco & Choco Donuts."

Frank playing the double two added, "Mama had coatings alright and her donuts with chocolate and nuts always sold out fast. She always said, "They may cost more to make but giving the donuts eaters a treat is her way of saying, "Thank you for buying my donuts."

Thinking back, I believe I was coating donuts with chocolate then sprinkling them with walnuts when I first met Betsy May outside of school. One thing I won't forget when she walked into Mama's Donuts and we made our first eye to eye contact for at that moment I fell in love with her." Then he gave Charlie a smile.

"Love at first site, you say" Charlie said while playing a two three on the double two before looking at Frank asking, "Frank, I've known you all these years and never knew how you ever got a date with Betsy May, I bet every boy in town had asked her out and she always said, "No."

Frank gave a laugh before saying, "That was when you two were hauling hay using your Dad's 52 Dodge truck and Milton your cousin took my place. I couldn't haul with you for I had sprung my ankle playing basketball forcing me to work in Mama's Donuts because I could barely walk."

"So you use the old sympathy method on her then," Charlie said with laughter.

Dwain after playing his double three asked saying, "Frank, why don't you tell us just how did you win over our sweet Betsy May's hand?"

"So you want to hear a story how I won her hand do you," Frank return while cutting the double three off his partner with a three five.

"Yes," the others answered almost as one causing them to break into laughter.

As they settled down from their laughter Dwaine asked, "Come on Frank tell us."

"It was not easy I'm telling you and not what you think," Frank answered before almost laughing again adding, "It was all Betsy May mom's doing."

"You're kidding right," Charlie asked before playing his double five being the only domino he could play.

Thomas counted with his four two off the spinner asking, "It was Betsy May's Mom fault?"

Frank cut the double five with the five blank making a nickel and as Frank played the double blank to make the same nickel he said, "Usually coating donuts is a two-person job and I was the only one doing the job at the time. So Mama placed Betsy May working with me for I alone could not coat fast enough and hot donuts were getting cold waiting on me."

"So what happen next," Charlie asked while playing on the blank his two blank.

"I kissed her is all I did and she returned it with more affection then any girl has ever kissed me so I married her," Frank answered leaning back before he added, "The kiss was the easy part but winning her hand was another thing."

"How did you win her kiss is what I want to know," Tomas asked thinking he wouldn't tell them when Frank said, "To tell you that you must understand how we first met."

"Well," Thomas answered.

"You want to play another game," Frank asked as he lean followed to shuffle the dominoes but Dwaine quickly answered saying, "Don't have the time Frank for another game so how did you get a kiss out of Betsy May?"

Frank lean back in his chair saying, "I first met Betsy May while limping around the Mama's Donuts around six that morning and upon seeing her beauty it caused me to spill the nuts out over the top of the hot donuts that I had just covered with icing. As I began to clean the nuts up she came and began to help and our hands kept touching till I pick her hand saying, "Did you know you have nice soft hands." That is when our eyes met and right then and there we connected and she turned my hand over and felt of it saying, "What strong and soft hands you have you big bad wolf."

Reaching and shuffling the dominoes again Frank, gave Dwain a sad look saying, "You sure you can't play another game Dwain."

"I would but I must go," Dwain answered as he stood and then with a smile added "For I just saw Nancy and Faith Sue walked by the door heading for the car."

But Tomas seeing that Frank was trying get out of answering their question said, "Come on Frank, and tell us how you were able to win a kiss from Betsy May?"

"Well, I can tell you it was not at Mama's Bakery," Frank answered before he reached and began to scuffle the dominoes letting his words set in before saying, "It was in the Delivery Trunk."

His words broke the spell and laughter broke out among them with Frank seeming to laugh the loudest.

Eventually they settle down as Frank continues with, "After we finished placing the Special donuts in boxes, she and I began coating the chocolate and sugar icing donuts and all the time as we worked learned all about each other and at same time our hands kept touching as we coated and boxed the donuts. After that was finish Betsy May help me load the delivery trunk and Mama asked Betsy May to go with me to deliver the donuts so that is why I say it is all Mama's fault I married Betsy May. She stuck us together in the Delivery Trunk."

Again laughter broke out among them and it settle down Frank said, "And before the Delivery was over I just asked Betsy May for a kiss and only Mama calling us on the cell phone did we part."

I WAS SCARED FOR SURE

LB finish shuffling the dominoes and as everybody drew their seven from the turned over dominoes when Wilber said, "It is your down Barbara? Now you just don't be afraid, I got you covered."

Barbara looked up at Wilber and as she played the Double Six, she answered, "I thank you, but I assure you I'm not afraid."

Rex as he played the six four asked, "Barbara, have you ever been afraid."

"I sure have." Barbara answered as Wilber played the double Four and counted.

While marking his twenty Wilber asked, "When was that if I may ask? When you were two?"

"When I was about sixteen," Barbara quickly answered back.

It was quiet for a second as LB counted with the four three and pointed his finger at Rex to mark it.

Barbara studied her dominoes a second before she said, "I been afraid that is for sure. I remember going home from a game at school about ten o'clock at night and was driving Daddy's old Ford with Lorraine and Rita in the back seat when we pass a work crew of Northerners working on the highway. When I passed them, a car pulled out and began following us."

Barbara reached and placed the double three on LB's three before she continued with, "That car got close to my bumper and the faster I went it stay right behind me. I got scared thinking it was a group of those Northerners following us."

"It is hard for me to believe you were scared of anything." Wilber asked as he played upon the double six with a six one.

"Well we were and when we got to the Whistle Stop to pull in, that car flowing us turn on their flashing lights and came to a stop behind us and

Sheriff Smith walked up to the car window and asked. "Just what were we thinking driving like I did?"

I just told him, "We taught he was some of those Northerner Men chasing after us."

He apologized for scaring us and let us leaved without giving me a speeding ticket knowing he had scared Lorraine, Rita and I. I mean we were scared.

Wilber seem to laugh as he said, "Well you do not need to be scared now. I still got you covered."

Barbara looked at Wilber and pointing to the score boards and said, "I guess it is too late to be scared now. They only have ten points to go out and we have seventy."

"I still got you covered," Wilber said with a smile. "Yea right," Barbara answered.

LEARNING LONG WORDS

Joey walked down the hall way not really wanting to be a sub teacher for the sixth grade English class. It was the farthest from his mind when he was called they needed a sub and now he be will be subbing for six classes a day for two weeks. That would mean he would have to actually teach instead of setting before a class handing out a pop quizzes.

If he didn't need the money he would have said, "No way. But two weeks' pay beats a day now and then any day."

As Joey walked into his first class, the room became quiet as Joey open his case and pulled out his needed documents, paper and pens on the he said, "My name is Mr. Joey Holgominery"

He wanted to laugh seeing the shock on their faces upon hearing his name before he said, "Rather you just call me Mr. Joey."

Looking up and across the class he then using his best command voice said, "Have I made myself clear so far. I will be your teacher for the next two weeks and I will do the best I can to make sure you learn something. Now first I need a head count."

Thought a second before he pointed to the girl in green pants and brown top ask, "How would you like to be my head counter?"

The dark brown headed girl pointed to herself having a surprise look on her face as she answered saying, "Me."

Joey held out the roster and a pen toward saying, "Are you not the prettiest Brown Hair girl in school."

His words brought laughter and a few "Yes's and No's and he could see the girl was blushing, so holding up his hands and walking around to face the class he said, "Hold on now. There more to this then what you think. I will be your teacher for the next two weeks and the person that takes the head count will be prettiest girl or the handsomest boy in school and will get a extra grade if they bring me the next day a short story that not over two pages story of being the ugliest Girl or boy in school."

Laughter broke out as his meaning became clear.

Then Joey look back at the Brown headed Girl and said, "Would like to be first to take up my challenge?"

The girl looks at this man before her and the way he expressed himself she said, "Sure, I'll take up your challenge and be the prettiest Brown haired girl in school."

Joey gave her a smile before wave an open hand her saying, "For today we have the prettiest Brown Hair Girl in school and I want everyone here to treat her as such all day long. I want you to go around bragging on her beautiful looks. I want you give her a vision of what it like to be such the prettiest girl in school that before I leave in two weeks she can write a great two-page story on being the ugliest brown hair girl in school."

Laughter exploded across the room with the added jabber among them and became quiet as the Brown Hair came and took the roster and as she did Joey stepped back and clapped quickly followed by the other children.

As the children calmed down with only couple friends joking, Joey turned his back to return to his desk, he asked, "Will couple of you guys pass out the dictionaries, please and as they do, please clear your desk of any writing material."

By the time he took his seat overlooking the children three boys had already passed out the Dictionaries and as they took their seat Joey said, "You are all wondering what this crazy teacher is up to now. It is written all over your young faces. For the next two weeks you are going to play in the big words."

Joey stood and walking toward the door thinking "Where are they" when suddenly through the door came a big giant TV Screen and a long table on wheels with six-word writer's units mounted on it and six chairs. The two guys pushing the stuff in said, "We been waiting outside didn't want to disturb the class." "Thanks," Joey answered.

It took them just a second to have everything was in good operation condition and Joey thanked them again as they left. Then turning to the class, Joey could see the children had what the hack written all over their faces.

He wanted to laugh as he pointed to the word writers then pointing toward the screen saying, "This TV Screen we have here can hold only so many words depending on the letter count within the words. Let me show you an example and you can understand clearer."

Joey call up a four letter display and there before the children was screen full of four letter words in rows one space apart and no commas. The children became mumbling when one of the girls said, "We are to fine 4 letter words in the dictionary and write the word we fine on the word writer?"

"No, no," Joey answered as he clears the screen he looking across the class room gave a big smile as he said, "Far bigger words than 4 letter you will be looking up."

Walking around the table he pointed to the word writers saying, "There a catch to this process. When you find a word, let's say we are doing ten letter words, you cannot bring the dictionary with you to write that ten letter word you found on the writer, you must do it from memory and if you spell the ten letter word right three different definitions will come up about the word and you must choose which one is correct. If you misspell the word you have 15 seconds to get it right."

Joey gave them his most wicked looked and as he turned back to his desk even gave them an old evil laugh while rubbing his hands which brought the classroom echoing with laughter.

As he sat down at his desk he said, "For the first day, I'll go easy on you and not require you seeking ten letter words. But to start this game, I will only have you seeking out seven letter words. I have six classes today and in each class they will also be doing the same thing and the class that can place the most words on the screen or fill it up will get a reward. What that will be has yet to be determined for I must go by school rules."

Joey left his seat and as he stood beside the Word Writers he said, "Today we will begin with only 7 letter words and I almost forgot I want all paper and pens off the desk with only the dictionaries remaining."

There was a few morning and complaining as they put their papers away and Joey could see some of the girls already had several words written down.

As their desks cleared Joey said, "It is now 8:20 so when the clock reaches 8:30 we will begin and I will stop you at 8:50 given the class 20 minutes to fill up the screen with 7 letter words if they can. We have six rows of desks and as you can see there are six Word Writers. Each desk row has a Word Writer and I believe you can understand why each Writer has a number beside it. It does not mean if one writer has no one writing on it, that you can write your 7 letter word on it. Remember you have only 15 seconds to spell the word right and check the definition and the class has only 20 minutes to fill the screen. You can only write one word down at a time and much let the next word on the writer be place by someone else. There be no hogging the writer and if you misspell a word you cannot change it for another until you have corrected the word you were trying to write. Remember if you fail walk back to your desk and find out what you did wrong.

There will be no talking, pushing, or rushing."

But as he returned back to his desk he knew those words went in one ear and out the other but looking back across the class room it did appear the children caught on to the game.

He took a deep breath as the clock neared the start time thinking, "Hope this works."

As the room became quiet, he let the clock do the talking as he watched the children and could see some were still searching the dictionary but most seem to have their 7 letter word ready to record and did he ever want to laugh as soon for as the clock bang out 8:30 the children left their seats rushing to place their word in the system. Some had it right some had it wrong. Some had the word but forgot what it meant but slowly the screen began to fill with 7 letter words but still was only a little over have way filled when the time ran out.

As the children morn regaining their seating, Joey stood saying, "Well done children and tomorrow I will tell you if you were the best for I have six more classes who will be competing with you on placing 7 letter words on the screen and I do hope you have learned something today."

Suddenly the bell to end the class rung out and the same boys that passed out the dictionaries collected them before they left.

As the last child left Joey cleared the screen to prepare for the next class before he leaned back in the chair, giving himself a pat on the back thinking, "That went way better than I thought it would. I never would imagine they would have found sixty-three 7 letter words in twenty minutes, but they did."

Joey glance as the first child who had entered for the next class Joey thought, "I wonder how many words they will fine next week when I make them find large words having the same meaning as smaller letter word."

As the room slowly filled with new faces, Joey stood to face them thinking, "When my two weeks are over subbing, I bet they never ask me to sub again."

When it seems the last child to sit had entered Joey wrote a name across blackboard saying, "As you can see my last name is hard to pronounce so call me, "Mr. Joey."

(Note: I made this one into a Novel)

RONNIE'S NEW JOB

"Hey, Ronnie, want to play a game," Sonny yell as Ronnie entered the Poolroom taking a sip his coffee as he did.

Dropping the cup from his mouth he answered saying, "Sure rack them up and let me fetch a Pool stick."

Ronnie quickly found his favorite pool stick and as Sonny finish racking he asked, "Where have you been? You haven't been by to play any pool in an over a month and you miss the last pool tournament over at Flipping last week."

"Who won," Ronnie asked as he positions himself to break.

"Who do you think," Sonny asked as he finished racking the balls. "William," Ronnie answered.

"Yea," Sonny replied as he took hole of his Cue stick to step away from the table he added. "Frank and William played for the playoff and William ran the table on Frank every game they played."

Ronnie laugh saying, "You're kidding right."

"Nope," Sonny answered adding, "Where have you been anyway?" "Working," Ronnie answered as he caulked his stick adding, "You know William would not play to win when he first started to play with us old folks. Not until Kelly sat him down and fussed on him. I mean she worked him over telling him to try to win and don't play favorites either."

"Well it worked and now everybody is mad at him now," Sonny added before laughing.

As the laughter settled down, Ronnie broke making the two in the left pocket but the Cue Ball ended hung up in the crowd. As he walked around examining the layout seeing if he could make another solid, Sonny asked him, "I heard you have been working, what you've been doing?"

Ronnie bent over seeing if he could shoot his Cue Ball into another and make a combo answered saying "Cleaning houses" just as he sent the cue ball into the 6 trying to knock the 4 into the hole.

It didn't work so as he left the table adding, "I saw an advertisement in the paper where someone needed someone to help them clean their house. Not doing anything, I called them up and offer my help and I just finish my seventh home yesterday."

Sonny sent the 4 into the hole and was set up on the five but shot the six instead but it left him with a hard shot on the five which he missed. As he left the table he chuckles asking, "Seventh you say. What did you do to go from helping one house to seven? I know it is not your good looks."

Ronnie having to shoot the strips sunk three of them before he answered saying, "It was old man Jenkins house and I know he must be 90 at least and was his house in a mess and needed some minor repairs. So Jenkins hired Doris Gray and he let her do most of the cleaning while I volunteered to fix what I could. When we were finished, Doris talked me into working with her in doing others round town."

Ronnie put the eleven in side pocket but his other ball's was tied up with Sonny's. So he called the 9 and banged away and as the balls stopped rolling nothing went so as Ronnie stepped away for the table and as Sonny took over he asked, "What the worst house you have work on so far, Ronnie?"

"Hard to say," he answered. "They were all bad but Doris and I worked with those that live there and tried to meet their demands and I believe we did a good job."

As Sonny was sinking the five into the corner pocket, Ronnie while walking to fetch his coffee said, "But the last one broke the union so I'm back to shooting pool and playing dominoes."

"What happen, Ronnie? Doris got mad at you or something?"

Sonny asked as he positions the cue stick to sink the one Ronnie laughed as Sonny missed the one before he answered saying, "It is nothing like that at all, Sonny. The last person I helped started to call me "Mr. Cleaning Man" just because she could not remember my name and Doris started to do the same."

"So you're saying you are no Mr. Cleaning Man," Sonny asked trying not to laugh.

"That is right," Ronnie answered as he took a drink of his cold coffee.

Sonny laughed and as he stepped away from the Table before he asked, "You sure?"

"Yes I am," Ronnie quickly answer and as he positions his cue still upon a Nine ball added "I've had many work names in my life but Mr. Cleaning Man is one I do not want."

Sonny laughed quickly join by the others watching.

THE SMOKER

Kim King was laughing as he leans upon the fence next to me saying, "It is not looking good for Marshall."

Then from the other side of Kim, Wesley answered saying, "I believe your right. The Clinton Track Team had a hand full of real fast runners and jumpers but the next event my favorite, the 3-mile relay and Marshall has won this race last two times these teams met."

I smiled knowing his grandson was starting the relay race today the last race of the day. I glance back upon the track and could plainly see the excitement within the young runners as they prepare themselves for the race. There was much cheering and yelling and with the drums beating and Wesley's grandson glance over at us once before concentrating of the race before him.

We yelled our support with the crowd and as the cheering and yelling quieted to start the race, Kim looked over at Wesley asking, "Wesley, do you remember Latham Jackson we call the Smoker back in the sixties who ran for Clinton."

Wesley almost at a laugh answer saying, "I sure do and I'll never forget what he did to me the first Track Meet we faced him."

Wesley took his eyes off the race and looked over at me saying, "William, he was the fastest kid in area if not in the state. None of these kids could match his speed."

"He was something at that," Kim added as he took his eyes off of the race and glance off thinking before saying, "Especially in this three-mile relay. In fact, Latham Jackson won every event he was in if I remember right."

Kin shook his head yes as he said, "He did at that, I remember their Coach always placed him as the last runner in this event."

218

Wesley laughed before saying, "Yea, and the Smoker was just a freshman when he beat me right here on this very track."

"He did at that," Ken laughed. "William, the first time we raced against him I was the second to last runner and we had good lead as I handed the Baton off to Wesley but that all ended when the Smoker receive the Baton. The Smoker took off and caught Wesley before the finish and passed him like he was standing still."

"That he did," Wesley answered then looking at me said, "I'll never forget that race, either. I was beat bad and I believe me that the last time Coach Horton placed me in the relay race."

Wesley laughed returning his attention back to the race at hand and added, "It looks like the race is about to start."

"They are at that," Kin answered. "I wonder who they got to run the last section of the relay for Clinton for it appears the coach got Cody, Marshall's speedster racing the last leg of the race."

"Him," Wesley said as he pointed to the young tall black he could see standing alongside Cody, just itching to get hold of the Baton as

Cody was.

NATE HATED FLOWERS

Suddenly Old Man Nate started to laugh and as he settles down said, "And that is how I created the Dead Man's Stretch along 27. Even sent it pass the house a mile or two all the way to Bill Waid's house who said, "No." Telling me his Freddie loves flowers and if he should agree to my deal his name would be mud and he rather keep it at "Come here lover boy."

Old Man Nate was a mean old man and flowers were not to be found around his house. I've seen him several times out in some field when I was going to town with Nelly Bay just chopping away on some early yellow daffodils and as he was whacking away he kept yelling, "Dam you. Dam you."

His hatred for flowers was shown in others aspects of his life and I've always known him as Nate but many call him using Mean Old Man Nate. Always rough talking in any action he took, speaking his mind freely, and in church would sit in the corner and watch. If anyone tried to say hello they would only get back a huff or leave me alone.

When I was new to the area I thought he was crazy seeing him out smashing a batch Daffodils and some of the other beautiful blooming flowers that grew along the road. I just figured something must have happened in the pass to cause him hated them so. Really thinking it was none of my business but I asked around anyway but only answer I receive that his wife and daughter were killed out collecting flowers for his birthday and ever since then he never would let a flower grow around him and he didn't.

I mean he wiped out every flower between his house and town and the trail became known as the Dead Man's trail and even I started to call it that and the flowerless trail even went pass his house a mile or two and not a flower was seen way into the woods on each side of the road.

But several days ago as I passed his house heading for town, Old Man Hate was sitting on his porch swinging slightly and before him sat a large pot holding one large pink Naked Lady in full bloom and I could see tears were running down his face.

I quickly pulled the wagon off the road into his yard and not sure how long I'll be and knowing Nelly Bay, if I didn't give her some oats she be cranky and nothing worst then having a cranky horse pulling a wagon and Nelly Bay was as bad as they come but I love her for she could ever pull a wagon load.

Afterwards I wonder slowly toward the porch not sure I should be here or not for I could see Old Man Nate was heartbroken and it had something to do with that lone Naked lady sitting before him. He has been my friend for over 45 years and in all the years I've known him I have never asked him why he hated flowers. There are some jokes around about Him like. "You know its springtime when you see Old man Nate out whacking the Daffodils." or "And careful traveling dead man trail for it may be raining flowers if Old man Nate is out swinging today."

There were others sayings but when I've gone about have way, off the porch came Pete and Gracie, his two Coonhounds to meet me wagging their big tail and off to the right I suddenly head several Rosters crow from his Chicken Pen and as grave Pete and Gracie a nice hello by getting on my knee and giving each a big hug, I notice in his rabbit cages located under the row of Cedar trees that they were full of young rabbits that he will sell to the fur company soon.

When I stood and walked upon the porch being chase by the dogs. Old man Nate with his tear stain face said, "I sure glad you are here, William. I need someone to tell my story too who will hear my story and not judge me and the Lord has blessed me with you."

While grabbing my favorite wooden chair I like sit in when I stop by and shared a bottle of his brew with him and I looked at the Pink Lady saying, "Nate, I can see something has happened and it seems you are very heartbroken over it. Now Nate old Buddy, if I am to be of any use to you, you are going have to tell me why you are so heartbroken and start from the beginning."

"The whole story," Old man Nate asked before he began cleaning his face with a nearby towel he keeps handy.

"Yes," I answered while leaning back in my chair to get comfortable before I looked Nate in the eye saying, "The whole story, Nate. I know it has something to do with this Naked Lady before us. I've never known over the years and not really wanting to know the reason you hate flowers. I always thought it was a very private matter and was none of my business. But seeing you crying over this Naked Lady here has me very curious and I as your friend will listen to your story and hope any suggestion I give will help."

Nate stop his swinging and leaning forward he open his hands over the Naked Lady saying, "I have been wrong all these years William. What you see here is the last Bulb my baby ever planted just before she was killed along with her mother when they went flower picking. But I remember that day so long ago as if it happened yesterday.

Today is the day it happened fifty years ago that I lost my two babies in a fog filled morning. But it is this flower before us that makes me think I've been so wrong over all these fifty years."

I wanted to ask why when Nate sudden stood picking up the Naked Lady saying, "Come William, let me show where I found the Naked Lady and you will better understand."

The dogs and I followed him and I looked back at my wooden chair wondering should I take it with me. We did not speak as we traveled and only the wining of the dogs wanting to be petted broke the silence. Slowly Nate led me toward the barn and as we passed by the Cedar Row of tree the smell of the rabbits filled the air and as we rounded the cedars I could see the old barn with more than one board missing but what caught my eye, I could see the old outhouse had been blown over during the night's thunder storms that had sweep through the area. It was a typical outhouse and I've use it more than once only on the over the women's area had a rough out storage bin had been added to clean out the potty area if need be.

I remember it always had that outhouse smell to it and way before we stopped before the blown over outhouse I could smell that same old outhouse smell.

Nate broke the silence as he stopped to the left of the outhouse and pointed to the area where the outline of the storage box had been sitting in back of the women's side of the outhouse and almost in tears Nate said, "That is where I found the Naked Lady. Right here where my baby placed the Naked Lady wanting to surprise me with its pink flower to show her love for me when I turned thirty and tomorrow I will be turning seventy-nine. So fifty years ago I was just turning 29 and she hide that Naked Lady waiting till next year when I turn thirty when it would bloom and she could surprise me with it showing what she grown just for me and she hide it in the only place she knew I would never look, the women's side of the outhouse."

Turning back toward the house Nate continues with, "Now you know where the Naked Lady came from and now I'm going to tell why I hate flowers. But first we must have a glass full of some of my home brew and I can say myself it is the best I've brewed up in a while. I can tell you William I'm glad you came by, you sure have ease my trouble mine greatly and when we get to house and over a good glass of home brew or rather you have a joint of the best Pot I've grown in a while I will tell you my story."

It was not long we were sitting under his porch and set between us was that Naked Lady blooming out of one those old plant clay pots I've seen around and I got to wondering why over the years there still was only one bloom as I took a taste of Nate's Home brew.

My thinking stopped as the home brew fill my mouth with a wonderful taste so I lifter my glass to Nate saying, "You're right Nate. This is the best brew you've made in a while."

"There a reason" Nate answered. "I've been letting Ricky make the brew on his own and he has never did learn the true touch on how to brew a batch. Always in a rush doing this or doing that and I left myself out of the picture and I mean I left dear old dad out if it. I tried to give some advice once and that went over like pulling a tooth. So this dear old Dad left himself out of the picture and I believe you have tasted the results."

I gave him another toast before answering with, "That I have, that I've had. But this brew is not the same as theirs what happen?"

Nate seeming more relaxed even giving me a smile as he answered me saying, "You know that last year's brew was so bad it had to be thrown out but Ricky took it somewhere and had a big party given it away in free drinks."

"Did you go," I asked as I took a good swig.

"No," he answered adding, "But I did hear it was a successful event."

I was feeling more relaxed by now and without thinking said, "Well I did and that was the worst tasting Home brew I ever tasted and it seems most of the drinks went back into the pot so your Ricky stood up and said, "I'm give a one no I'll make that ten dollars to anyone that can drink three glasses full without the added sugar to sweeten it to made it drinkable. This brew is no different than the others we done over the years and you all know we make the best brew this side of the river and we believe only someone been sabotaging us and putting some kind of bitter weed in the brew when we are not at home."

What happen then," Old Man Nate asked having a clear smug look about him that exploded across his face.

"Well," I answered given him a small laugh before I continued with, "Many took up his bet but only twelve guys and three girls did all three glasses but most gave up after a sip. I do remember the heaving and gagging that went on with them trying to drink that stuff and did it ever make them drunk."

My laughter seemed to eased Nate's trouble mine as he join me saying, "I'm sure it did."

As I settled myself down I looked at Nate asking. "What did you put in his brew to make it taste so bad anyway?"

"I did nothing," Nate answered, "Ricky made that brew all by himself only he use barrels he made brew the year before and you must wait as lease four years letting the barrels sit around and let the ants clean them out. Leave that old brew in the barrel sure makes a bitter brew and last year was the second year he used the same barrels and you tasted the results."

"I sure did," I answered busting out in laughter. But as I took a good drink of his fine tasting brew asking, "Then where this great tasting brew come from."

Old Man Nate just smiled before he said, "Use an old barrel that been sitting around for several years and was well cleaned by the ants and brewed myself a barrel full is all I did. I think it is the best I ever made and been thinking maybe four years over an ant bed not been long enough or I just got lucky. There is no doubt in my mind that this is the best brew I think I made in a while."

After drinking the last drop of Nate's nice brew, I lifted the glass into the air saying, "Here a salute to you Nate. I have tasted a glass full of your brew every year for over forty years and I agree with you. This is by far the best you have ever brewed up."

He just gave me his old man Nate's smile and I still could see there was sadness in his heart for when he looked back down at the pink Naked Lady his eyes became sad as he said, "Did you know it was my dad that taught me how to brew. I would gather everything that went into the barrel and I did the same thing to each barrel and when I was done with that I had to double check my work making sure all the ingredients where in place and let me forget anything, I got punished for it. Daddy's method was not perfect but I learned to make a great tasting brew."

Then he looked out across the road and saying, "I wonder do Dad's teach their boys like mind did. My dad was in his forties when I was born and was a wonderer. Work at many jobs and I took right after him. I still miss him even thou when I needed him he was not around and had to live with the pain alone."

"Here now, you not going to go sad on me again are you," I joked.

When Old Man Nate did not return a response, I could not help myself and said, "If you're going to be this sad Old Man Nate again, might as well tell me story of why this beautiful pink Naked Lady was hidden in the outhouse and get it off your chest."

"If you promise to not interrupt me," Old Man Nate asked as he reached down and as he took hold of the Naked Lady's pot picking it into the air saying, "Did you notice the writing across the pot."

"No," I answered as I left my seat and there sure enough written by a child's hand were the words, "Happy thirtieth birthday daddy. I grew this just for you to tell you I love you. Kay"

The words brought tears to my eyes and I guess the brew helped and we both cried. I just could not help myself either as her words seeming so innocent so simple yet the message she put forth was a heart killer written as if she at any moment could come in and hug his neck.

Nate sat the flower back down beside him saying, "William, on this day fifty years ago Sharon and Kay was killed. I admit is was partly their fault for it was one of those real heavy foggy mornings and whenever Sharon needed to talk private with Kay they would go walking away from the house well of my hearing and mostly I stayed inside the house making sure I knew nothing of what was being said.

But that morning it must have been important for they went walking in the worst Fogs I ever seem. I mean it was as bad as a fog can get in the woods. When they left the house they went right instead of left which is the direction of Holquist's pig farm that Sharon uses to make a point when giving her talk to Kay. But that morning they went right where the Daffodils had started to bloom where the My houses' old homestead use to be and all that left was their Daffodils to indicate it was a homestead.

Now Sharon like flowers but Kay became obsessed with growing them and she loved running around collecting them also. Of course Sharon had to help her and I became their tool with words like build a bed there are move that bed to there and bet I move rocks a hundred times from one end of the house to the next and the yard was always full of flowers sometimes all blues or all yellows or all reds or everything in between. But that morning was a cold very foggy morning and they should not have been walking on the road. I heard the screech of breaking tires and I heard the two rumps as the truck slam into their bodies. I ran up the fog filled hill and there smashed underneath the truck were the mangle bodies of Sharon and Kay. I looked in shock upon them when I notice the hand full of Daffodils still in their hands that even in death they did not let go and as I stared at those flowers hate began to boiled up in me not seeing the truck driver at fault for their death it was the flowers that killed them.

So I remove all flowers around the house up and down the road I started to carry a weed killer around with me and I bet I have murdered, smashed, and several times mowed whole fields of flower laughing as the blades chopped one flower after another. I think most of those times I was drunk." He stopped and gave laughed adding, "Yep I was drunk alright from trying out a new brew. If I can't get drunk on it, it is no good which I can honestly say never had a bad batch, no never. Then drunk I am off chopping the heads off the flowers."

His words were funny and I couldn't help myself and laughed causing him to glance over at me saying, "Well I was."

As our laughter settled down Old Man Nate collected his thoughts before saying. "William, I bet I have killed over ten million flowers and I've forgetting all about the special gift that Sharon and Kay had made to give me on my thirtieth birthday. I was too busy killing out the thing I thought had killed my two babies. In my mind the vision of those daffodils in their hands was the cause of their death. I lost sight forgetting the so many little things they showed their love for me, forgetting the times they reached for my hand, but most of all forgetting the meaning behind the flowers they grew."

Old man Nate stood and way his arms around his yard a second saying, "I forgot why the yard sometimes just full of blue flowers or yellows flowers and could not understand just why they made me move flower beds around. I have forgotten seeing the many colorful blooming flowers around my house singing out the spirit of their love for our home.

My hatred blinded me and I made sure anywhere I went I saw no flowers. You know between here and town there not a house or field has a flower around it. I pay them not to plant flowers and I have permission to cross their property and kill any darn flower I see."

Somehow I felt the Nate sadness was all gone a he busted out on laughter.

Then Old Man Nate suddenly became serious as he sat his drink down and calmly picked the Naked Lady saying, "William all these many years I've been so wrong, oh so wrong have I been."

He became quiet as tears filled his face. I said nothing for the vision he shown me fill my heart with heartache as strong as his but before I could help myself I asked, "What have you been wrong at," and after I said it I thought, "You done it now," but I already had a good notion what it was.

Nate raise his finger at me as if saying wait before he set the Naked Lady back down on the ground and as he stood said, "Before I answer, we must have another glass of my Home Brew don't you think?"

"You bet I would," I answered holding out my empty glass.

As Nate pored my glass full he said, "It is not what you think. I can tell you that."

After he returned to the swing with a glass full of brew for himself, he looked at me before saying, "Fifty-five years ago William I was struggling to make ends meet. Had a house note, a car notes, Utilities and a wife and daughter to feed and the bills piled up and among all this was the flowers. Get that plant food, get that fertilizer, get us some dirt, put that rock here or put that rock there and not that I did not love flowers, I hated having to spend hard earn money on them. Then to die over flowers was too much and I cross over to the Devils side and anything that reminded me of my two Babies I remove from my vision, my life and that was flowers. Hated what they represented. For when I see a flower, I live over the nightmare of seeing my babies tangle bodies."

"I can understand your reasoning," I added taking a good drink of my brew.

Old Man Nate shook his head as he looked down upon the Naked Lady saying over and over, "I have been so wrong, I have been so wrong."

As he became quiet, Old Man Nate with tears just a flowing down his cheek looked up at me and with a smile said, "William, it was their love for me they grew flowers and it was not flowers that killed them it was their desire to show me how much they love me and here I was thinking it was their love for flowers all along. Every breakfast, dinner and supper there always sat a vase in the middle of the table filled with colorful flowers showing me how must they loved me and even going out into the fog to gather a few flowers for the breakfast table seeking out a simple I love you to display.

I's about to add my two cents when Old Man Nate slapped his legs saying, "William, the first thing I'm doing is destroy Dead Man Stretch and fill it with flowers and I'll I think I'll even place an aid in the paper to see if anybody wants to help me."

"I'll help," speaking proudly. "I may be old but I can drive down the road tossing hands full of flower seeds into the wind as I went."

"Good idea," Old Man Nate said as he stood. "We will do that right now. I didn't tell you but beside the Naked Lady was a large plastic bag full of spring and fall wildflower seeds. Sharon had found the seeds at the Farmers Market and I had forgotten all about the seeds but I can still remember Sharon words as I paid for it, "Kay is just going love growing these all of these flowers."

Nate reached behind a closet door and pulled out a big bag of seed that must have weighed twenty-five pounds and as he set it before me, "William will you help me in spreading these seeds that I can returned to the world the message "I love you that Kay's flowers was showing the world that I could not see."

MY AUNT FLOSSIE

My Aunt Flossie was my Daddies' father's youngest sister who had become blind at a very early age. Now before she went blind, Aunt Flossie had a boyfriend and were to marry which ended when her blindness over took her. Her father who was my Grandpa arrange for us to live at the homestead if they would take care of Aunt Flossie and him. But Grandpa died when I was very young which left Aunt Flossie who we all love dearly.

Does not mean we did not have fun with her and her being blind and hard of hearing to go with it. She liked to listen to St. Louis Base Ball and Soap Operas upon the radio and often had the sound so loud you could hear it all the way out into the barn. We would often sneak and change channels and even sometime hid it when one of her favorite programs were about to come on. She would rant and holler what she was going to do to us if she caught us and away we ran just a laughing. Especially, if it was the time for one of the mystery stories that she was caught up in.

But really and truly she was everybody's Aunt Flossie. Everyone at church call her their Aunt Flossie. Visitors to the house did the same. She may have been everybody's Aunt Flossie but she still had some ways about her that were strange to us children. Now as I think back on the times she would walk out onto the front porch face southwest and Holler loudly at workmen building her Mansion. Always telling them whom we could not see what she wanted in the Mansion we also could not see. But I guess she did, for she would holler, "I want the extra rooms for friends over now," or she would say, "Looking good, well done." As I watch her and hear the words she would yell and say, I, who was most of the time sitting in the rocker in back of her and would rock trying to imagine the Mansion she was building. I promise myself right then and there that I was going to visit her in her mansion when I get to heaven. I will I assure you.

But when I was in my early twenties and no longer living at home her health became such Mom and Dad had to place her in a nursing home and it so happen there was her boyfriend, Cephus Choey living there that she was to marry many years earlier. Then during her last few months of her life, he would sit in her room and hold her hand for hours on end. He told me he had lost her when they were young because she did not want to burden his life having to care for her. He told us she forced him to move on in his life and leave her and by holding her hand for hours he wanted her to know he could have taken care of her when she became blind. He also wanted to show her in her last hours that his love for her has never change and would been proud to have had as his wife if she had only let him.

But as children Lorrain and I slept with her and I was always in the middle. What I remember most that no matter how bad we were to her in our play, she would always put me to sleep starching my back.

She was my Aunt Flossie and will always love her and believe me, I will be visiting her in her Mansion that she may know what I looked like that is for sure.

BICYCLE BUILT FOR TWO

Bill Jr was thinking of the bicycle built for two as he left the library and was wondering if he could make one by putting two bicycles together. He had been wondering around the Rice Universities Library by himself for Bobby family had gone somewhere when he had come across a Bike Magazine called, "Easy to Ride." In it, they had covered the many different kind of bikes built for two there had been over time. The images he saw in the magazine made him think by using Bobby's bike he could made a bicycle for two.

He couldn't get Paul or Carl for they'll be gone a month or more visiting their Grandmother over in Dallas area which they did after school has been let out every year.

He placed the western novel in the carry all basket on back of his bicycle and headed home. The image of the bicycle built for two never left him causing him to be thinking how he could make one all the way to the house. Even dodging the cars through The Rice Village did not remove his vision and Judy's bike came to mind as he entered Amherst. "Yea," he said as he stood to pump the bike harder, "Judy's bike."

He slid to a stop in the backyard the way he liked to do and he has goof a hundred times doing it, but not this time, as he pulled the kick stand down he glance down at his bikes wheel bolts before entering the garage and begin examining Judy's bike which had a heaver frame painted with girly pink and blue designs, wider tires and even had a pink seat.

He spoke loudly to himself saying, "Shoot, I could take her front tire off and easily bolt her front end onto mine."

"You can do what," he heard Judy loudly say behind him.

"Judy," he answered before holding his hands up saying, "Judy, do you think you can help me make a bicycle built for two by bolting your front end onto my bike and see if we can ride it?"

"What you talking about," Judy said looking on her brother with her hands on her hips like she does when she figuring her wild brother was up to no good which he seemed to be always doing.

"Listen Judy," he answered leaving her bike and grabbing the small tool box from the floor. "I want to make a bicycle built for two and I think I can bolt your front end onto the back end of my bike and when I'm done we can see if we can ride it. What do you say? Will you let me?"

Judy looked upon her brother using his best lines to sway her into letting her do this. But she thought to herself, "It might be fun to try." "I want hurt it, promise," Bill Jr said for the third time still in his best begging routine Judy has heard a thousand times when he wants something.

"You promise," Judy still concern he still might hurt it.

"Yes, I promise," he answered as he took hold of her fancy handlebars by its hand rests having red and blue tassels hanging off the end of them and brought the bike out of the garage placing it beside his. Open his small tool box and as Judy watched he remove her bikes front tire and without any problem had her bike attach to the rear bolts of his bike.

Smiled as he finished saying, "Well there she is, a bicycle built for two. Think you and I can ride her?"

Judy surprised him as she pushing him aside saying, "Only on the side walk, as she headed down the driveway."

Her words perked his excitement as he kicks the kickstands upped and climb upon his bike and using his feet he moves the bikes down the drive to follow her. As he walked the bike forward and feeling confident he pushed himself forward weaving a bit before he settles down mostly in control as he rode pass Judy who stated to run after him but slowed down as he came to a stop beside the sidewalk.

"You better not hurt my bike and specially me." Judy said with some force in it as she took hold of her handlebars and placed herself in position behind her brother just knowing they were going to smash for sure and hoping they didn't.

Bill Jr looked back at his sister and waited till she seems ready before he almost yelled saying, "One for the money, two for show, three get ready and go, go, go."

Together they push the Bikes forward and after a little weaving back and forth with both their feet working to keep the bike upright started down the sidewalk a little ways till into the grass they rolled stopping their forward motion and causing them to end up upon the grass just a laughing.

"We almost had it Judy," Bill Jr said as he gained his feet and then helped Judy get up.

"I do not know if I can do this," Judy answered having her doubts. "Come on Judy, we can do this," he pleaded as he began to pull his bike off the ground and seeing Judy's bike was not going to stand right, "Help me Judy get our bikes back on the sidewalk."

Judy gave in and it was not long they were in position with Bill Jr repeating, "One for the money, two for the show, three to get ready, go, go, go."

Being more careful, Bill Jr was able to keep it on the sidewalk and the bicycle built for two was traveling nicely down it until at the end of the block he pulled onto the grass to help stop her and again they ended up upon the grass just a laughing.

"That was fun," Bill Jr said sprawl out upon the grass.

Judy, still on the grass only said, "I think we need to work on our breaking method myself."

Back and forth down the sidewalk they practice. Sometime Judy was in front and sometime Bill Jr. They ended upon the grass edge several more times before Judy surprised Bill Jr by pulling up into the driveway saying, "Bill Jr, I need to go inside, Right Now."

As they parked their wonderful bicycle built for two in the back yard, Judy left running toward the back door. Bill Jr watched her go knowing she want be back for she been helping Mother fix the evening meal and it was getting close to supper time. He undid the rear bolts and it was just a short while both bikes were back to normal and parked in the garage. But as he walked toward the house Bill Jr smiled hardly believing Judy actually let him use her bike to build his bicycle for two and even had fun with her as they learned to ride it.

Then as he opened the back door to the smell of his Mother's cooking he thought, "Playing with Judy was fun and that don't happen very often."

BILL'S FIRST BIG FISH

"Mother, is there any tea made," Bill asked as he enter the dining room after changing from his wet clothes.

Grace looked upon her tall young son saying, "There a some in the fridge. How did your fishing trip to Mr. Jean's pond go? Got rain out I see."

"I sure did," he answered as he entered the kitchen and took the tea jug from the fridge. Then as he about to open the cabinet for a glass said, "I almost caught a big bass today. But my line broke."

Grace gave herself a laugh as she set the book she was reading upon the table and looking over her reading glasses into the kitchen said, "Come tell me all about it."

She could hear him getting ice thinking, "This ought to be good. I let him fished Mr. Jean's pond at least once a week and I've fixed us a fried fish meal out of the small fish he brought home. But this heavy rain shower has change things today and I guess there will be no fish meal for supper today."

Bill entered the dining room taking a big drink of his ice tea before grabbing a cookie off the counter saying, "Mother, I had a big one on my line today and lost it all because of this hair oil I used."

"Well what happen," Grace asked taking a sip of her glass of ice tea as she watch him take a bite of the cookie before he sat down across her.

He laughed after a drink of his tea before saying, "I had arrived at Mr. Jean's pond when I saw that it was going to rain. Well Mr. Jean told me best time to fish for the big ones was while it was raining. So upon getting there, I put a one of those lures Daddies gave me on my line and started casting out into the pond. Trying my best to keep it off the bottom where it would hang up if I didn't."

Bill took a drink of his tea before he continued with, "Anyway, when the rain hit and believe me it was one of those real heavy down pours and about my third cast I hook a big fish. I mean Mother it was a big fish."

"Big," Grace asked, "How big was it?"

Bill set his tea down and using hands saying expressly, "It was at least this big."

"Well, what happen next," Grace asked as she watched him take another bit of his cookie and drink of his tea before he answered saying, "I was trying hard to make sure that big fish would not break my line when this hair oil I have been using began to get into my eyes from the rain hitting my head. I mean it got so I could not see from it and in my struggle between my eyes and the fighting fish, my line broke and the fish got away and was I ever mad."

Grace, knowing her son asked, "Then what did you do?"

Bill ignored his Mother's stare as he said, "I got so mad I threw my rod down on the ground, it bounced and into the pond it flew. Being already wet, I went in after it and washed my hair and eyes while I was there. That hair oil hurt my eyes and it was not till I was almost halfway home before it stopped hurting."

"I guess there be no fish supper today," Grace said as she picked her book she was reading from off the table.

"I guess not," Bill said before standing while finishing off his cookie. Then grabbing his ice tea said, "Maybe next week I'll do better. I know one thing, Mother. I am never going to use hair oil on my hair again that is for sure. It hurt my eyes."

Grace watched him leave letting the screen door slam behind him and laughed while checking herself from yelling for the hundredth time, "Don't let the screen door slam."

MY SEEING CREATION

Professor Wilson set the very old rusty sword upon the table before me saying, "Is this worth anything?"

I glanced over the rusty sword a second before I answered him as he walked over to fetch himself a cup of coffee by saying, "I believe it could deliver a great deal of money if I think this is walk I think it is, "An old Spanish Sword."

"Good," he said and after a taste of his coffee Professor Wilson said, "It my last auction pieces I'll be bringing you. I'm going on eighty and my old body saying enough. I found this sword close to two miles out Galveston beach and it almost killed me fetching it from the bottom for it was buried about three feet down in the sand."

I reach for my camera and place some our standard forms before him to fill out concerning the sword its beginning value and just had to asked, "Professor, now that you are quitting, I just got to know how you were able to fine such artifacts in the mud and sand. I've action whole Armors you discovered to a hand full of jewelry. There must be a secret here for I know there not a seeker out has ever discovered what you found over the years."

He just smiled at me saying, "I have at that. Haven't I?"

"What is your secret," I asked putting the sign documents in my briefcase.

"I use nature is all," he answered.

"Got to more than that then just nature," I asked lean back in my chair looking upon I've learned was quite a brilliant man over the years. I heard he had been quite the inventor for Space Industry. But now he is over eighty, and I always secretly assume, he was using some invention he created and kept for himself.

"I guess it is a little more than nature," he answered before taking another sip of hot coffee.

He gave me a serious look before saying, "I guess it want hurt if you knew."

I answered serious saying, "You know us Auctioneers are a close mouth bunch unless it will help in selling a product to make it more valuable."

Professor Wilson appear to look off in the distance before he said, "I worked on a project for developing a system that could analysis the reflection of radio waves as it travels into the Earth and determined all it properties. I formed a team and we after couple years had a functioning operation in theory only the computer systems were not fast to analysis the Data enough to bring forth a visual image or any information at all. So they scraped the project and I took what we have developed home until computers operation speed became capable to analysis the Data. I modified the system to work with a Laptop. It is simple enough. I just send a strong radio wave into the Earth and through trial and error I learn how to handle the Radio Waves Data. Using my programming basically able to removing water, mud, and sand's radio reflections till only what I was left brought forth an image I could see like rings, swords, and lots of just types of material. You never know how many bottle caps or under the beach sand for example. That where I started. I mean I started walking the beach and I found rings, necklaces, bracelets and even guns which you know of one that brought us over fifty thousand."

"I remember that one alright," I answered. "So, that how you find things you bring here using space industries developments."

"That was at the beginning I did," Professor returned taken a drink of his coffee before continuing saying, "I then tested it upon the bay waters and discovered my radio wave went farther into the ground than expected. I'm talking close too fifty feet of water and two feet in the mud or sand bottom and in shallow water close to ten feet in the mud or sand. I mean I found lots of goodies way to deep for me to bring into the boat. I can only gather as long as it is not too deep in the sand or mud. This sword was in ten foot of water and close to three feet in the ground. It about did me in getting it out of the mud. There was more metal around the sword like an old suit of armor but I wanted the sword and it about did me in getting it too."

"You do have the movie documentation of where and how you dug it up," I asked handing him his copy of our agreement.

Professor Wilson set the coffee cup upon the desk as he took the documents saying, "That I did. You can find it in the envelope on the sword."

"Thanks," I answered as I watch him leave. I open the envelope to discover a video chip and wondering what I'll see as I plug it into my computer and call it up.

It began with an image of its outline on the bottom which I now knew was from his image device before I find him starting to dig which cause a cloud of muddy water hiding the Professor. Slowly the tide pushed the muddy water away and we find Profess or Wilson holding his chest and I'm thinking heart attack. It appeared to take a deep breath of his air supply before bending over and reaching way into the hole he had dig and slowly brought out the Spanish Sword trying not to disturbed the mud. Then he calmly brought the sword toward the camera for a close up view of the sword."

After I pulled the video chip from my computer, I marked it with a yellow M and as I place a C on the five copies, I got to wondering about Professor Wilson and his invention. I wonder if it will die with him or will he make sure it lives on. At lease it has made me quite a bit of money over the last few years.

OLD RUM

"What a day I've had," Elaine said as she dropped her bag off on the table beside the door before adding, "What a mad house it was getting out of Marshall. There must have been ten thousand or more there to see the car show."

"How was the car show, anyway," Barbara asked with William from the kitchen adding, "We forgot all about it. By the way, what you want in your coffee?"

"Just black," Elaine answered as she took a seat on the couch next to Barbara. Then as she settled, took the cup of coffee said, "Woody and I walked around admiring the many cars when I swear we didn't come across Old Rum."

Barbara sat up quickly in her lounge chair saying, "Old Rum, wow, I haven't thought about her in many a year. Do you think she'll still there? I would like to go see her."

"Don't know," Elaine answered as she set her coffee cup down standing. "But we can go and see and I'm driving."

By the time William could follow them out the door Elaine was already in her car and Barbara called out while pointing toward the Van saying, "William, Elaine is going home after we see Old Rum. Why don't you follow us with the van so she will not have to bring us home?"

After Barbara settled in, Elaine quickly had her Nova to move onto the road but the highway was full of cars and trucks leaving Marshall which allowed William pulled the Van up behind her and even quickly followed her out upon the pavement when a break came within the traffic.

Elaine drove fairly fast while she and Barbara randomly talked about the family and how they were doing and those they knew that had passed away lately. But upon entering town Barbara's thoughts turn to Old Rum saying, "I hope Old Rum is still there."

"I believe she still there," Elaine answered as she found it was easy to park for most of the visitor's cars were gone.

William parked beside them and quickly join them walking toward the Antique car display and they could see that most of the many antiques cars shown were gone. But as they walked passed Daniel's Hardware Store, Barbara caught a glimpse of Old Rum sitting beside a car trailer being pull by another antique bright red ford pickup and the closer they got the more excited she became untilled she took hold of William's arm and made him come with her as she quickens her stepped toward the old Chevy and as they drew closer he saw a small blue and white standup display with the car's picture which read, "58 Chevy Sudan painted turquoise and white."

William stopped near the car letting Barbara rush ahead and with hands on her hips stopped and as she looked the car over, gave him a glance before looking at Elaine saying "It's Old Rum alright" and William's think, "So this is Old Rum, a 58 Chevy Sudan painted blue and white and here I was thinking it was something like a truck.

Barbara stopped and turning back toward William, "Do you know why it is called a Sudan?"

But before William could answer she continued with "It is not because to have 4 doors it is because it has a hardtop so the name Sudan means hardtop."

"Oh," is all William got out before Barbara turned away and started to walk around the car admiring the outside motioning for William to join her saying, "Elaine, I do believe this is Old Rum. But it doesn't have all the dents and I see the damage rear has been fixed and new front bumper for the one on Old Rum was well used. But I always thought it gave Old Rum this, "I can take a beating but I keep on ticking look and now, she perfect as gold and not one dent in her at all."

She patted the car top a second saying, "William, Old Rum here was Daddies and Mothers first car the two of them ever own and believe me, Daddy and his drinking gave it a rough go around but Old Rum took good care of him as he weaves all over the road putting a new dent in her now and then."

William laughed saying, "I can understand that."

Elaine added, "But Daddy had a car before mom and him got married."

"Not for long, so it does not count," Barbara answered before she poked her head into the driver side window examining the interior and William asked, "How old were you when they got Old Rum."

Barbara not looking away from her examination of Old Rum's interior said, "Twelve or thirteen."

"Really," William asked before poking his head through the back window looking inside he added, "then how did your Mom and Dad travel around?"

"Catch rides," she answered.

Elaine poked her head through the passage window saying, "We sure did but mostly with one of the cousins. Momma would wait on the corner of the driveway for a ride and she did not take us with her if she could not help it accept on Sundays. Catch a ride with Cousin Joe and Mary and their three kids. Pile into the black Ford Truck Bed with bales of hay for us to sit on and when we all rode together Dam boys would pick on us poor girls," Elaine laughed as she ran her hand across the seats.

Barbara lifted her head back out the window saying, "They sure did and the worst thing was they put hay in our hair and I'm telling you William, it bad enough getting that hay out of our clothes, we had had to get it out of our hair also and here we were just out of church and all the way home fussing with the boys trying to keep them away from us."

Elaine following Barbara out of the car saying, "I always thought Joe put that hay bales back there for us to sit on for the boys to torture us girls."

"Me too," Barbara added before she suddenly reached out and punched William on the shoulder.

William quickly moved away from her holding his arm saying, "Way you do that for."

"For being a boy," She answered.

"But I didn't throw hay on you," William added stepping back out of her range.

Barbara took a step forward acting like she was going hit him again saying, "If you been there you would have done the same as the other boys."

William with a frustrated face said, "Girls." "Boys," Barbara answered.

Loraine by now had walked around the Old Rum car and broke William's and Barbara 's joking saying, "Barbara, I remember it was on one of those Sundays when Daddy made us all go to church with Mom and when that happens you know we always got in a hay fight with the boys and I remember upon arriving home, there standing beside Old Rum was Dad and even had a blue ribbon an several balloons tied to the antenna singing, "Happy birthday to Momma, Happy birthday to you," and then did a bow to us.

"Yea, I remember. I watch Momma began to cry upon seeing Daddy and Old Rum parked before the house," Barbara added before giving a small laugh before saying, "Old Rum got Mom and us kids around when we could afford to put gas into her."

Elaine lifted herself from looking into the backseat saying, "But Daddy and his drinking got her eventually."

"I would say it did," Barbara added before walking to the rear of the car and pointed to the left side corner saying, "Right here it was all smash end."

"Smash," William asked jokingly.

"Yes smashed," Barbara answered seeming frustrated with William. "One day when the School Bus stopped to let us off, the other children started pointing and there down the field was Old Rum sitting against the old man Jenkins' rock wall and it seems Daddy was asleep in it. We started to move toward the car when Mother yelled for us to leave him alone. It appeared he was backing out and just kept on backing till he hit the rock wall and smashed Old Rum's right here in rear corner.

"I can see that happening," William said before he smiled at saying, "I guess Old Rum did more traveling weaving on the road then driving straight and is that why you call this 4 door Sudan, "Old Rum."

"No," Barbara answered. "Daddy liked to drink Rum and I had to remove many empty Rum Bottles before Mom let us ride in it. Many bottles had lot of Rum in them and splash over the car so it began to smell like Rum so we started calling her Old Rum."

William stuck his head into the car taken a good sniff before as he pulled his head out saying, "It does smell a little like Rum."

"I thought it did also," Elaine added. "Daddy started to take Russell with him when he went drinking and Russell who must have been not over 8 brought Old Rum home with Daddy passed out in the back seat. He could barely see over the steering wheel and it seems Russell had taken some scraps of wood and tied them to his feet so he could drive her."

"Russell sure did," Barbara added walking toward the rear of Old Rum to opened the unlocked trunk wider saying, "Russell brought him home several times and leaving Daddy asleep, he would run from car afraid Mama would catch him."

Then pointing to the trunk said, "Now the trunk was another story."

Elaine quickly joined Barbara saying, "And that saying it mildly for the trunk smelled like rotten fish."

William gave a small laugh as Barbara gave William him a smile saying, "It sure did and when Mama went shopping she never use it." "I guess your Dad like to take Old Rum fishing," William asked wondering what their answer would be when Barbara answered saying, "He sure did and we had many a meal off them fish he brought home thrown into the trunk also and sometimes those fish never did make it home."

"I bet the inside really did stink," William bending down to take a good smell of the trunks interior saying, "It does have fishy smell to it."

Then as he stood, Elaine almost at a laugh said, "Daddy would take Old Rum fishing at one of his fishing holes as he called them. Get drunk and several times he upon leaving be so drunk he back or drive Old Rum right into the creek. Old Rum had to be pulled out of a creek more than once and those fish sit in her till she was pulled out too."

William stepped away from the trunk saying, "I can see why it stunk for sure."

"If sure did," Barbara added and while reaching to close the trunk said, "I think we all had to clean the trunk out but Mama made Russell and Reynolds clean the trunk most of the time but we never could get the smell out,"

Elaine was almost laughing as she reached to help Barbara close the trunk saying, "I was thinking of the many times I threaten to lock Russell or Reynolds in this trunk if they did not stop bugging me."

They were laughing as Barbara opened the back door and took a seat inside saying, "This is where I sat when we went anywhere in her."

Elaine opened the passage side back door and also took a seat saying, "And this was my side but Mom mostly went by herself. Old Rum had its key broke in the lock and its overdrive was breaking. It began to rattle and bang more and more as Daddy did put more and more dents on her but she kept on running. I mean we had to put air in the tires to get old Rum started toward town and put air the tires to get her back and sometimes had to put air in one or more tires as we went."

Barbara just shook her head saying, "Before Old Rum disappeared from our lives she was getting to really look like it was on its last leg. I mean, the muffler was dragging and tires were bold, dents and scathes all over its side and the poor front bumper look like it had hit a hundred fence posts and it had started too smoked."

Mom would fuss on him and he always would say, "I'll get it fixed."

Barbara lifted herself out of backseat and closing the door said, "William, you never could guess what did Old Rum in?"

William looked at Barbara thinking blown motor but she said, "Two bullet holes."

He stepped back asking, "Two bullet holes."

Elaine answered saying "That is what Uncle Joe told us" just before she suddenly bent over saying loudly, "What have we here?"

Laughing she reached under the front seat and pulled out one of Daddies Empty Rum Bottles.

William and Barbara quickly join her in laughter as she handed the bottle to Barbara.

Who after examining it a second and as Barbara was handing the Rum Bottle to William, from the right came an old man in a wheel chair saying, "So you found the little gift I left for you."

Barbara had to push William away as she exited Old Rum saying, "Uncle Joe, you're the one that fixed Old Rum and made her look new again?"

"I sure did Barbara," he answered as he wheeled to a stopped before her. "Had her stored away after Harrell and Tommy left Old Rum in the yard and were they ever drunk. I got them to sleep it off on the porch and that morning I bought Old Rum off of your Dad for $50 bucks. I had gone out and looked her over while they were sleeping. I was sure they had burn up the motor, the two tires on of right side

were flat and when I examine the front of the car I found the front windshield was all cracked from a bullet hold through it and the reason they burn the motor up for I found another bullet hole in the radiator."

"So you got Old Rum off of Daddy for fifty dollars," Barbara asked.

Uncle Joe gave her a big smile before he answered saying, "I sure did.

I got the tracker and drug her to a hay shed I was not using. Then when I had extra money had something fixed about her. I like Old Rum the first time I saw it when Tommy stop by to visit right after he bought it. I asked him if he ever needed to sell her come see me. Then when he broke down I saw my chance and got it off of him."

Then pointed to the Rum Bottle in William's hand said, "I found that bottle under the front seat and upon repairing the interior seats I put the bottle back. Old Rum would not be Old Rum without it."

His words brought laughter among them and as they settled down William asked, "You said two bullet holes did Old Rum in. Do you know who put them there?"

"I pretty sure Tommy did over some Bear he was seeing from their porch is would seem while they were drinking," he answered.

Barbara almost laughing added, "I remember that Uncle Joe. Daddy was always seeing a bear out in the yard and I heard him tell Mama that more than once. Mama always parked Old Rum different to unload her groceries and that night when Daddy went on the porch the shadows across Old Rum gave him the appearance there was a bear sneaking around. But I don't remember him shooting Old Rum."

"It was on Friday your mom had taken you all to see the football game," Uncle Joe answered as he repositions himself as William place two chairs before Elaine and Barbara.

Elaine said, "Thanks" but as Barbara took her seat she said, "Uncle Joe, I remember that day. Uncle Harrell and Daddy been out hunting and when we left for the football game, they were out back cleaning the rabbits for tomorrow's supper. Uncle Harrell and Daddy been out squirrel hunting and came home with rabbits. We joke about them rabbits sure didn't look like squirrels."

Barbara gave Old Rum a glance before giving her a pat saying, "I believe that was the last time we saw her Old Rum. Sometimes for days she would stay gone before she would come weaving home with another scrape and it was hunting season and I always thought he got it stuck somewhere and left it in the woods somewhere and never went back for it."

"He left it alright but not in the woods," Uncle Joe said with a laugh. "He left it on the left side of my house and I bought it off of him."

William, still looking into Old Rums interior asked, "So you saying their Dad shot Old Rum thinking it was a bear."

"Yes, it appears that is what he did," Uncle Joe answered as he pointed at the window added, "Old Rum must have been parked along the fence for he placed one rifle shot across the front glass and out through the driver's side window and placed a rifle shot into the radiator and believe me Old Rum was a mess when I pulled her into the shad. It seems they were drinking out on the porch when Tommy said, "I think I see that old bear sneaking around again." Then Harrell handed Tommy his rifle and he took two shots at that old Bear and would have shot more but on the second shot he heard the bullet hit glass." They got a flash light and while checking out the damage, Harrell said he needed to go home. So they climbed into Old Rum and was she ever smoking and knocking when they left her at my doorsteps. But I always figured the main reason he brought Old Rum to me to buy it off of him for I believe your dad did not want to answer any questions why there was bullet hole through the windshield."

THE CHURCH BASEBALL GAME

It was a blessing to have cool weather for our Mother's Day Barbeque at the church after morning services allowing me to sit and visit being spoil by the men folk as they brought us plates full of delicious Barbeque chicken or ribs, mash potatoes and corn on the cob.

Out in back of the church was a large pasture and someone had made a make shift baseball field out of it and when the teams were formed one team was one man short and the only boy left was Wesley who was begging to play anyway and they made him the catcher.

I watched them hit the ball and run around the bases. Run in to Bat and then back out with lots of lots of yelling and screaming between the teams and even those running the bases whenever the ball was hit.

As the game finish old WT Treat was smiling as he walked by me saying, "Going be a fight when they get home."

I answered "What else is new" as I watched Billy who was behind WT stopped before me seeming all frustrated, threw his glove down beside the ice chess, saying, "Sometimes Wesley makes so made."

I look out into the pasture and I could see Wesley and Matt Armstrong wrestling each other before I just ask, "What did he do now?"

"He caught my foul ball for one thing putting me out." Billy answered while opening the ice chest and pulling himself out a soda.

Then as he closed the lid added, "Mom, he was just a big show off what he was and everyone was patting him on the back saying well done."

I could tell Billy was jealous and to let him get Wesley off his chest, I asked, "Billy, what did Wesley do that was so great?"

Billy took a big drink of his soda before seeming to angrily saying, "He caught every foul ball that was near him and that includes mine. Then he got on base and was able to make the other team a run and I was put out every time I went to bat and we got beat by one run and that was Wesley's run that did it. That what I heard Clift Ragland say."

"His one run," I asked seeing the silliness of the situation and sure wanted to laugh.

But Brenda saved the day as she took a seat beside me saying, "Billy, if you just knew how silly that sounds."

Our laughter only seemed to make Billy madder for a second until he suddenly understood Brenda's words and quickly joined our laughter.

WHAT COULD I DO?

When Bogie first showed up at 207 W Campus here in Marshall last summer in 2013 it was when our female name Princess came into heat and Bogie just fell in love with her. We found out whose dog it was from the children and we tried but could not get hold of Peggy. So Barbara call her brother Reynold, who happen to also be Peggy's son in law and got him to tell Peggy to come get Bogie and she did it once and Bogie was back the next day and she never came after him again. No amount of calling did we get a response. It appeared she had abandoned him and after several months and I was sure of it after Barbara had complain to her brother about his biting and asked him come get him and he said "No." and I guess Peggy said, "No" like wise.

I met Peggy during Christmas over at Reynolds and she went straight into attacking me claiming Princess's only puppy was hers because Bogie was its Father and she had all rights to it. I politely told her to her face she needed to come get Bogie and he was not the Father. She did not like my answered I assure and she did not come and remove Bogie from our house.

In the last days of May 2014, I had to take him to Wesley's, it made 9 to 10 months Bogie has been abandon living at and around the house at 207 W campus and not one time have we claim Bogie as ours but we still ended up feeding him and that was not until the winter months did I start by giving the other dogs more than they would eat.

In the beginning Bogie lived on the pouch and would steal our dog's food but mostly ate the dry stuff our two spoil dogs Princess and Peekaboo hardly ever touch.

When winter came in October on cold nights we felt sorry for Bogie and on real cold nights let him come inside and he stayed in back by the wood stove. I just point to the door and out he went in the morning. I let him in and I let him out and when it warms up a little, more outside he stays then in.

I get up early in the morning for Barbara went to bed at seven each night because of her breathing problem and I would go to bed with her and get up around 3 in the morning and write on my Novels. I learn real quit to throw Bogie out when I do get up otherwise he would pee on the bed corner and leave a load going into the bathroom for Barbara to step in. It does not mean that Bogie when it was real cold at night did not stay outside at times and I was hoping he would go home.

Well Princess went in heat around February and Bogie was the only one to mate with her and she did not have one pup. I considered then that it was true what the local girls said to me he could not have pups. Where they got the info I do not know. Peekaboo, he was not able to mate yet. Thou he tried.

From the beginning Bogie's biting kept causing lots of problems and Barbara called Reynold her brother up about Bogie several times about his biting and even asked him to come get him more than once. He didn't and neither did Peggy and when he came for a visit, Bogie tried to bite him as he did anyone.

I do not know how often Bogie tried to bite or nip at the ankle of someone important that came over. It mostly depended on if he was on the front porch, if he was on the couch out back he did not bother anyone. The only ones I know he really bit hard was the two young girls across the street and the boys and that was when he first showed up around the house and I told them they need to go see Peggy or call the law if they wanted too. They did not. It also tried to bite Wesley and Billy that came to visit and any delivery man or women that showed up. He would chase cars, bikes and bark at walkers. Been kick several times for trying to bite I assure you. It only made him madder at that person.

Barbara tried more than once to get me to haul him off, but, I did not know where and anyway, I could not catch him if I tried. She would call her brother who she thought was the path to Peggy and he said, "There was nothing he could do about him."

So we left Bogie alone and let him eat and live among us and it got so I could even pick him up without him growling at me around October. Barbara never could. But dealing with Bogie came to a head when Sandra, who delivers Barbara's lunch five times a week from the Senior Community Center, was attacked by Bogie and he catch hold of her shoe in his attack. Kelly at the Center demanded we get rid of the dog or Barbara will no longer receive food. Barbara called her brother and he said, "There was nothing he could do" and receive no answer from Peggy either.

I felt my only choice was to take Bogie to the country and let him stay at Wesley's till I could come up with something to do with him. Wesley told us Bogie bit two friends that came by and would sit in the girl's lap. But Bogie only stayed there a short week even though Wesley was feeding him. He said that he looked for him but where he went is unknown. He said maybe someone he was chasing on the dirt road picked him up or just left we do not know.

You may lock me in jail if you like, but Peggy in my eyes had abandoned the dog. I never lock the dog in a cage and Bogie stay outside 75% of the time and that was every day and all day. It was free and she was free to come and pick Bogie up at any time and believe me Barbara tried a number of times for him to be returned to no avail. Peggy did not come get him and she knew where that dog was and I bet "She plan it that way." That is why she been claiming Princess's puppy were hers, that she had all rights to them to sell the pup claiming some kind of right as a dog owner. Bogie came to us without a name tag or markings to indicate it was her dog in the first place. If it was not for the chasing of children that he did, was his name even known among them and it was from them we learn his name was Bogie and where he came from.

I have chased Bogie with sticks. I have thrown small rocks at him. I have run him off the outside furniture every morning and he would never leave and "Now," that we are no longer are taken care of him or he is in our procession, this Peggy suddenly wants him back who I feel abandon him and left him with us for over nine to ten months and is seeking to lock us in jail claiming we stole her dog. I believe her whole intent in doing this is she can get you the Judge to say we are Bad People and find us guilty, I believe she then can go to civil count later and sue us. Others that know her say she just doing this for meanness. I can only guess.

You may lock me up or whatever, I figured there a lie here somewhere and if you as our Judge believe the lie that Barbara and I deserve to be in put in jail so be it. I have not been in jail in a long time. For in Peggy's eyes, William Ellis and Barbara Henry should be found guilty for her own unknown personal reasons. But to Barbara and I, we see it as removing a biting dog, name Bogie, that threaten to have the community services that provide a health service to the house for Barbara Henry stopped which I could not let happen for Barbara happens to be disabled and needs their help.

Barbara and I also see Bogie as a dog who did not claim Peggy as its Master and as a dog she would not come and fetch back to her house when asked for I'm pretty sure she knew that if she did, Bogie would not stay there and return and I figure the real underlining reason for leaving and abandoning Bogie like she did was obvious when she yell at us claiming any pups our Princess gave birth too was hers to sell because she had all rights to them. She told us so in no uncertain terms and she'll probable present this argument in court when we meet.

I personally think it is not vengeance she after here for a dog name Bogie that would not stay at home and did not make her money or Pups. I believe and don't quote me with this, "What she is seeking by going and trying to make the world believe we stole Bogie who was not making her money and could not have pups. Peggy figured by getting Barbara and I arrested and thrown in jail she'll have the opportunity to sue us later and it will not cost her anything to do so, for a Judgment of guilty has provided her winning case already with providing a cost free door to do so. Sneaky and evil is she, ask anyone that knows her."

Your view and Judgment is important to both Barbara and I and your Judgment will be fair and just I'm sure. Only thing we are worried about is, we believe your Judgment has for more implications than we may know for we really do not know for sure "Why" she is doing this?

I do not know her and only met her twice or maybe three times and I am telling you I do not like Peggy at all. It appeared to me as if we were part of some scheme to make money with Bogie and each time I have met her she would fuss and accused both Barbara and I of wrong doing claiming that the only pup Princess had is hers. I'm pretty sure that while she fussed and hollered accusing Barbara and me of wrong doing, I asked her directly to her face, "Come get Bogie and take him home and keep him away from us" and she did not.

The only time Peggy came to fetched Bogie was when he first came to the house in the early summer and that was only after we called Reynold. When she came Peggy just walked up onto the porch and picked Bogie up in her arms and carried him off and bet that is when she saw Princess. Thus, there is not a reason in the world she could not catch him and take him home. I couldn't get near Bogie nor could anyone else as well catch him, until he had been around the house for several months. Eating just what he could sneak from us, Bogie began to become a quite a skinny fellow and still would not go back home to Peggy's? I think he was deeply in love with Princess at least that is what I think.

A question came up by Sandra what if Bogie had bitten a health worker that came to the house. Barbara's has several aids and there are several that come and check up on her each month. What would have happened? Sandra delivering food told us he tries to grab her shoes every time she came and Bogie did catch her shoe and she had to almost kick him off her foot. Barbara's aid from AAA, Hidie always had to protect her feet when she walked upon the porch to enter the house. The question is if he had bitten either one of her aids and broke the skin we did not know who would be liable, us or would it be Peggy? That is when I made the choice with Barbara's support to obey the ordered by Kelly at the Senior Center to remove Bogie away from the house and what else was I to do since Peggy would not come to fetch him or answer our calls and for as I can tell never would even though we tried to get her too.

THE DAY THE DRAIN LINE CLOG

Wilber set the Chess Board and Chess Pieces upon the table before holding out his two hands saying, "Choose?"

I hit his right hand and there inside was black pawn and he said, "You're black."

I began to set the black Chess Pieces on the board saying, "I feel like you are going to slaughter me with what I had to do yesterday."

Wilber sat down and began to place his white pieces on the board saying, "What happen?"

"The drain line clogged," I answered, "Discovered it the other day where the vent comes out the ground for the drain."

"How could you tell," Wilber snickered as he played the King's Pawn two squares. "Did smell or something?"

"Toilet paper around it how and some of our leftovers with it," I answered while meeting his pawn with mine.

Wilber brought out his king knight before he smiled asking, "I bet you had a mess getting that unblocked?"

I looked the board over for a moment before bringing out my Queen's Knight saying, "Barbara told me I could get a clean out tape from the city which I did. Ran a water hose and I pushed that tape in but it had a bent end and got hung up. So I figured away to straighten it using a large wrench and channel locks. That did the trick."

I stopped to move my Queen Bishop Pawn for two squares and Wilber said, "Well what happen? You get it unclogged?" "Nope, the city did." I answered.

"The City?" he questions moving his queen pawn to cover his other pawn.

"Yes," I answered while studying the board. "I ran that tape till it

254

bottoms out where it enters the city line. I tried and tried and on luck so to the city I shouted needed help and they came out and found something wrong which I did not want to know about and suddenly left having some kind of problem they had to run to. I went back to the city hall and asked what happen and she said they would be back. Well that night around seven they returned and ran their 5000 pond water pressure hose into the drain line and blasted the clog away."

Wilber move the White Bishop asking, "Do you think it will be back?"

"Yea," I answered moving my Queen Pawn out to protect the other two. "About ten feet from where the drain line enters the main line there a spot where I could not get over with the sprayer attachment on the hose. The paper will build up behind it and one-day break loose to clog it again."

"I guess you well have to clean it out again then," Wilber asked as he Castel his King over.

"Probably, but I'm still not finish yet," I answered, "Cause the commode to leak and after lunch I'm going to go put on a new wax ring on her."

Wilber taking his usual long time before he moved studying the Chess Pieces said, "I feel for you, I really do."

After his moved, I set my mind upon the game and as predicted he just plain slaughtered me.

FAT MEN ARE PROPHETS

Whenever I went to the VA in Little Rock, on the way home stop I loved and to stuff myself with Chinese food or any of the other all you eat places in Conway. There was a small operation that I really liked but was expensive. I mean it had shrimp fixed ten different ways and even thou it cost $29.00 sometimes I just could not resist myself from stopping and was I ever stuff when I left.

Well, a few years ago I stopped there and after I've gotten what I wanted I found the only empty table was by two very young Fat Men that looked like twins. Above was the only lighting in the room and all around them were plates stacked and even some stacked on an empty close to them from the many times they've gone back to the food line.

As I took a seat I just could not help myself and asked, "I see you two were hungry."

"That we were," the one on the left answer. "More like staving," the other added.

After chomping down on a Shrimp and again I could not help myself asked, "It seems nobody wants to sit around you."

The one on left was almost laughing as he said, "You would too if you heard us eat."

I was shocked at his answer and busted out in laughter and as I got control of myself I had to ask, "I bet it cost you a fortune to eat if you had to pay for every plate full."

Then the young Fat Man, turned the other saying, "Bob, you answer him, you paid this time."

"Sure Bobby," he answered back before turning toward me with a chubby smile said, "$29.00 for each of us."

I could not help myself again busted out in laughter almost losing the

Shrimp I was eating for he spoke the answer so proudly and as I got control of myself asked, "I guess the owner must like you?"

The Bobby bend over closer to me and whisper, "The Owner thinks we are Prophets who has come to test his love for his neighbor, so he lets us come in once a month and eat all we want for $29.00 dollars." "He thinks you two are Prophets," I asked wanting to laugh.

The Bob quickly answered saying, "Not so loud, others may hear you and want to worship us."

By now I was getting low of Shrimp and thinking of going back for some more but these two large young Fat Men being called a Prophet had me wondering so I asked, "How come he thinks that? You heal someone or did some kind of miracle or something?"

"It is not that at all," Bobby answered before looking over at Bob asking, "He thinks we are a blessing isn't that right Bob?"

"We sure are," he answered before looking back at me to say, "We bring business."

Laughter busted out between them and their belly just wiggled as they did suddenly laughter busted out all across the tables, including me.

As the laughter died Bobby said, "Well Bob, it looks like it is time for us to leave."

I caught the "leave" wondering how they got here, but as I grab my last shrimp I seriously asked, "Why would you two think that?"

Suddenly walking around me came five waiters pushing several empty food carts and a small Arab like man dress in a cook's outfit following and as the waiters started to grabs the many plate from the tables, the Arab turned to me saying, "Bob and Bobby are Prophets because when the people of Israel and the Arab world have need of a Prophet, God always sends the sign "He will be born Fat."

His words cause both Bobs, to burst out into laughter causing their jelly belly bodies to wiggle with one saying, "We was born fat. That we were."

Their laughter caused the waiters to laugh and I quickly followed for their attitude about being fat was getting to be real funny.

The Arab left me to stand beside the Bob and while placing his hand on his shoulder said, "I've known Bobby and his twin brother Bob since," stopping he turned to Bobby asking, "You was ten when I first let the two of you come in and eat all you wanted or were you nine."

"We were eight," Bobby answered laughing causing his belly to wiggle but Bob countered with, "No, we were seven. Don't you remember? It was on our seventh birthday Uncle Huey brought us here to eat to celebrate for he didn't think we would live to see seven or eight or nine and it was after our ninth birth day we started to eat here once a month for $29.00."

"That is right, Bobby," the Arab answer before turning toward me to say, "Mister, it was after their ninth birthday that I started to let our Prophets eat all they wanted on the fifteenth of each month and stay all day if they liked and my decision has given my place a name and a blessing for when they here hundreds come just to watch them eat. Bring their kids and let them watch and you never heard the noise a room full of kids would make while watching them eat and the gagging should they ever fart."

Laughter again busted out across the tables and got worst as Bob said, "We don't mean too, it just happens" with Bobby agreeing with a wiggling belly.

Then Bob looked at me saying, "Did you know we had a contest to see who could eat the fastest and I just barely beat Bobby today."

"It was close and I still don't how you did it," Bobby asked.

"Easy, I just ate faster than you, is all," Bob countered causing Bobby to burst into laughter followed quickly by Bob and did their bellies ever wiggle as they did."

I was going too asked, "Who won," when a morn sweep across the tables causing me to look to see two very strong men in a white uniform walking toward them when one on the left said, "Bobby, Bob it time for you to leave."

Without another word they took a position behind Bobby and Bob and as they started to push them toward the exit door, Bobby motioning them to stop and looking at me before me saying, "I see in your life that all you have sought for is to find out just who you are. You sought out knowledge seeking the answer. You tried love, it failed you. The only constant in your life been Christ and our Lord said, "If the Son has set you free you are free indeed and you should live as such."

I was shocked at his words and staying quiet, I watched the two big strong men wheel them out of the restaurant before turning to my empty plate I noticed the Arab had also watched them leave, so I asked him, "Who won the eating contest?"

He turned to me saying, "Bobby does most of the time but Bob won today."

As I stood to fetch me another plate of Shrimp, I asked, "And all they win is an apple pie?" That is when I notice the tables were beginning to empty and as the Arab said, "Yes" a Tall Man needing a shave and haircut came up saying, "I believe I'm the winner of the contest."

The Arab took his ticket and glancing at it said, "It looks like you finally won, Alex."

"After ten years of trying I think it is about time," Alex answered. The Arab just laughed saying, "Wait here Alex while I'll fetch your free meal tickets and get my gang to start cleaning up the place."

As I followed the Arab looking for another plate full, Alex followed me saying, "Might as well get me a plate full also. I've been eating here enough to know once he gets in the kitchen, he'll become busy for number of reasons and I've known some winners that had to wait over two hours to get they're winnings."

As I set my dirty plate on one of the tables still needed cleaning waited for him to catch up asking, "You won four free meals. So, how did you win them?"

Alex not stopping almost laughing said, "Its Easy, for five dollars added to your Bill you can bet on how it long takes Bob and Bobby to eat a huge plate full of fried Shrimp and you never heard the cheering on from those watching, getting Bob of Bobby to eat faster or to eat slower depending on the time one had guess."

I busted out in laughter for the image he gave me was quite funny and as I calmed down to grab a clean plate asked, "How long does it usually take them to eat the huge plate of fried Shrimp?"

As Alex began filling his plate full of different Shrimp dishes answered saying, "The time depends on a lot of factors when it comes to Bob and Bobby eating Shrimp or any of the other goodies."

"Factors," I asked while filling my plate full of fried Shrimp.

Alex waited for me to get some Tartar Sauce saying, "Lots of Factors and the main one is they wanted Fried Shrimp and had the eat Boil Shrimp or oysters or mixed or wrong drinks or and they do love Apple pie and loser gets a half of an Apple pie."

Then as I followed him he said, "I guess the average time is between 5 to 15 minutes and I won guessing 12 minutes 22.5 seconds."

As we reseated ourselves to eat I asked, "Why the half seconds." Alex wiped his white hairy face before answering saying, "I learned that half seconds comes in handed for I lost because I was guessing just the minutes and seconds and had not thought about the half second the timer uses. So after losing by a half second I have now always use a half second in my time guess."

"I guess it worked, you won," I said as I stuff another mouthwatering fried Shrimp in my mouth cover in Tartar Sauce.

We became quiet as both began to concentrate on eating for a second and as Alex lean back in his seat saying, "Man can they ever cook Shrimp here. Been eating here going on twenty-five years. Way before Bob and Bobby started coming. My Dad likes Shrimp and when he had a client he needed to empress he brings him or her here and I know some times his bill was over three hundred dollars more than once. He also took me and Mom if he could once a month whenever my three sisters were with Grandma, Dad would load Mom and me into the car and here we came to The Forty Shrimp Delight and ever since then, I been coming once a month on fifteen of the month and years ago when I had the money would bring Edward, Joey, Diane, Melody, and Mary now and then when I had the money to spare."

"There your kids," I asked wondering.

Alex looked across the now clean tables with only a couple guys mopping the floor and still having a far away as he said, "No they were my adopted family so to say and now their scatter from here to there and I'm staying out their lives and I hope they don't find me. You might say I love them too much to stay."

"I guess I can understand that," I replied before taking a good drink of my coffee.

Alex face became "Their Mother had Polio when she was a child had four kids early and were grown when she started a raise a second set of Five kids and I so happen rented a garage apartment across the street from the where they lived. Now I like to play basketball and Edward I guess he was twelve then also played and I remember the first time I met him he was sucking on his T-shirt's collar watching the blacks play and I could see he wanting to play. But you needed three to play and none of the blacks would let him play with them being a kid.

It was the first time I been to that park and it was full of good players.

Now back then I was bad to the bone player and I loved to play center and after couple wins, the black playing guard on our team had to leave so needing another guard or quit, I called to Edward who was now shooting and dribbling around one of the empty rims saying, "Hey kid would you like to play a game. We need a guard."

"Was he any good," I asked.

"A lot better than I thought but we still lost," Alex answered with a laugh.

I liked Alex as I left him, wondering back to my table and as I sat, I saw a waiter bring Alex his winnings and as Alex left the restaurant he waved the four tickets for his free all you can eat Shrimp meals at me with a big hairy face smile.

But the words of the Arad still were with me as I ate that good tasting shrimp when he said, "Prophets are born Fat. That almost never happens among the women of Israel unless God has sent a Prophet. Being fat enable them to seek God when fasting demands, it and being real fat enable them to fast for many days seeking an answer from God and Bobby and Bob were Prophets in his eyes and in his heart and his business has benefitted from them greatly ever since they walked in when they were seven."

THE MEAN LOOKING PROFESSOR

"I'm going to be rich with this mind control device," the mean looking Professor said as he held the mind control device up before him.

"I've increased its power to a thousand times. I've just been using it on rats and I don't care if people have been saying, I look like a rat. I had rats doing all kinds of tricks and I'm tired of that so I'm moving to people."

Patting the helmet on his lap, he gave his meanest looking smile saying, "If you can work them rats you can work on people. Yea you can, Ha, ha yea."

Then the mean looking Professor began wringing his hands together with even a more joyful hackle said, "I'm going to be rich. When I going put you on, I'm going have people put money in my account. That is just the start Ha, ha yea. I'm going have girls knocking at my door. Not just any girl either and she will love me and that I will make sure of Ha, Ha and few more ideas I've been thinking of doing."

Glancing over to his rat cages, it as if every rat was sitting at its door wishing him lots of luck as he placed the helmet on his head. Look down and fingered the start switch and with a Ha, ha yea, he pushed it.

The large blond headed intern pushed the hospital bed into the large teaching auditorium and placed the mean looking Professor under the light clearly showing his long hair that made headlines for although he was asleep no one cut his hair without gagging and hog tying him and there was not an intern around that would tackle doing that for mean looking was mean looking for the Professor looked the meanest now and then would holler "Ha, ha yea" had everybody scared to get near him. Someone said he had over 35 different interns that started to watch him but everyone only lasted a week.

Quiet fill the Auditorium as the six foot ten, Doctor Mr. Know It

All entered and stood looking down on the mean looking Professor said, "Look at him, isn't he the meanest bad ass looking Professor you ever seen."

Look upped at those gather said, "We have here and unknown problem, physically there is nothing wrong with his body or his mind accept he was a mean Professor. Made all kinds of strange devices and experiment on rats with some kind of mind control device and the local reported he experimented with some kind of mind control device to use in controlling people's minds and make them give him money." Then the Doctor started to walk around the Bed with hand over the body saying, "His last invention placed him in this state. How it was built is a mystery for if it was destroyed in the fire it caused when he turned it on and placed him in this state of mind."

Leaving the body, he opened his hands outward as if he was pointed to those gather above him calling out, "Who here will save him. We have done all we can for him and in one week he will be left alone to die."

Then pointing toward the mean looking Professor said, "You have one week to come out of your shell are else?"

But unknown to the Doctor, the mean looking Professor was trying to find his own thoughts for when he turned on his invention, the thoughts of everyone around him came into his thinking and that included the rats and the only thought that was his was "Upps wrong button."

ANDY'S CUE STICKS

When I returned home from a month visiting with my brother, the first thing I heard about was the Senior Center had been given a new Pool Table. After I settle back home, I got up early and by 8:30 I was walking into Center to see this new table for myself and sure enough as I entered the pool room, there set a brand new Pool Table in place of the old worn out table that needed new everything. I mean the old needed new cloth, new bumpers and new pockets Grabbing a cue stick, I walked around the table feeling its new cloth and even sent a few balls rolling. But just as I started to really get serious, in walked a white haired man wearing a shirt having Best Pool Tables writing on it pushing a golf cart full of cue sticks caring a briefcase saying, "Hello, I come to check your new Pool Table and make sure it is perfect working condition."

Walking away from the table, I Place my stick away asking, "My name's William what's yours Mr. Best Pool Table?"

"Just call me Andy," he answered as he parked the cart neat the Table then carefully placed his briefcase on the table. He looked over at me asking, "Did you pay for this?"

Shaking my head fast no I answered saying "It wasn't me and don't know who bought it."

Leaving the cased he walked around the table examining the bumpers and as he walked back to his briefcase saying, "The floor seems solid enough and now let us see how level you are let us level her."

As he opened his brief case he said, "This table is seen only in your big Pool Tournaments. It is design with the ability to adjust bumpers and level to within less than 1% of being perfect and the first thing I'm going to do check the level."

Out of the briefcase he pulled what looked like a large white ball, with #1 written across it and carefully rolled into a pocket but could only fit between the entrance bumpers. Did the same to #2, 3 and 4 and as he pulled #5 and #6 and placed them at each of the side pockets he asked, "I guess you are wondering what I'm doing with these balls?

"I was thinking something like that," I answered.

As he turned back to the briefcase he pulled out some kind of control said, "These balls are lot better than what had to use before. With them I not only am able to level the slate I can also adjust the bumpers opening of the pockets."

Then he held up the control saying, "All have to do is press this big red button and it is done atomically but first let me hook up the power cord."

Going back to his golf cart, I watched Andy pulled out a computer power cord that looked like it was twenty-five feet or more. Coming back to the table he bent over with his left arm resting on the bumper plug the cord into a power plug under the table.

As he said, "With this system the table will adjust itself to within .1% of being perfectly level."

Looking over at me asked," Would you me honor of pressing the big red button?"

To my surprise the table immediate began to morn and bang and even now and then I could hear a light bong. I could see nothing happening to the table top when the morning and groining stopped as five short bongs rung out.

As he reached under the table to unplug the cord, Andy said, "That's all she wrote and now comes the fun part."

I wanted to laugh as I asked, "It plays balls by itself?"

Smiling he answered saying, "Who ever bought this table paid a lot of money for this and it has all the bells and whistles."

"I bet they did from the looks of this table," I answered moving out of his way.

"Does make one wonder," he answered as he began rolling the cord up stopped and looked me saying, "Aligning the table is the easy part but aligning the bumpers with the pockets is another story. You see the table has every bumper in place but they are not aligned within 1% requirement. Now with a lot of trial and error I came up with a method using a ball and cue sticks that works."

After I watched him placed the cord away, he stood and removed one of the very short Cue sticks and across its tip was mounted some kind way to shoot a pool ball with springs.

I wanted to ask question but instead remain quiet watching him work.

Placing the Cue stick on the table, he carefully replaced all the large corner balls back into their carrying case and pull out a very white pool ball, close the case and set it out the way next to the golf bag. Then began walking around the table tossing the white pool ball in the air talking to himself saying, "That one wants do and neither will this one."

After several trips around the table he stopped at the topped right bumper section saying. "To align it right I need a one bumper section to be my base and I believe this one will is the best one to use. Not that I've been wrong several times.

Setting the white ball on the table, he mounted the shooting contraption to the bumper saying, "Around this table at various points are metal slots that allow me to place my tool in the perfect position to shoot for testing."

As he walks back to the golf bag he continues saying, "Now you wondering how hitting a ball I can make these bumper perfect."

"I can imagine," I answered.

Removing a thin narrow metal strip with marking he walked around the table and place it across the left pocket opening saying, "This tells me how far I'm off left or right."

Moving where I could see it better it had markings with zero in the middle with small measurement markings running on each side outward Pulling back to the cue stick he place the pool ball into position, pulled the cue stick back and when he let go it sending the pool ball into the bank and as came to a stop resting against the metal strip.

"Three marks," not bad he said as he replaces the pool ball and did it four more times before adjusting the position of the bumper. Repeated the procedure until the ball hit the plate on the zero.

He removed the cue stick holder and move to the one he just aligned and repeated his procedure adjusting the bumper. Several times he repeated the procedure until the white ball were hitting the pockets in the center.

Then he started cross banking to corner and then the side adjusting, repeating till all seem well before he started on the side bumpers with three rail banks into the side pocket.

I spoke not a word as he worked but as he felt satisfied, he pulled the cue stick out of his device placing it in the golf bag, he as he pulled out another he broke the silence saying, "Now this time I will adjust the height of the railings. The spin played on them is as important to the players as none. For unless the cue ball hits the rail exactly in the center of the ball with the spin a player places on it the ball will not come off the rail as expected."

I answered saying, "I agree with that."

As he placed the new cue in his device, he looked at me saying, "These other cues in my bag took me a long time to fine having a crooked end that worked better than any cue holder I could make, for I just could not get the spin I wanted off the ball mostly because a player does not start with the cue stick in position to shoot the spin. I tried making holder after holder and could not obtain the correct spin I wanted. So I visited the pool halls around and after many trail and errors I found what I needed."

Smiling, he mounted his device on the table, went back to the golf bag and pulled out a folded up ruler and placed it on the table using the slots he used for his aligning the bumpers.

I could see the ruler had several zeros on it and he when he was satisfied he had the ruler on correctly went to his device and when he hit the cue ball sure enough, the ball spun left and when it hit the bumper spun off and hit his measuring tape several notches to the right of zero.

Walking to the railing he knell down and watch him make and adjust to the railing having no idea how he made the adjustment. Repeated the procedure till the cue ball hit zero on his tape.

Then he changed cues for one that spun the ball right and after several minutes he change railings and around and around the table he went placing his device on the other railing and his device until in he was satisfied all railing were within the 1% requirement.

Then he brought cues that he could spin the ball harder and faster testing and adjusted if needed and by now I had taken a seat to watch thinking "What a table someone bought for the Senior Center."

Placing his cues and device back into his golf bag he pulled out some paper work asking, "Will you please sign this paper work that you have witness that I have set your new pool table up to specifications."

"Sure," I answered.

After signing, Andy asked me to follow him out to his Van and as we exited the Center, I could see Rex sitting in his truck eating a McDonald breakfast sandwich.

At the van, he opened the rear saying, "I have a couple items that go with the table."

Reaching in he handed me a new ball polisher and a large briefcase saying it was full of tools for maintaining the table and the new cue sticks that should be delivered by UPS in the next couple days.

Closing the rear, Andy climbed into his Van then giving me a smile, he said, "Enjoy."

As I watch him leave, Rex join me asking, "Who was he?"

THE CHOCOLATE CUPCAKE

Barbara set down into recliner as Elaine placed a coke on the table beside her asked, "How do you like our new porch?"

"This is wonderful, Elaine," Barbara answered. "Why from here, with a sling shot you sure can keep the peace when the Grandkids come over."

As Elaine took a seat in the other recliner was laughing saying, "That will not work. I'm so slow I'm sure they will be able can dodge anything I can shoot at them but my mouth hits dead center very time."

Barbara joined her laughter for a second before saying, "I think I can agree with that from hearing you call the cows at milking time." "It was lot easier then rounding them up when were we little girls," she answered with a laugh.

Barbara glanced over at Elaine asking, "I heard one of your granddaughters has started first grade?"

Elaine seemed sad as she said, "One of the babies already in the first grade. I'm telling you Barbara, time is just flying."

"I agree," Barbara answer before saying, "I was thinking, do you remember what we ate for lunch in the first grade?"

"How can I ever forget that," she answered before laughing saying, "Mothers chocolate rolls."

Barbara wanted to laugh as she said, "I remember when Mama only had one sack and put both our chocolate rolls in the sack. I ate first and I sold your roll to Steven for a nickel and went and bought me a Popsicle."

"I remember that," Elaine said, "and Mother never again left you in change of her chocolate rolls she gave us for our lunch."

But Barbara countered with, "But Elaine that was the best tasting Popsicle I ever had."

Only laughter was their response.

COCONUT-GUMDROP COOKIES

From William Ellis

1 cup shortening or butter

2 Cups white sugar

4 Tablespoons of molasses

2 eggs well beaten

1 teaspoon of vanilla extract

2 cups of flour

¼ teaspoon of salt

1 teaspoon soda

1 cup of coconut

2 cups of uncooked oatmeal

1 cup chopped pecans or peanuts (optional)

1 cup or more of gumdrops chopped as best you can.

In a large bowl cream together shortening, sugar and molasses, add eggs and vanilla and mix well. Mix in the flour cup at a time. Then add oatmeal until it appears all is mixed well before adding coconut, nuts and gumdrops.

Drop batter by spoon full on baking sheet several inches apart. Bake at 400 degrees for 10 minute until lightly brown. Make sure center is done.

Note: Add 1 teaspoon of baking powder for raised cookies. Use 1 cup brown sugar instead of molasses.

TO ALL THAT WORK AT THE NURSES STATION

Barbara and I want to thank you for your great feeling of Love you have for those that lay before you seeking help. Barbara is one of a kind and you were suckered in on her displayed of weakness which she has learned well to performed since sixteen. But as

Barbara barely sat in the chair, she looked upped at me and calmly said, "I am dying." I need not say more.

As one grows old we begin a battle as our body telling us, "You are on the way out." You as a group of Nurses enter that battle and help hundreds win. Not always perfect and if God is really calling them only tears remain to lead the way.

That is why I suggest on your Banner "United We Stand" for you group of Nurses functioned with one mind as you reach for the ones in pain, hurt in ways only you see and sorry to say, "Must live with."

My hat is off to you and all nurses that took up their cross and shown the world what winners in this battle to live looks like. Thanks.........

UGLIEST BOY IN SCHOOL

When I was born, I was born into a family that was at war with the neighbors you might say being that we were the only white folks that choose to live in the roughest part of town. It had something to do Daddy's drinking and Mama's fighting. You see Mama was an Alligator fighter and if she wasn't fighting them she be whipping up on someone around town. I'm sure you heard of her, Alligator Women, the greatest Alligator fighter in the whole world. She works down at the Joe's Alligator Farm on highway 27.

I was ugly before I was born. Mama had a fight with Crazy Betsey and Betsey had a knife on her and she stabbed Mama in the belly and I was inside Mama and was stabbed also. It made me look like this ugly creature you see with its hunched back and all. Mama tells me I'm going to be famous after I told her about some movie director wanting to put me in his movie. It has something to do with me being so ugly.

In school, for a time I was not happy. I was called ugly, humped back Kid and many more names especially if I mess up in a game we were playing. Sometimes I wanted to smash their face in but Mama told me to take the insults because they were right, "I was the ugliest boy in school."

It got so I was even making up a few names for myself like "Ugly and handsome" and my best was "Ugly Crazy" and one time I went home and Mama heard me say, "Ugly Crazy is home." All hell broke loose and Mama fussed on me for calling myself Ugly with a Crazy to go with it and went on and on about loving myself and love others and I'm thinking why was Mama talking that way, for to know Mama, she would rather give a black eye then a hand shake. I even heard Daddy say, "When you see Mama walking down the road you best run especially if she wearing her war paints."

Now in school, I was always being used to scare the new kid in class. Ever since kindergarten, Carl and Paul would hide me and when the girl or boy came to answer their calling, I would jump out and say "Hi." It usually made them give a little scream when I did and that was when I learn girls can hurt for most of the time I ended up with a black eye for scaring them and that black eye only made me uglier. Still it was funny to watch their reaction upon seeing me.

Another thing I liked to do was go on School trips for on them I get to see the world around and meet so many people and I liked to see their reactions upon seeing ugly me. The last school trip was when we had that last Earthquake. This trip we went to Hero's Playland Park and the Earthquake broke the foundation of the Fairest Wheel. Bobby my friend was riding it and was knock out of his seat like some others and like Bobby, was left hanging and screaming "Someone help me." I really don't know what happen I just reacted and quickly using my hunchback abilities, I climbed up onto that Fairest Wheel saving Bobby and six others.

Mother told me that is when my true self showed itself for by knowing how ugly I was. She said words and insults mean nothing because I am an ugly 12-year-old boy so I should not be ashamed for showing off and use my Hunchback abilities and save my friend."

Well must go I hear Mama calling and I hope some of you Reporters are still here when I come back. I'm leaving for a meeting with my director today and he is going to show me," then he hunches his back showing his ugliness and discussing self before continuing with, "the ugliest kid in school, I am about to become famous. Bye now."

THE UGLIEST GIRL IN SCHOOL

As I hobbled into the kitchen letting the screen door behind me, I said, "Mother, I was happy when I walked up to Mr. Joey to obtain the ugliest girl in the sixth grade award."

"When they start giving out Awards to be ugly," Mama asked as she turned from the sink drying her hands.

As I slide myself into my favorite chair at the kitchen table answered saying, "It was Mr. Joey's idea and I won it."

Mama watching me sit she added, "So you won the ugliest Girl award. Why don't you tell me all about it?"

"It started yesterday," I quickly answer eyeing the apple on the table, fighting the ergs to eat it before saying, "Yesterday, Mr. Joey had us enter a name on a computer who we thought was the ugliest and when a name was enter ten times it was listed on the voting screen and ugly Francis Big Butt thought she was going to win but I won by a landslide."

Mama was laughing as she placed a glass of tea and cookie before me saying, "To them your ugly but to me you're my sweet thing and how ugly you are makes me no different."

"Aah Mama," I answered and as I picked the cookie upped, I very frustrated said, "You don't understand. I proud to be the ugliest girl in school, it was Charlie and Bill and some other boys were calling me the prettiest girl instead of the ugliest girl and I wanted to whip up on all of them."

Mama wanted to laugh as she said, "I have to admit you are ugly and I can see that boys had no right for calling you beautiful and knowing how ugly you are. I think it would make me mad also."

Not sure how to tell Mama so I decided just to confess, took a deep breath before saying, "Mama, mad really is not the word to use. As I was walking by Charlie's desk he said, "Hey, beautiful" and I just went crazy and hit him and left the class room just a crying."

"Wow, you sure were mad at Charlie," Mama asked watching me consume what was left of my cookie.

Looking up at Mama I gave her a smile saying, "I wasn't mad at Charlie for him calling me beautiful Mama. I was angry because Charlie saw beauty in me I did not think I had any and I sure didn't want to be call beautiful for sure. I like being ugly."

As Mon set another cookie before me she laughs as she said, "I've been telling you what would happen if you took a bath, comb your hair, put on clean clothes what will happen?"

"I had too," I replied.

"Why," Mom asked returning to the sink.

"I smelled so bad even the dog wouldn't get near me is why," I answered as I consume the cookie looking for another.

"That bad," Mom asked.

"I sure was," I return wondering will I get another cookie before saying, "At school when I walk down the hall the other kids were gagging and holding their noses and I knew I must need a bath. I don't mind being ugly but smelling I don't like."

"You know it comes with being an ugly girl," Mom returned. Standing, I open my arms saying, "Mom, just look at me. I must wear a pair of Dad's shoes my feet are so big, I have a knock knee walk, my butt is so big I must sit on two toilet seat to pee, I can't wear a brassier for I have no tits yet, buck teeth, very large nose, three eye brows over one brown eye and only one over my blue eye, hair that want stay combed and sticks out everywhere, one arm shorter than the other with one hand way larger than the other and what really makes me ugly my skin has white, brown, black and blue makes covering my face and my hairy ears are large and rounded and stick out facing forward and I weight over three hundred pounds."

As I took a seat back at the table, Mom just smile as she said, "That may be what you look like but your still my sweet little baby." "Aah Mom," I returned.

NUMBER THIRTEEN IS SEX TIME

I stood looking out the 4th floor apartment window and below to my surprise looked like a giant orgy of some kind was going on. For beside a lightly flowing water fall and pool, many of the local inhabitants having sex and were covered with some kind of grease and both the Males the girl looked like they enjoyed what they were doing.

Turning back toward my local guide asked, "What is going on below? It looks like a giant orgy?"

"Sir, it is the mating month and below is where girls can have open sex with anyone to become pregnant," he answered standing tall and old at the same time old Vickie continued with "and we have just entered into the thirteen month and right now there is only a few mating but soon there will be no free space below."

I looked down on the orgy asking, "I was wondering of all things, give a young Vickie a month of free sex and no more the rest of the year is that what I'm hearing?"

As I turned back to my guide, he motioned for me to sit down saying, "Have a seat and let me tell you a little of us Vickie's."

"I think I should and don't tell me the juicy stuff, I saw that below," I answered as I took my seat.

As I left the window the old Vickie took my place and as he looked below said, "Our society has been around for millions of years and it came a point of having to regulate the population of the world and develop a system that maintains a fairly level population, it was decided babies were to be born at the same time and it be the only baby a girl can have so over time these orgies areas where establish."

I look at the old Vickie asking, "Why the orgies and not private sex?"

"The orgies are part of what we are as Vickie's," he answered with a smile if you could call it that.

I Looked at him with a good confuse looked as the old Vickie continue with, "In our society there is no marriage or girls and boys living together. We live in a well-organized society and have separated girls and boys that the population will remain somewhat stable and we have chosen that on every thirteenth month, girls and boys during a certain age period are free to have open sex and these giant hotels like here are just one place providing for girls that want babies can have one. Not that there is not some private sex going on also somewhere."

Leaning back in the chair asked, "I can understand what you are saying and I bet it is well regulated?"

"That's for sure," he answered before saying proudly, "Any one that has a baby outside of the time period, the Baby, Mother and Father is put to death is how important a baby's age is in our society is and maintained."

The old Vickie as he looked down upon the sex happy bodies said, "Most are here for the pleasure and a baby is far from their mind and there are always more girls than boys but not always."

Looking back at me said, "But it did not change society. The rich girls only have children with the rich guys and the poor with poor for there is a factor one has to pay to have a child."

Suddenly he said, "Come and looked upon the orgy below and as you looked understand, both the boys and girls will be taken responsibility for the child care. The boy will be place with the male and the girl will be placed with their mother using advance DNA methods taken at birth."

Not getting up, I said, "I don't need to look but I do understand what you say but my first question is "How is the baby kept until given to their parents?"

The old Vickie still looking below said, "Within very large Mother groups until they are four.

Opening the soda drink I was given earlier, I look at old Vickie saying, "I have one more question, "Why is it, every thirteen months is your orgy time and not twelve?"

There was quiet for a second before he left the window saying, "A long time ago it was every twelve months but then everybody had the same birthday month that was born and it became a problem with jobs,

277

housing and maintaining control with couples using that time to have babies that was not warranted and live as couples which was against the law of propagation that was establish."

Then given me a smile, if you could call it a smile, he sat back down at the window seat before continuing with, "So it decided that by making the orgy time at thirteen it would cause the birthdays to change the month each year and it seem to correct most of our society problems dealing with the month one was born separating even the age that one can enter the orgy."

Taking a good drink of the soda I looked at old Vickie who was still looking below watching the orgy I asked, "Do you think I could go down and join them?"

Laughter was his answer.

THE NEW STORE

As Bobby was dropping the stack of mail on the kitchen table, he heard Uncle Joe say from the open door, "Welcome back Bobby."

Turning catching his breath for his sudden appearance had startled him but quickly said, "Hello Uncle Joe."

As Uncle Joe entered, Bobby noticed he was carrying a small ice chest in his left hand and a can of Sille's beer in the other and as he got near made him take the beer saying, "Your Mother told me you would be back today so I thought I catch you and we have a couple beers and you can tell me everything that happen in Hawaii before you go and meet the family. You know you have been all over the Newspapers along with your new girlfriend whose has name so happens to be Bobbie."

"Met her dancing," Bobby answered as he took the cold can of Sille's beer from his hand open and took a drink letting the coolness and taste of the beer prepare him for Uncle Joe who has always been his friend has always wanted to know all he did ever since he was a kid. He thought I could become a great Artist and open a path for him to follow and here he was bringing Beer to fine the truth from him what really happening in Hawaii and dig out of him information he did not know he knew. But two can play that game and lots of the time he just made something upped which Uncle Joe believe but not always.

"She a beauty I do say," Uncle Joe said as he placed the ice chest on the table and quickly pull out a beer and sat it on the table as he sat saying, "I don't want to know about her but that you love her for the Media News has given me all I want to know about her. But something is about to happen so now you are old news."

"I bet they will be back for an update for I telling you, I'm followed everywhere by them," Bobby answered as he sat down reaching into the

279

sack for one of the letters while thinking of the ten more sacks he still had out in the car.

Uncle Joe lean back and ran he hands across his short air before he reached for the cold beer on the table saying, "I've been watching the news and what I have come to understand is these Outer Space General Stores that just showed upped out of the blue in their Huge Space Ships and wanted to know did the people of Earth want to buy some Goods from around the Galaxy. But to land, they were charging a fee of One Dollar Bill that every nation on the Planet will own and it will be the bond between them and the people of Earth giving them permission to land for they came to sale to Earth products from all over the Galaxy and they will give the Planet Earth one rotation around the Sun to come up with this Dollar are they will be leaving."

Rubbing his chin, he looked hard at Bobby before asking, "What I want really want to know is how did a thousand or more artists decide to use your Dollar Bill design. The News never said, nor did your Mother who always had her two cents into your life."

Bobby did not answer him but just toss the letter onto the table saying, "Job offer number ten thousand," and looking down into the sack of letters added, "I bet they are all job offers."

Uncle Joe just laughed before he said, "You better think twice before throwing these Job offers away. If you are going to be marrying Bobbie, you will need to find a job somewhere and I can tell you nobody has ever come knocking at my door wanting me to work."

"I guess you're right," Bobby answered before saying, "It all Bobbies fault I'm getting these job offers. For before her, I was just one of the artists. But I also believe I was thrown to wolves to keep the Media out of lives of the Artists. Me and Bobbie tried to played hide and seek game with them and somehow here come the reporters wanted us to act like they are not there filming away."

Laughter broke out between them and the second they settled down, Bobby took a good drink of his beer emptying it and as he threw it in the trash, Uncle Joe set another before him and as he closed back the ice chess Uncle Joe thinking it was funny asked, "Did you know they showed on TV you kissing some girl at a some dance a thousand times and it was not Bobbie."

"I didn't know that," Bobby answered as he opening his beer saying, "I always try to get at lease one kiss out of a girl thanking her before we parted out on the dance floor. That girl was a setup. The first time I dance with her, she tried to get me to kiss her after every dance we danced. I would dance with her only on the Waltzes for she was good at it. I always love a good dancer and try to dance to a girl's ability. Anyway, after a great waltz dance I had to give her a thank you kiss. Knew I was doing wrong for I did hear about it from Bobbie."

"She gets mad at you," Uncle Joe asked.

Bobby wanted to laugh as he gave, "Steaming is a better word and that was when we first started dating and believe me she did not talk without wanting to whip up on the girl I kissed."

"Does she still do that," Uncle Joe again almost laughing.

"Not now," Bobby laughed, "I think she's been wanted the girl to drag me off the last few dances?"

As their laughter settled Uncle Joe, "You get her mad at you again?"

"Oh no," Bobby quickly returned before saying, "I think it's jealously for getting all this attention over my Artist work and drugging her into it?"

"I would never think Barbara was shy," Uncle Joe asked getting himself settled from his laughter.

"It's the darn questions they ask about our private life that she don't like to answer and she tells them so," Bobby returned laughing.

Opening a new beer bottle Uncle Joe leaned back asking, "I guess they're be moving in with their robots and fancy doodads for I heard they accepted the dollar you drew up with all one hundred and ninety-five nations name on it forming a beautiful design with none written bigger are smaller than the other."

"The Nations accepted it alright," Bobby answered before with pride said, "I think it was because I was the only artist that sent a drawing in that representative every nation as equal."

After a good swig finishing off his getting warm beer he continues with, "Did you know even with all the chaos not one nation refused to place their name on the Dollar Bill especially after they began showing ads on the TV what they had to sell to the people of Earth. But the design of the Dollar Bill came from many Artists from all over the world and I just took their strength and gave the world the image of what the Dollar should look like from them and I was surprise how fast it was accepted."

Seeing Bobby's beer can was empty, Uncle Joe open his ice chest and while handing Bobby another Sille's Beer asked, "What they going to do with your Dollar bill. I heard so many stories about what they could do with the dollar so I've come to the one that should know?" while giving his sneaky smile.

Seeming to know this is what Uncle Joe has been wanting from him, Bobby said, "So you brought beer to loosen my tongue for a truthful answer."

"I couldn't have said it better," Uncle Joe answer and still serious asked, "Well, what are they going to do with it."

Bobby thought a second took several drinks of the beer before saying, "What I have heard these creatures are just as human as we are and it seems before selling their goods their buying, using this dollar I have created as payment. And in the future when enough money has flowed into the market they will open their doors and using this same dollar we'll be able to buy from their store. I imagine with a little profit and take our products and I guess they sell to other planets."

"Sounds like good business dealings to me," Uncle Joe answered quickly surmising wondering what product they wanted to buy figuring it was food but a question of them looking like Humans had to asked,

"I was wondering why you say they look like us?"

"They do exactly look like us," Bobby quickly answered. "That sounds impossible," Uncle Joe returned.

"It does sound impossible, Uncle Joe," Bobby countered with, "I've seen them myself and they look just like us."

Uncle Joe became quiet thinking for a few seconds before saying, "If that is so, it has to do with Man being God's greatest creation so on every planet where us humans could live, God placed a version of his greatest creation us humans and gave them strengths that they could survive and grow."

Agreeing Bobby said, "That may Be Uncle Joe but I feel I was thrown to the wolves to keep the media out of the Artist Teams giving me all this credit."

"Why you say that Bobby," Uncle Joe asked while opening another Sille's Beer.

Before Bobby could answer the phone rang stopping him for there was only a few people knew this number and Mom was one of them, looked at Uncle Joe saying, "It's Mom?"

"Better answer it," Uncle Joe quickly returned.

"Hello Mom," is all Bobby got out for his Mother, almost yelling said, "Turn the TV on quickly" before she hung up.

Setting the phone down he found the remote and there on the screen was the three local seated newsmen saying, "We take you live to the location where one the Ootash huge space ships..."

Suddenly the TV flickered and a long white breaded old man standing behind an all-white pulpit wearing a beautiful robe of blue and white with yellow outlines having a large collars having a Sun set image across it and behind him hung huge curtains having a drawing of a produce wagon being pulled by some very powerful looking beasts of burden.

His image caused Uncle Joe to instantly say, "Now there is a King."

The first words this King spoke in a language they couldn't understand for several minutes before suddenly he spoke in English saying, "I guess the interrupter is now on," waited a second before saying, "Good."

Turning his vision toward the camera the King said, "My name is King Ootash and I am proud to report the people of Earth has purchase a membership into the Ootash Trade and Barter with this outstanding Dollar where every Nation on Earth has equal ownership and now being a member of the Ootash Trade and Barter Company you have rights to purchase any item from our great selection of produce from all across the Galaxy."

The King seem to shuffle some papers and things on the Pulpit before continuing with, "Ootash Trade and Barter will first begin buying any and all dry grains using a copy of this Earth Dollar as payment and if we buy a million tons we will be paid in a million of these Earths Notes that will be sold to the public for grain payments and these Earth Dollars will be the only currency one can use in our stores."

The King looked down on his notes for several minutes before looking back into the Camera saying, "You must understand first an utmost we have not come to rule, outside of our Trade and Barter Space ships, the

Ootash Family does do not care what kind of government there is. Earth has been off limits to us traders for you did not have the communication systems you have now and the Ootash tribe is just the first trading family to arrive."

Leaving the Pulpit, King Ootash's walk and the colors in his robe made him look younger and stroking his white beard with one hand said, "All us Trader Family's live under very strict rules. You are our customers and you will be treated as such with honor as we expect you to treat us."

Walking back to the Pulpit he held upped the Earth Dollar to the camera saying, "With this, you have given us permission to land our trading vessels. Let me the first to say, we do not sell weapons of any kind. If you made any of our items into a weapon you will do it on your own."

Seeming to stand taller King Ootash gave a smile before saying, "As a gift for letting us land, you will also be given you Space Travel. In the Galaxy, there's billions and billions of planets just like your planet with us Humans living as the dominate life form on every one of them for God created man the same way on each planet to survive against all kinds of beasts and creatures and some of the wildest weather you have ever seen. But no manner what their skin color is or what their face looks like all of mankind throughout the Galaxy looks the same, beard and all."

Pausing for a second, he looks on the Pulpit for another second before continuing with, "You have white, black, browns and the in between races on every planet and some are tall, some are short, some very strong and their beaches on every planet where their fun in the Sun."

Seeming to want to laugh King Ootash said, "Sorry my mind wonder on what was on all the planets and I do like to visit the beaches and let me tell you there some worlds have beautiful beaches and after we land I'm going swimming."

Again he pulled on his beard and taking a deep breath said, "But that's getting off the subject isn't it?"

Looking down on the Pulpit, the King seemed to study it a second causing Bobby to think, "He got a computer screen on the Pulpit." Looking back at the Camera the King said, "In the beginning we will be buying using only your Earth Dollar and introduce it to the public where it will be sold a dollar for a dollar to pay for the produce we buy."

Holding up a Ten Dollar note, he smiles through his beard as he said,

"After several million one dollar notes are sold, we will start selling these Ten Dollar Notes having the same design as the One Dollar Note only the Capital of each country is written instead."

As the King became quiet, Uncle Joe glance over at Bobby and there was shock written all over his face and it even become more shocked at the King held up a fifty-dollar note having the image of Earth opened to show the Continents and Oceans saying, "We will also be introducing this Fifty Dollar Note with continents drawn out using the names of animals living in each using the language of the people that live there."

Setting the fifty back down he looked back at the camera saying, "I want to thank Earth for providing probably the best image on the Dollar we have ever gotten."

Quickly holding the Earth Dollar up, he pointed to it with the other hand saying, "You have here is the entrance fee to all Traders giving them permission to land and Barter and once this Dollar image is shown to the Galaxy, there will be Traders coming just to get this Dollar image into their data banks."

Placing the Dollar back down on the Pulpit, the King rub his white beard and the way to the end before saying, "We have tested all your grains and our Grain Bends will be landing at each location designated at the central point many produce region in the next few days to begin the process of buying your grain and there will be a website showing what we have to sale on Google."

Suddenly the King picked up the Dollar bill and took a bit bite right out of it chewed on it and after swallowing lifted his head up as if was analyzing the flavor looked at the camera and said, "That's has the sweetness of the Whatdoyacallit berry from the Planet we visited that showed us show to make paper out of nut and Grains and all our paper is eatable add a little sweetness and we have the very eatable Earth Dollar Note."

Took another bite off the note before holding it out toward them saying, "I bet you've been thinking I took a bite out of the new Earth Note and I can tell you that until there's a chemical change you cannot make a scratch on it, you can't cut it with a knife are do any physical harm to it whatsoever but after a year you can eat it and on are around the fourth year it will look like this."

Slowly King Ootash lifted into view a limped Dollar note almost like a limp cloth or rag hanging off his hand.

Replacing the limped Dollar back on the Pulpit, King Ootash lifted a small jar half full of a bluest colored liquid that was very slimy like saying, "And by the fifth year rolls around this is all that left."

Watching King Ootash replace the Jar back into the Pulpit, Bobby could see a smile in that hairy face of his as he said, "So thinking of saving Earth Dollars for the next Trader Family, I suggest you think again and spend like crazy every Earth Dollar you get, steal, or work for."

FISHING WEST BAY

Galveston's West Bay was one of my playgrounds ever since I was a small boy till life moved me inland. By the time I was thirty I knew it almost like the back of my hand. West Bay was really a gift from my Father. He kept it in my life even after we had moved into town far away from the bay. For there, sitting in the backyard sat a turn up aluminum boat Daddy's had which waited for him when he came home from the traveling the sea's on a Cargo Ship name Shirley. One of Like's Brothers liberty ships built during War World II. He would come home and would, oh let me not forget his white truck that also never moved until he got home from traveling the sea.

He would load that boat with his fishing gear and go fishing and he would always fish alone or he pick up somebody, I do not know. Why he never took me I always thought I was too young and I may never know.

When I turned 14, we moved to Waller and my life went upside down. I never told Mother the abuse I got at school but that was when Milton Thomas came into my life, my age, my height, and my weight but wore glasses a mile thick. I became a part of Waller and knowing me, I went looking for jobs dragging Milton alone who got us some more jobs which were all temporary like hauling hay or mowing a pasture, picking water melons or other vegetables.

When we move to Waller, Huey my older brother's playground still was West Bay and when he had no one else to go fishing with him, he got me to go with him to fish for the big Gafftop Catfish on the Intercostal Canal and taught me the bay and even shared it with Milton once.

In fact, if it was not for my brother I might have gone another path in life instead of fishing for the fun of it and cooking what I catch. But by my middle teens in our move to Waller, I was becoming a Cowhand. Specially reading ever Western I could get my hands on from the school Library.

Now Milton Thomas had become my best friend. He was a good Christian boy who was born with very bad eyes and had to wear glasses a mile thick. I lease that what he often said when we were hauling hay and I guess those big glasses would get heavy at times.

My brother by this time was fishing around Jones Lake which was a small lake leading off of the West Bay divide by the Intercostal waterway and built him a place to stay at night. He had gotten himself several free sections of the wood crate frames from where he worked as a heat exchange drafting job learning about Heat Exchangers before graduating college and become a Mechanical Engineer in the field at the same company.

What he had gotten was sheets of wood made up using doubled 1x4's nail together and with theses sheet, he built a small 8x12 cabin using them as plywood and the camp was very heavy.

When he was done and time to place the camp on poles he came and got me and I got him to let Milton come along and now over fifty years later the memory of that trip is still fresh in my mind.

Now this was first and only trip I made to the camp with my friend Milton and with him having bad eye sight I do believe he had the most excitement and fun doing something he never imagine he be doing, "Went Floundering."

Huey had come to the farm to get Daddies Pickup and he talked me and Milton to go with him to take a few things to his camp out on the bay and help him a little. Yea Right, we loaded Daddies trunk with telephone poles and what else could fit back there. He told us he had gotten the poles from along the road left there by the telephone people. I believed him then and knowing him I'm sure he would have bought them. Even today, when I think how he was able to drive Daddies trunk, loaded such as it was. The front end was almost off the ground and the poles sticking out the truck bed would hit the road in back now and then. Me, Milton and Huey in front with our arms sticking out the windows looking like we had not a care or worry in the world as this rocking, waving, banging truck travel down the road.

When we got to the Boat Lift on Highland Bayou we unloaded the poles by the water's edge and fetched the boat at a boat storage site and it was not to long we left the dock with Huey taking his time with the over loaded aluminum boat with a forty horse motor pulling the two poles behind us.

As we traveled down Hall's bayou, Huey pointed out stuff about the marsh to me and Milton and as we exited from the calm waters of Highland Bayou into the wind blown waves of Jones Lake and I'm sure it gave us a trill. There were even white caps. But that did not stop Huey and many times, I sure we would get wet but that boat road the waves out and as we cross the Lake, Huey pointed out the camp he had built sitting on what he called, "The Dumps" which were the dump sites when they dug the Intercostal Canal years earlier.

Huey was a one of our nation's top Engineers and being such he had a plan to raise the Camp into the air using telephone poles with two of them being pulled behind us. We found he had already dug the holes for the poles during earlier trips to the bay where he would to go fishing along the Intercostal shore line where he would catch very large Gafftop Catfish about as big as they get using cut bait on the bottom. Back in the fifties the Intercostal was only used by a few Tug boats. We were lucky to see even one pass in a day of fishing.

But fishing for me came later for Waller was hundred miles from Galveston Bay and Milton and I being only fifteen or sixteen at this time the only fishing I did was the small lakes if Milton and I wasn't swimming in them. So as we slowly dragged those telephone poles behind us, we traveled across Jones Lake and believe me, Milton and I was excited.

After arriving and working together, we had the poles up to the camp and in their holes that Huey's had already dug around the camp and by dark, had the camp couple feet off the ground and I was excited for we were going foundering. Now Milton and I have never been but it is not that we didn't know all about going Floundering and back then I had yet realize at full Moon, the Stingrays come and bed down in the shallow waters along the shore line and luckily it was only half Moon so that night there was only a few early ones.

Now after we got the poles upright in the holes, Huey told us that we were to raise the camp and set it on the slots he had cut out on the pole ends.

Eagerly Milton and I took up the challenge and discovered a problem, the jacks which were the kind you screwed and can life a ton, but kept sinking into the ground and it took until night to get the Camp House high enough to bring wood support into play and I bet it took twenty turns on that jack to move it up an inch and worst of all, had to put with those pesky swamp mosquitoes.

As night time fell and covered with some kind of anti-mosquito spray with a two prong gig in one hand and Huey's only two gas lanterns with a reflector mounted to a long circular handle we went Foundering.

Milton chose not to carry a lantern giving me the responsibility and as we settled in the boat, Milton and I had our first ever ride in a boat at night.

The night air hitting my face, what waves there was almost gone for the wind had died at sunset. Huey had a spot light and down the Intercostal canal we went with him shining that light now and then and eventually, we travel inland, parked the boat on a spot he liked to fish at and as the moon shined we walked across the hundred feet to the shore line of West Bay and with Lanterns in hand we went Floundering and instead of Flounders there was stingrays bedded down.

Now Milton with bad eye sight and the stories of what being stung by Stingray can do made the walk through the shallow water rough on him and several times, he, I thought he wanted to walk on the water when we come across a Stingray and after a couple hundred yards dodging them, gigging only two flounders, we came across a stingray that had a tail I bet was ten foot long and Huey decided he had torture us enough and back to the camp we flew talking about those Stingrays and Milton and I was glad we did not get stung.

By 3pm the next day, we had the camp using boards on the posts as support had the camp on those telephone poles and locked in place and I bet I turned these jacks getting that camp up on those posts ten thousand times or more.

Milton never went fishing with me again but the Galveston Bay never left me and by the time I gotten out of the Army, Huey had built a floating camp and parked in at the end of Halls Bayou among the other camps and into the West Bay I started fishing with Huey whenever I could.

Huey liked to fish for Gafftop Catfish off the Intercostal banks with cut bait and in a day of fishing maybe catch us five or more. After I got out of the service, I move into college leaving Milton in Waller for Mom and Dad had moved back to town because of Mother's Health.

Got a 14-foot use fiberglass boat with a forty house outboard and I needed a fishing buddy. I got a job in the Psychology department and met a graduate name Dave Stump and talked him into going fishing with me, How I did it was one day I was talking about those swamp Mosquitoes and Dave bragged that Mosquitoes never bother him because of his native Indian blood in him and I of course countered saying, "Come fishing with me and we'll see."

That Friday I picked Dave upped and after putting the boat in the water at the Halls Bayou boat ramp and store and after the thirty minute ride down the Bayou, I parked the boat asking Stump to tie the rear and I'll get the front. I wasn't thinking about the Mosquitoes until I started to tie the boat and those pesky Mosquitoes must have been waiting for they started to attack immediately and as I was finishing, I heard Dave start to holler and I heard him jump into the water. Not knowing what happen I called out, "Dave you ok?" as I ran to the other end of the boat and Dave in the water called out, "Those are not Ma- quitoes. They are Man-quitoes."

He changed clothes and inside we joked how Ma-quitoes still don't bother him but those Man-quitoes is another story.

Using the cast net the next morning, I caught us some bait and down to the Intercostal I took us and I had learned Gafftop when they strike they strike and if I'm not careful will do it so hard and yank my Rod into the water.

Dave had brought his fresh water pole with him which was nothing compared to my large salt water rigs and he had cast out into the waters and left the pole on the ground without securing it from a Gafftop strike.

I was telling him so when suddenly something hit his rod and into the water it flew with Dave following and I was amazed he catch it and as he stood in the waist deep water holding pole up in the air and whatever was on the other end was strong enough to keep pulling the lines from his rod and him crying out, "What should I do?"

I said, "Let it run."

But Dave tried to stop it and the line broke and was he disappointed. We had a good laugh about hooking his first salt water fish and losing it.

We fished a few more times off the Bank before we moved out into the

West Bay drift fishing and away from those pesky Mosquitoes and never went back to fishing the shore line for in the open waters of West Bay, we caught way more than just catfish.

I remember one time, I hook a stingray and I swear it was larger than the width of the boat before my line broke or was cut on the boat's bottom which is what I think happened and was I glad at the same time.

Well I eventually graduated and couldn't locate a job in Houston so I fell back on my Military background and got a job using my Electronic Technician skills. Move out of the Dad's and Mom's house and renting an apartment and met Edward, a 12year old basketball player who became my guard and when I went to play ball, I'd take him with me and he became a really good player in the three on three game we played at the local park.

We were playing and another white player started playing who on seeing how good Edward was, recruited Edward to play for the Lutheran Private School and paid his tuition and I watch him play ball when I could and by now I was involved with his whole family and by this time in my life, I no longer went fishing on the bay and never went back as I moved into a work life, left my job and at the Well Logging Company and got one operating a Scanning Electron Microscope at Texas Instruments.

But Galveston beaches became my fishing hole and I'd take all the kids with me and let them swim and I would fish. It was simple enough using a light rod. I stop and buy a pound of fresh dead shrimp and put it in a floating bait bucket and drop into the waves using a fish stringer to hold it and that bucket of Shrimp after ten minutes would start to attract the small fish and I would catch twenty in no time.

Teas Instruments for some reason, started to lay people off and close certain operations and the Boss of the Failure Analysis group came and took my Bosses place and I went out the door and Galveston Bay disappeared from my life as I got a job in Tennessee working as an engineer in a Failure Analysis Lab for IBM. Met a girl, got married and became an expert in this field of telling why electronic components fail. I bet I've written twenty thousand reports with photos and my opium.

As I write this history, I can look back and remember the times I walked the muddy banks of Jones's lake sinking in the mud with Huey gigging flounders to catching those big catfish fishing off the

Intercostal and I will never forget, Huey's Jesus shoes that allowed him to walk on top of the mud and as I followed sinking to my knees but they muddied the water as he walked so he only used them once but they did work. I really think they were hard to walk with was the main reason.

My brother is now 82 and still goes fishing but no longer uses a boat but fishes off the Catwalk beneath his and Bobbie's fancy house he built on a canal among a group of them and I heard he was trying to sell the place for million bucks. Now, I just have the memories, for at 72, I now live in Arkansas Ozarks Mountains and don't go fishing at all.

THE GARDEN OF FUN

"Hey Frank, what's been going on," Thomas asked as he entered almost hitting the sign not watching where he was going which Read "Dominoes being played tonight at The Card Garden."

"Same oh, same oh," Frank answered as he pulled a set of dominoes and set them on the table to use and glancing over at the Winners Circle displaying the pictures of pass winners said, "Tomas, I've been thinking of closing this place down. I look over at the winner's circle and many of those winners have gone on to be with the Lord and I feel I'll be there soon. Going on eighty-eight now and my bones feel it.

Tomas slipped himself between the box of Dominos sets and Frank saying, "Let me passed them out for you."

"I was doing just fine, mine you," Frank returned with a sneaker. "I'm not saying you are not doing great," Tomas answered as took hole of the box of domino sets and when he started to place a set on next table said, "But still being on table #1 for ten minutes is not moving at all. You've been waiting for me haven't you?"

"Now why would I just do that," Frank returned as he found himself a seat behind in one of the covered lounge chairs and was just getting comfortable when Thomas return with the empty box asking, "Isn't this the last day of the Domino competition?"

"Last day, that it is," he answered before adding, "And the house is going to be packed for the two couples paying tonight are both good players."

"Better than you and me." Thomas asked as he placed a coffee cut under the auto coffee maker and press "Mild."

"Get me a cup also," Frank commanded before saying, "Frank looking back if I remember right, you and I lost every game we play as partners.

I mean we tried Pinochle, Hearts and Dominos and not one game have we ever won."

"Oh but we did against Bill and Paul," Tomas returned as he set Frank's coffee on the table beside him.

"That don't count," Frank answered after he took a drink of his hot coffee and as he held the cup close to him added, "They were only ten are eleven years old at the time."

Tomas took a seat having a question running through his mine, "I've had known Frank going on four years and although Frank never stops talking I've never had the chance to get him to talk about the how Garden of Fun got started."

Glancing over at the clock and seeing it read 8:25 also thought, "It will be hours before the many gamers begin to show up and since Dwain and Charlie is not here yet when did you open this place?"

Frank took a drink of his coffee and after he set his cup down, he rubbed hands across his face adjusting his glasses and feeling better Frank said, "It wasn't me, it was Betsy May that really started the place, I was just along for the ride."

Thomas still digging asked. "Betsy May, and how she does that and where has she and Judy gone off too anyway?"

"Yard sales," Frank answered, "It is Saturday and Judy always drags Betsy May off to go with her and they always come home with more junk. I mean just look around at the window shaves and all the crazy looking glass and pottery figures displayed and it is always changing. They would come back from yard sales and replace one thing with another and fight over where to place the item for an hour wanting everything just right."

Thomas added saying, "What I like is the item of the day on displayed at the far end. They place an item in the lighted display and write what it was and who made it and how old it was. It amazes me they can find out that much info on the items?"

"You don't know them two as good as I do," Frank said almost laughing. "If Betsy May or Judy do not have any info on what they are going to display as the item of the week, they would make it up. Dates, who made it, who own it on and on most of the items the age was always a guess."

"Still, what they say about the item is interesting," Thomas countered before standing and picking up his coffee cup asked, "I think I'll get a refill before Dwain and Charlie show up. Want a refill?"

"I'm Ok," Frank quickly returned and while watching Thomas pour himself another full cup of coffee said, "Thomas, I was going on 65 when I met her. After my wife died I was alone and in the loneliness I learn how God felt after he had to place Adam and Eve out of the garden and when Betsy May entered my life she was like a savior and I fell in love with her and she own this here building."

Thomas was laughing as he refiled Frank cup with coffee and just had to say, "Are you sure it wasn't a three story building you fell in love with and it came with a Betsy May."

Frank look at him cockeye as he quickly answered saying, "It was all Betsy May. I met her out dancing and we just hit it off. We dance until our heath became such. I guess you never seen her dance either. She is one of the best."

Pointed toward her picture by the door waving goodbye to the players as they leave saying, "That's Betsy May and what she looked like when we first met."

Thomas walked over to the picture he has seen a thousand times but never really gave it much thought. He noticed right off that Betsy May had not change and still a heavy set women wearing a nice white and blue flowered blouse, dark blue pants and light blue sandals. Her face was round and smiling and wore her hair as she does today and as the other women around her age do, easy to take care of.

As he returned to take a seat, he took a drink of his coffee before he said, "Your right Frank, she was and still a knock out. I think I would have falling in love in a heartbeat. You say she was a good dancer and I know she can cook, I do believe when you found Betsy May, you found a winner."

But Frank returned, "I found way more than a winner for we are two friends who are spending their last years of their lives together." Thomas was laughing as he said, "I guess you two have been shacking up together like me and Margie? That is what she and I are doing. Shacking up, so here you are shacking up with Betsy May and now where does this building come into play."

Frank thought a second trying to remember and even took a drink of his coffee before he said, "I found out about the building while doing

Betsy May taxes. It seems her Dad had willed it to her on his death that year being the only child. She asked if I wanted to check it out and there set this here three story building and as we entered the building we found the setup as you see it now. It appears her dad had been running a big poker gaming hall and law came and shut him down so he willed the building to Betsy May free of any debt and taxes paid up for twenty years."

"So this place was a Poker hall," Thomas asked looking around thinking it would have made a good one at that.

"Still is," Frank answered before adding, "But Tomas, when we first walk into this building Betsy May and I walked around and using flashlights went upstairs and check each room out and of course I tagged along checking them out also and did the place ever needed cleaning."

Thomas now more curious then ever asked, "Whose idea was it to start this Garden of Games anyway, yours or Betsy May's?"

Frank stood to fetch a refill of his coffee saying, "It was all Betsy May's idea and I think she came up with the Idea but in the startup it was touch and go for a while."

As he finished filling his cup he asked, "Like a refill?"

"I'm OK," Thomas returned before asking, "I bet this place must have wild life at one time from the stories I've heard."

"It has a History alright," Frank answered causing him to laugh as he took his seat. "You know the sound proof Stage Room where camera system is set up for those want to perform on Face Book. Did you know it was a striptease stage during Betsy May's Dad days of running this place? Same set up as now but the pay to view web site is gone and Betsy May made me put the Camera on one of those Story Time Websites and today it's on Face Book."

"You are talking about that Red Door where one must place couple poker chips in a slot to enter," Thomas asked before saying, "I never been inside in the four years I've been playing cards games here. But I heard they get their money back if they leave the place clean."

"It was a trick," Frank answered and feeling cocky added. "I left a sign saying, "They could not take the money without cleaning the place up before they leave for the eyes of Face book is upon them. It worked like a charm and I never did have to clean that room. There even been young men and women will come and actually clean the place to show how good they could work seeking a Job using face book."

"What's it like inside," Thomas asked catching Frank thinking back to the day Betsy May and him walked into the Stage Room and the mess it was in.

So as after he took a drink of his coffee Frank answered saying, "The room is nothing more than a large stage before a wall full of cameras, lighting and now thanks to the some organization from the better tomorrow groups, my small computer screen was replace by a giant TV screen and they upgraded the camera system and using the latest thing going using the Cell Phone to control what image they want to display upon the giant screen calling up songs, scripts or even their Ex hoping she still loves them."

"But what was it like when it was used by Betsy's Dad for the striptease act," Thomas asked.

"When Betsy May and I first entered the Stage Room we found was on the left side of the room was a large camera mounted halfway up a wall surrounded by stage lighting and before the stage what was called at that time the teasing couches just out of camera view where a guy could come and really be tease. There were curtains dividing the room and a change room on each side of the stage for the strippers to change clothes or put some on."

Still digging Thomas asked, "Is that why they close him down."

Frank took another drink of hot coffee thinking before he said, "No, it wasn't just the strippers. It was the whole operation. I think her Dad had his hand in every illegal operation in town and opening a Gambling Hall in the middle of town brought in some rough looking characters and a shooting now and then. But not the stripper show. I heard the Mayor at the time was one of Betsy's Dad best customers on the Tease Chairs which Betsy May said her dad had them steamed cleaned every week."

"Ooh, I can imagine why," Thomas spoke trying not to visualize what action could be going on happily on one of those Tease chairs so he asked, "Speaking of Betsy May and Judy, where are they?"

"Out running the yard sales," but as Frank answered he notices Dwain entering the game room so he called out, "Where's Charlie?" "Coming," Dwain answer stopping by the coffee pot and began filling the white coffee cup he brought with him.

Frank looked over at Thomas saying, "If you want to know about Betsy May's dad, Dwain and Charlie can tell you, they worked for him." "Charlie and I did that alright," Dwain answered as he took his coffee and headed for the Domino table with the only yellow painted chair in the place. It was Frank's Chair and whatever table it sat at would be the game table. But after playing every table in the Game room Frank settled for a table near the coffee pot saying "I've played them all and not one lucky table among them" and Dwain was glad he did for as he took his seat and gently scattered the dominos out across the table made getting Coffee refills easier.

Dwain was shuffling the dominoes as Frank and Thomas join him each turning over a domino and Charlie was high and Dwain was his partner then as everybody was seated Frank began shuffling for Charlie to start the game being high man.

After drawing their seven dominoes, Charlie started the hand playing the double five and Thomas followed playing five blank with Dwain following with a double blank. Then as Frank was thinking Thomas asked, "Charlie, did you and Dwain really work for Betsy May's dad?"

"We sure did and right here in this building," Charlie answered. Dwain added, "We were young men back then and we made money off of tips fetching drinks or smokes or Mama's donuts." "Mama's Donuts," Charlie said as he places the double six for twenty. "I forgot all about her and those great donuts she made."

Thomas passed and as Dwain counted again with the six one he said, "You didn't know them but Betsy May's Mom and Dad ran this place like a business and Betsy May was always off to some girls' school and never set foot in the Club unless her Mom needed help making donuts because some worker quit."

Frank play the five one which was the only rock he could play and Dwain made another twenty with the six Five finishing the hand by domino-ing. After counting the losers' rocks, Dwain began to shuffle saying, "Thomas, it is not what you're thinking. To work in the Poker club, you had to pay to get in the door to get a job and if you played it right and dress well and being good looking young man helps, one could make over fifty dollars in tips and of course that could include a good tip for some after hour play. But to work in Mama's Donuts, you were paid to make and deliver donuts and that included several of the local stores with a sign over the boxes saying, "Mama's Donuts always fresh"

As they drew their seven dominoes Charlie said, "But donuts were not the only thing we delivered out into the poker rooms. There were peanuts, beer, liquor and cigarettes and anything that was use in and around the poker and slot machines and we had to keep the place clean and quite often I remember getting a big tip by some winner saying thanks."

Thomas played the six four to start the new hand saying, "Sounds like Mama was the supplier and Dad had to pay her for the things he used in the poker hall making his money stay at home and I bet Mama Donut's was making a good profit too."

"Hard to say," Dwain answered but as he played the six one making five points added, "But they sold out every day and night."

After Frank played the double four, Charlie played the double one making ten asked, "Have you and Betsy May talked about reopening the poker hall."

Frank spinning one domino over and over answered saying, "Not really for the same thing that close her down has not moved and now the church has double in size and I being a member I don't think it will not go over well. This place is almost a type of Senior Center. The money we make is just enough to pay the utilities. But Betsy May has been talking about reopening Mama's donuts but the startup cost is beyond our income."

After Thomas played one two making ten he added, "But I check the equipment and Mama must have had the equipment clean after they closed down for I'm pretty sure I can get it up and running again."

Charlie, while looking over what he should play looked at Frank asking, "Does Betsy May have Mama's recipe book of the icing she used."

"I'm sure she does, "Frank answered.

Deciding on cut the four with the four three making a nickel before looking at Thomas saying, "Thomas, Mama had many donut coatings. She always had us make plain and chocolate cover donuts and then she had her special of the day coating that could be anything and everything you can eat with chocolate. I always like the coconut and chocolate one myself she named them "Mama's Coco & Choco Donuts.""

Frank playing the double two added, "Mama had coatings alright and her donuts with chocolate and nuts always sold out fast. She always said,

"They may cost more to make but giving the donuts eaters a treat is her way of saying, "Thank you for buying my donuts. I was coating donuts with chocolate then sprinkling and walnuts when I first met Betsy May. I will never forget our first contact eye to eye and it was love at first sight."

"Love at first site," Charlie said while playing a two three on the double two. Then look at Frank asking, "Frank, I've known you all these years and never knew how you ever got a date with Betsy May, I bet every boy in town had asked her out after Tim was killed in that car wreak and she always said, "No."

Dwain play his double three and Charlie ended the hand with a six/three asking, "Come on Frank tell us just how did you win sweet Betsy May's hand?"

As Charlie shuffled for the next hand, Frank lean back in the chair wondering should he answer or not and when he leans forward to draw his dominoes said, "Really it was MaryAnn's fault we met?"

"Maryann's fault," Dwain asked as he started the hand with a six/four.

As the hand continued Frank said, "When I first move here thirty years ago, Barbara Jean and MaryAnn had become friends and about a year after Barbara Jean died, MaryAnn called me and asked would I like to go dancing with her and George."

"So MaryAnn was the match maker," Dwain asked as he played the double one making a nickel.

"Not as you think," Frank answered playing the one/two making same nickel.

Thomas played the double three as Frank continue with, "I've always been a good dancer and while dancing, I'd meet some girl who would sweet talked me into going home with her and her house needed repair. So I fix it up and when I was finish the girl would kicked me out and I'd never see her again."

Laughter spread around the table for a second and as Frank played on the spinner, he looked at his friends saying, "I did this twice and was thinking I'd just quite going dancing when MaryAnn found out I was back home. Called and that was when I met Betsy May. It seems MaryAnn had been picking up Betsy May to go dancing while I was working and while sitting with Betsy May in the back seat of their car, we became friends and I dance every dance with her and rest is history."

WILLIAM'S COLLECTION OF SONGS

Dear Reader,

I have not written many songs and the ones I have written I wrote for our Lord for basically saving my Soul. Being "Born again" and filled with the Holy Ghost brought the Kingdom of God into my life that I will stand before God without fear. I tried to be a Minister got all my prudential's and register myself at the Court House but God had other plans for my life. I have tried to be faithful and now that I'm over seventy and looking back I see nothing but ups and downs and Victories and Failures. But my love and hope has not changed no matter what path I'm following that day or year. If you wish to use any song be free to do so. Love William.

SONG OF THANKFULNESS

I gathered myself together and stood before the Lord
I was lost oh so lost in my sin
I was sure I was so stain within
And I was sure God knew where I've been

I'll never forget the moment Jesus open my Soul
I knew not what happen as I fell to the floor
I only felt I was giving a great change within
As his present I felt as my soul became Born Again

TAKE YOUR CROSS AND FOLLOW ME

By William Gaillard Ellis Jr

Chorus:
Take your cross and walk the hillside with me
I can hear Jesus calling as he struggled alone
Don't you know there are souls to save? Take your
cross and walk the hillside with me

On a hill side long ago walked our Lord with a heavy load
A crown of thorns on his head for all to see
And the crowd was cheering on as he staggered under the cross
He was carrying to save our souls

On top of Mount Calvary he placed the cross upon the ground
Now the strips on his back could be plainly seen
And the crowd was cheering on as he lay across the cross
He had carried to save our souls

High above Calvary they lifter the cross into the air
Now the nails in his hands could be plainly seen
And the crowd was cheering on as the blood fell cross the cross
He had carried to save our souls

From the cross to the tomb there Jesus was laid
Yet in three days he roused from that grave
But high on Calvary there a cross that remains
Calling for you and for me

DON'T RUSH THE MUDDY WATERS

By William Gaillard Ellis Jr

Chorus
Don't rush the muddy waters don't rush it my friend
For the gates will stand open until we all enter in
Don't rush the muddy waters don't rush it my friend
For the water been muddied by us children rushing in

When life seems in danger and you know eternity is near
On the shore of old Jordan we'll stand waiting to hear
For the Trumpet will sound and our crossing appears
The waters will muddy by feet that are so dear

When the multitudes start crossing it will be a wonderful sight
We'll see the Pearly Gates where there is no night
Our eyes will be on Jesus our hearts full of his light
For in the muddy water our wings will shine bright

Don't rush the muddy waters walk slow and enjoy the show
For the millions that know Jesus it is time for us to go
Take your time crossing take it easy and take it slow
For each step is a victory what joys we will know

ME AND JESUS STICK TOGETHER

By William G. Ellis Jr

I don't care if it rains or freezes as long as I got my plastic Jesus
Riding on the dash board of my car
Thru all kinds of stormy weather, me and my Jesus we stick together
Riding on the dash board of my car

Chorus:
On the dash board, on the dash board
Jesus keeps me safe riding there
Thru the storms of life may falter but my plastic Jesus never alters
Riding on the dash board of my car

I don't care if I'm cold with sneezes as long as I got my plastic Jesus
Riding on the dash board of my car
Thru all kinds of sickness, I'm better, for me and Jesus we stick together
Riding on the dash board of my car

I don't care who I pleases as long as I got my plastic Jesus
Riding on the dash board of my car
Friends may leave friends may gather, but me and Jesus stick together
Riding on the dash board of my car

WHAT A STRANGER

By William G. Ellis Jr

Chorus:
Yes, God only knows what a stranger has done.
Only God knows who that stranger to be
I was lost and undone until he came along
And the kind words of this stranger set me free

I was so lost in the swamp feeling all bog down
Million of Mosquito's seem to be pushing me down
When this stranger's words echoed as I was about to drown
And I'll be blessed, if he didn't place me upon solid ground

As I lived and played between the save and the lost
Wondering between my cross and his crown
And no matter how far I wondered when peace I did sought
And I'll be blessed, if he didn't place me upon solid ground

Now my feet want to stray with all my wondering ways
But wonderful bright lights are now shining my way
Now I see clearly how much for my soul he had to pay
And I'll be blessed, if he didn't place me upon solid ground

I SUNK TO THE BOTTOM

By William G. Ellis Jr

Chorus
Yes, I sunk to the bottom Way down to the bottom
Thinking I could walk on water
But when I will step out onto the streets of gold
There will be no sinking to the bottom

Now I stood there looking down upon that pond
Thinking I could walk upon water
But when I took a step out onto that pond
I'll be darn if I didn't sink to the bottom

Now I sat down beside that dirty old pond
And for ten days I prayed and I fasted
But when I took a step out onto that pond
I'll be darn if I didn't sink to the bottom

I just laid myself back down beside that dirty old pond
More days I prayed and I fasted
But when I took a step out onto that pond
I'll be darn if I didn't sink to the bottom

IN A MANGER LAY

By William Gaillard Ellis Jr

In a Manger lay little boy Jesus
And he smiled as he looked all around
For there was Mary and there was Joseph
And looking up his Father was found

Chorus
And there was his Father looking down upon him
As he laid among his creations
The joy he felt filled all of Heaven
Until every Angel was singing

The Manger was warm and cozy that night
With many animals Josephus had to shoo
There were cows a mooing, chickens and horses
And even a goat or two

The Sheppard's came from across the fields
Wondering what they would find
And as they entered the little manger
In Mary's arms little Jesus whine

Three Wiseman saw the light that shined
For it shined both day and night
Gold, Frankincense and little Myrrh
They gave baby Jesus that night

I'LL WALK AROUND HEAVEN

By William Gaillard Ellis Jr

I met my Lord and Savior one day
I met him on my Knees
And he made this promise and I do believe
That I'll walk around Heaven someday

Chorus:
Yes, I'll walk around heaven I'll run around Heaven
I'll see the hidden things untold
For we have been set free that is you and that's is me
And we'll going to walk the streets of Gold

I went to a friend and told what had happen
How the Lord had save my Soul
Now he is walking the straight and narrow
And together we'll walk the streets of Gold

I met a stranger and said why do you run
When Jesus has so much for you
He is alive and he gave us this promise
That you will walk around heaven someday

JUST GET ON YOUR KNEES FAITHFUL PILGRIM

By William Gaillard Ellis Jr

Chorus:
Call him up faithful Pilgrim Call him down on your knees
He will then hear your mournful Cry
Call him up faithful Pilgrim Call him down on your knees
He will lift you that you can stand on high

When trouble and strife is all around you
And nobody seems to care
Just get on your knees faithful Pilgrim
Call him up Call him up Call him up

Don't be mistaken about our Lord above
Don't think he does not hear our cry
Just get on your knees faithful Pilgrim
Call him up Call him up Call him up

I never seen the righteous forsaken
I never heard him turn one away
Just get on your knees faithful Pilgrim
Call him up Call him up Call him up

We often wonder and stray from our Savior
We sometimes forget about our brother

Just get on your knees faithful Pilgrim
Call him up Call him up Call him up

I never seen his hand short to answer
I'm sure he'll never run from danger
Just get on your knees faithful Pilgrim
Call him up Call him up Call him up

It makes no difference what life you have walked
It does not matter where you lay your head
Just get on your knees faithful Pilgrim
Call him up Call him up Call him up

COME TO ME SONG

By William G. Ellis Jr

Chorus:

Come, come, come to me   Come, come, come to me.

Come, come, come to me   Jesus my Lord cried.

Peter stood on the bow of the boat searching the waters for Jesus
The wind was howling the waves were swashing, and clearly he heard
Peter cried, "Is that you Jesus" "If so, bid me come to thee."
The cry that came was low the waves were swashing and clearly he heard

Peter did not stop to think over the side he went
Upon the waters he stood the waves were swashing and clearly he heard

In Peter's wonderment he slowly began to sink
To the lord he cried the waves were swashing and clearly he heard

Suddenly Peter felt a hand and upon the water he stood
But still echoing in the wind the waves were
washing and clearly he heard

TO THE CROSS I GO

In this world of sin and sorrow
In this world of hate and woe
There a place where I can meet Jesus
It is to the cross to the cross I go

Chorus:
To the Cross, to the Cross, to the Cross I go
When I'm in trouble it's to the Cross I go
To the Cross, to the Cross, To the Cross I go
Jesus will meet me at the Cross I know

When my heart is torn and broken
When my life is thrown to and foe
When it seems that my life not worth living
It is to the Cross to the Cross I go

When I see a family member is hurting
When I see a friend in great need
When I've done all I can on my own
It is to the Cross to the Cross I go

HE IS MY VERY BEST FRIEND

When I was a child I did not know I just knew that Jesus save souls
When I grew older I wondered in Sin for Jesus was a stranger
Yes, Jesus was a stranger till I met him one
day and he opened my blinded eyes
Yes Jesus was a stranger I knew him not But now he my very best friend.

CHORUS:
Yes Jesus was a stranger now he is my friend
and gave me that peace assurance
He changed my life, gave me new hope, and became my very best friend

As I grew older I wonder this world Oh so alone
I fell for all of Satan's tricks until I felt my soul was gone
Then upon my knees one day Jesus entered my lonely life
Yes Jesus was a stranger I knew him not but
now he is my very best friend

Now wondering this world gave much joy but I had no peace within
This stranger was calling, calling to me to come out and be with him
I answered his call though I knew him not
now the Holy Ghost lives inside
Yes Jesus was a stranger I knew him not but
now he is my very best friend

William Gaillard Ellis Jr

If you are walking this world all alone and you are feeling OH SO Blue
This Jesus who's change my life he can change yours too
For Jesus came into this world to bring the love of God to you
Yes Jesus was a stranger I knew him not but
now he is my very best friend

LONELINESS

By William G. Ellis Jr

I can't get away from the loneliness it hangs over me like a cloud
It follows me like a stray hungry dog it waits for me in a crowd
It used to pant and claw at my door I resisted but I knew it would win
It found the key hidden under the mat and now it just lets itself in

The loneliness latched onto me a long, long time ago
I never could hide for I stood out like a black crow
The loneliness rapidly become part of my physique
I watched as we grew old together, my loneliness and me

Now looking back over my life with loneliness I do recall
If it hadn't been for loneliness, I'd have no companion at all
Now that I'm old and gray my heart has awoken to a new song
I had a glimpse of Gods Glory and my loneliness was gone

WHAT A DAY FOR THE SUN NOT TO SHINE

By William Gaillard Ellis Jr

Chorus
What a day for the Sun not to shine
What a day for the rain to come down
They had taken her son and he was being crucified
What a day for Sun not to shine

Mary and John was walking the hill called Mount Calvary
John held her as they climbed the lonely hill
The echo of a hammer rang across the mountain side
They had taken her son and he was being crucified

Now Mary was weeping and John was weeping too
Jesus was her son and John friend too
Arm and arm they struggled up that lonely hill
Then the hammering stopped and everything got still

When Mary and John arrived at the Hilltop
They saw three crosses and solders drawing lots
John did not understand why Jesus had to die
But when Mary saw him she cried "My God My Son"

Now Mary and John drew close to Jesus
He looked down at them and he smiled
Then he said, "John behold your Mother"
And to Mary he said, "Mary behold your son."

Now Mary and John left that lonely hilltop
For her son was no longer alive
For they heard him cry out with a voice so clear
"Father it is finish," and then he was still

WORD FROM THE LORD

Friday May 4 1984

This word of our Lord came by tongues and interpretation of tongues through Sister Patty.

1) From the house of the Lord, I say unto these people tonight, if thou will come and repent, I the lord will forgive thee and will help thee through every trial even I'll make away for escape with ever temptation, say the Lord.

2) I shall help thee for there are those here this night that need help and I the lord have come by way of my Spirit to help thee, to deliver thee and set thee free.

3) I say unto thee even lift thy hands this night it praises you, for the Lord does dwell among its people, Yea, come, see only my Idol, kindly, says the lord. Oh taste and see that I am good.

4) Oh see, see and evil hour and evil power, I see and evil power and even a time shall come as never been in any generation that an evil work of iniquity, oh shall abound upon this earth.

5) But I say unto thee that I am greater, shall even abound thee more.

6) Oh, if thou will come unto me, I'll help thee and my grace will be sufficient to take thee through the hour that shall be dark before thee. For darkness is covered the earth and gross darkness covers the people

1. and who shall even able to stand in this hour. For only those, yea, who prepared themselves, only those who have called out upon me that my Spirit rest, yea, in their Temple shall enter in

through the door I have set, oh, even I the Lord have set before thee and open door.

7) As I Messiah has spoken in my work, The Harvest is ripe in the labors of Eden. I say unto my people this night that pray, Yea, even that Lord of harvest will send more laborers into the Harvest for many is not willing to work. Oh, for the Harvest is past and some remained and were not saved.

8) Some are not sowing the seed and some are not reaping the seed that has been sowed. But, I the Lord will call a people that lived Holy and, Yea, that will sow and that will reap for surly the Harvest says the Lord is ripe and the laborers are few.

9) But know ye not that I shall turn to a people that will Praise me. I will rise up a people for my name sake that has come forth and they shall do the work, sayeth God, that I have commanded them. They keep my Commandants and they love one another.

10) Oh, come this night, says God, come unto me and I shall heal thee.